ADC LXXXVI ART DIRECTORS ANNUAL

THE BEST OF VISUAL COMMUNICATIONS AROUND THE GLOBE ADVERTISING DESIGN INTERACTIVE ILLUSTRATION PHOTOGRAPHY

ADC L̲X̲X̲X̲V̲I̲

Editorial Director
Myrna Davis
Managing Editor
Kate Farina
Design
Giampietro+Smith:
Rob Giampietro,
Kevin Smith,
Darcy Jeffs,
Leslie Kwok
DVD Title Design
C&G Partners
Editorial Assistant
Joe Saphire
Publisher
RotoVision SA
Route Suisse 9
CH-1295 Mies
Switzerland
Sales & Editorial Office
Sheridan House
114 Western Road
Hove, East Sussex
BN3 1DD, United Kingdom
Tel: +44 (0) 1273 727268
Fax: +44 (0) 1273 727269
sales@rotovision.com
www.rotovision.com
ADC
The Art Directors Club
106 W. 29th St.
New York, NY 10001
United States of America
www.adcglobal.org

Design Software
Adobe Creative Suite 3

ISBN
978-2-88893-012-9

Paul Lavoie

The Art Directors Club is committed to honoring the past, celebrating the present and empowering the future like no other industry organization. This year's activities are proud testimony to these goals.

Timely dialogue and debate were alive at events like Big Brand Talks featuring Neil Powell, Chief Creative Officer, MargeotesFertittaPowell (New York); Terry Lee Stone, Principal, Terry Lee Stone Design Management (Los Angeles); and Colin Drummond, Group Director, Cognitive & Cultural Studies, Crispin Porter + Bogusky (Miami), who shared insights on repositioning brands and jumpstarting ideas. "Designism," initiated by board member Brian Collins, was a contemporary echo of an ADC goal originally expressed in 1920, "to contribute in some way to make the world a better place." The role of design, to this end, was discussed by panel members Milton Glaser, George Lois, Tony Hendra, Kurt Andersen, James Victore and Jessica Helfand.

The Young Guns showcase, now in its 10th year, recognizes young talent under 30, and is a core mission of the ADC. The brilliant work submitted from around the world was showcased at the ADC Gallery and featured in a special edition volume published by Moleskine.

In addition to these events for members and community, the Art Directors Club itself honored the past and empowered the future in a milestone leadership transition. Myrna Davis, Executive Director since 1993, passed the torch to Ami Brophy in April.

Myrna Davis' significant role in shaping the club includes finding our gallery and home on 29th Street in New York, promoting the ADC globally as a multidisciplinary hub, and initiating many outstanding educational and professional programs along the way. Myrna was tireless in her devotion to the club and her resilience in the face of the obstacles inherent to running a not-for-profit organization. We thank Myrna for carrying the torch with such grace, wit and style.

We are delighted to welcome Ami Brophy to the role of Executive Director. Most recently Executive Director of the Clio Awards, Ami began her career in publishing at Copley Newspapers in California, participating in the launch of L.A. Weekly and L.A. Style going on to become VP/Publisher of Adweek Magazine. Articulate and passionate about our industry, Ami takes on a dynamic agenda to deliver the four pillars that are the cornerstones of my mandate as president: to increase the relevancy, visibility, currency and financial health of the ADC.

This exciting year has also produced the exciting volume you hold in your hands. The work featured was selected by a jury composed of remarkable talent from around the world and led by outstanding chairs. Tony Granger, Chief Creative Officer, Saatchi & Saatchi (New York), chaired the Advertising jury, and Rei Inamoto, Global Creative Director, AKQA (San Francisco) - not long ago an ADC Young Gun, chaired the Interactive jury and led the Hybrid jury. Design, illustration and photography juries were co-chaired by Adam Eeuwens and Rebeca Méndez, Founding Partners of Rebeca Méndez Design (Los Angeles). The selection was unbiased – and tough. And we salute them especially for the vigilance in the latter thereby preserving the high currency of an ADC Cube, and delivering a stunning annual.

Enjoy!

Paul Lavoie

Myrna Davis

ADC's 86th Annual Awards Competition drew 11,177 entries from 55 countries, a record number. 347 winners made the cut. Also a record were the number of international judges who gathered in the ADC Gallery in New York for several days of intense review, looking at every single entry and selecting from among them the great innovative work documented in this volume—the year's best in integrated media, print and broadcast advertising, design, interactive, illustration, photography and other aspects of visual communications worldwide.

Since 1993, when I became Executive Director, the communications industry has seen enormous change. ADC, the oldest creative membership organization in the world, has always been poised for the future, embracing, right from its auspicious start in 1920, advertising, design, art and culture. I am proud to have had the opportunity to help ADC grow into the 21st century. Many outstanding signature programs have been put into place, among them the ADC Young Guns biennial showcase; the Invitational Portfolio Reviews for top graduating talent; the Saturday Career Workshops for promising high school students; the Paper Expo, Photography and Illustration reviews, Big Brand Talks, the ADC Hall of Fame exhibitions and archive; and, most recently, Designism, an initiative for design activism. Our facility, which accommodates all these activities, the judgings, and more, is spectacular. Membership is attracting leaders with broad interests at every stage of their careers. None of us, or these activities, could flourish without the proceeds from ADC's core program, these Annual Awards.

This edition of the Art Directors Annual is of special note to me, providing the chance to officially congratulate for one last time the winners who are now part of this incomparable history of the industry, and to express my gratitude to the exceptional board members, ADC members, winners, and colleagues with whom I have worked during the past fourteen years. The time seemed right to turn over direction of this legendary organization and competition to the next generation, and I am pleased to welcome as my successor Ami Brophy, whom I wish every success as ADC enters its 87th year. Thank you all.

Warmly,

Myrna Davis

Elin Ankerblad
Interactive

Frank Anselmo
Hybrid

Jerome Austria
Hybrid / Interactive

Rob Baird
Advertising

Giorgio Baravalle
Graphic Design

With a decade of experience in interactive branding, Elin is one of the founding partners and Client Director at Doberman in Sweden. Elin has degrees in management and communication from the Chartered Institute of Marketing in London, Nordic Brand Academy, and the pioneering design school Hyper Island in Sweden. Throughout her career, she has gained extensive experience from managing global interactive design projects in both the US and Europe at agencies such as Razorfish in NYC and Lateral in London. Her references include award winning interactive projects for clients such as Levi's, EMI, Mars, Nationwide Building Society, Vodafone, Panasonic and Volvo.

Frank Anselmo's creative work has been recognized by every major awards show in the world including The One Show, D&AD, Cannes, ADC, Clios, etc. As an Art Director/Writer, Frank has worked on high-profile accounts such as Guinness, HBO, FedEx, Pepsi, GE and Ebay. Frank is credited for winning BBDO's first One Show Gold Pencil for an unconventional media concept in 2001. Other career highlights include being honored as an ADC Young Gun, and working on a music video for John Lennon. Frank is also an alumni turned instructor at The School of Visual Arts in New York where he founded and currently teaches the world's first documented class focused on creating unconventional/guerrilla advertising. In 2007 Frank opened his own advertising/design/invention company KNARF. You can see the work at knarfny.com.

Leveraging a diverse background in the visual arts, engineering, writing, and filmmaking, Jerome Austria has quickly established himself as a world-class creative force in interactive advertising. Currently a creative director at AKQA NY, Jerome's career client list includes some of the world's most recognizable brands such as Coca-Cola, Nike, Estee Lauder and IBM. Jerome has collected over fifty international awards from some of the most prestigious competitions, including Cannes Lions, One Show Interactive, the London International Design and Advertising Awards, and the Clios. His work has been featured in Creative Review, iD Magazine, Communication Arts, and HOW magazine.

Rob Baird is an art director at Mother in New York, working primarily on Virgin Mobile and Milwaukee's Best Beer. Prior to his 3 years at Mother, Rob worked at Fallon NY on Starbucks, Virgin Mobile and Timberland. He's also spent time at Arnold Worldwide on the "truth" anti-smoking account, at Bartle Bogle Hegarty NY, and at North Carolina boutique The Republik on clients you'd only recognize if you were from North Carolina. Rob has been lucky enough to have his work featured in every major advertising awards show, as well as earning several solo exhibitions on his mother's refrigerator. He was raised in Texas, and considers his passion for the University of Texas football program a very close second to his passion for advertising.

Giorgio Baravalle was born in Torino, Italy. He moved to San Francisco and in 1992 graduated from the California College of Arts. Drawn to the naturalistic approach of Japanese design, he embraced a clean and minimalist style. In 1995 Giorgio moved to Milan to work with the design office of 21 Investimenti, the holding company of Benetton. Then, in 1997 de.MO was born in Milan, a design and publishing firm that seeks to explore subjects thoroughly and communicate an unconventional and passionate ethos. In 2001 Giorgio moved to Millbrook, New York, and since then has published thirteen books and continued his award-winning design business.

Tim Barber
Hybrid / Interactive

Dave Bedwood
Hybrid / Interactive

Masayoshi Boku
Hybrid / Interactive

Irma Boom
Graphic Design

Keith Butters
Hybrid / Interactive

Tim Barber is a creative director and designer. For the past ten years, he has specialized in creating entertainment and marketing productions for new technology platforms. Tim currently serves as a principal and creative director with Odopod in San Francisco. Odopod is widely recognized and awarded for its work in two areas: software product design and online marketing. Tim's creative direction draws on a unique combination of technical expertise, entrepreneurial spirit and critical design sensibility. At Odopod he leads creative engagements for clients, including Nike, MTV, Red Bull, Target, Yahoo and Google.

In February 2004 Dave Bedwood became one of the founding partners in the advertising agency Lean Mean Fighting Machine. Dave has worked with his creative partner Sam Ball for 11 years. Initially from a traditional background they moved into online advertising 7 years ago. Together they have won numerous industry awards including D&AD, Clio, One Show, Cannes, Revolution and BIMA. In 2004 they were voted into Campaign's Top Ten Creative Directors in London across all disciplines as well as Campaign's Faces to Watch. In 2005, they picked up Campaign's Young Achievers of the Year Award and were voted by their peers as the number one creative team in online advertising.

Masayoshi Boku is the Executive Creative Director and the President of Bascule Inc, an interactive creative production based in Tokyo, Japan. Since its establishment in 2000, Masayoshi continues to pursue the possibilities of new web interactivity which goes beyond the boundaries of generations and languages. Currently, he studies various interactions of the next generation youth on the web through the works for Pokemon, one of his major clients. He also finds this as an opportunity for learning more about fatherhood, as a father to a 6 year-old son and a one year-old daughter. Boku's work has been noted by ADC, D&AD, Cannes Cyber Lion, London International Ad Awards, Clio Awards, One Show, and AdFest.

Irma Boom is an Amsterdam-based graphic designer specializing in book making. For five years she worked (editing and concept/design) on the 2136-page SHV Think Book 1996-1896 commissioned by SHV Holdings in Utrecht. The Think Book was published in English and Chinese. Irma Boom studied graphic design at the AKI Art Academy in Enschede. After graduating, she worked for five years at the Dutch Government Publishing and Printing Office in The Hague. In 1991 she founded Irma Boom Office, which works nationally and internationally in both the cultural and commercial sectors. Clients include the Rijksmuseum Amsterdam, Paul Fentener van Vlissingen (1941-2006), Inside Outside, Museum, Boijmans Van Beuningen, Zumtobel, Ferrari, Vitra International, NAi Publishers, United Nations and OMA/Rem Koolhaas, Koninklijke Tichelaar, and Camper. Since 1992 Boom has been a critic at Yale University in the US and gives lectures and workshops worldwide. She has been the recipient of many awards for her book designs and was the youngest-ever laureate to receive the prestigious Gutenberg prize for her complete oeuvre.

Keith has over 10 years of experience conceptualizing, designing and developing interactive projects. He has focused his career on creating immersive online experiences by amalgamating graphic design and usability, with animation, video, and server-side technologies. His work has won many major design awards, including Clios, Hatch Awards, One Show Pencils, and Cannes Lions. Most notably, his work on Burger King's subservient-chicken.com earned him a Gold Lion, and his efforts on Method's come-clean.com won a Grand Prix at Cannes. His work has also been featured in publications such as Communication Arts, Print, and HOW.

Andy Clarke
Advertising

Anna Coll
Hybrid / Interactive

Mimi Cook
Advertising

Lars Cortsen
Hybrid / Interactive

Paul Davis
Graphic Design

Originally hailing from the UK, Andy wins the award for greatest number of miles traveled over his career. He spent his early years as an Art Director at Euro RSCG London before being seduced by the mystique of the Orient and working for Euro RSCG Singapore. Other stops in Singapore included Batey Ads and Saatchi & Saatchi before returning home with Saatchi in their London office. But the travel bug hit Andy, his wife, and three kids once again. Tempted by the outdoor lifestyle that Minneapolis has to offer and the adventure that comes from exploring a new country, he packed up and moved to Minnesota joining Carmichael Lynch as Executive Creative Director. Over the course of his career, Andy has worked on some of the world's biggest brands, including: Compaq Computers, Mitsubishi, Mercedes-Benz, Sony, Tiger Beer, Singapore Airlines and the Singapore Tourist Board. He has also made great work for Burger King, Hewlett-Packard, Toyota, Carlsberg Lager and T-Mobile. His bookshelf is adorned with Cannes Gold Lions, One Show Silvers and Clios.

Anna was born in Barcelona in 1973, and graduated as a graphic designer at ESDI (Escuela Superior de Diseño) Design School in 1996. She started her career in McCann Erickson Barcelona in 1996, and at the same time began doing some freelance work for FAD (Foment de les Arts Decoratives, a design collective) and other companies. In 1999 Anna joined the creative team at DoubleYou as a Graphic Designer, after a couple of years she was promoted to Art Director, the position she currently holds. At the time she joined, DY was a small interactive agency. It already stood out though for its high creative standards and for its good grasp of what online/interactive communication was. This profile has been maintained until now and it's been valued by some of the biggest brands in the Spanish market, which have trusted DoubleYou to help them translate all their brand imaginary and emotional values online. Anna's experience at DY has involved work for clients like Nike, Arbora&Ausonia (part-owned by P&G), Audi, Seat, etc. During 2005 and 2006 Anna had the honor of being invited to participate on the interactive jury at various festivals such as One Show, Eurobest and the Webby Awards.

Career testing during high school indicated Mimi was uniquely qualified for a future in either lounge singing or real estate. Luckily for bars patrons and homebuyers, she instead began a career in copywriting at Chiat / Day and continued on until attaining her present position as ACD at Goodby, Silverstein & Partners. Her office shelves contain a few awards, pictures of her two daughters and many books in which she likes looking at the pretty pictures.

Having graduated from the Danish School of Advertising as Art Director in 1995, Lars Cortsen spent his next 5 years working at traditional advertising agencies. Framfab Denmark instigated his switch to interactive, asking him in November 1999, if he'd be interested in working on a pitch for Nike. Even with no history in the digital arena, this rare opportunity to work with one of the world's biggest and most exciting brands was far too good to pass up. Lars has worked on a number of award-winning campaigns, picking up statuettes at Cannes Lions, London International Advertising Awards, One Show, Clio, Epica, Eurobest, Arnold and Guldkorn. He has been part of various juries such as Cannes Lions, Eurobest, London International Advertising Awards (LIAA), Clio, Scandinavian Advertising Awards and various national award shows.

Work featured in Creative Review, Time Out, Graphis International, Print (US) , Barfout (Jap), Dazed & Confused, Self Service (Fra), Illustration (Jap), Bibel (Swe), Doing Bird (Aus), Independent On Sunday. I.D., Arena, Blueprint, Clear, Eye Magazine, The Believer, PPaper, and Varoom. Books include: Blame Everyone Else. Us & Them. Marketing Photographs. God Knows and Lovely. Exhibited all over the place including London, New York, Tokyo, and Stockholm. Agrees with Steinberg that boredom is the enemy.

Lorenzo De Rita
Advertising

Pablo Del Campo
Advertising

Kathy Delaney
Hybrid

Dean Di Simone
Hybrid / Interactive

James Dive
Advertising

Lorenzo De Rita is currently CCO at Euro RSCG Netherlands (Amsterdam). He previously worked at Colors Magazine as Creative Director and before that at Fuel Europe (Volvo), Kesselskramer (Diesel, Do, The Column), 180 (Adidas, Dunlop, MTV), Wieden + Kennedy (Nike, Benelli), DDB (Volkswagen, Audi), McCann Erickson (RAI). In the course of the years, Lorenzo won a few awards for his clients (amongst these, 13 Lions at the Cannes Festival, including a Titanium Lion for the Volvo "Life on Board Project"). Lorenzo is also a lecturer at various Universities around the world. He's the Director of The Soon Institute, an observatory on the near future for the United World College of the Adriatic.

Pablo is the most awarded Argentine creative of the decade and the second in the whole Iberoamerica Region. In January 2000 he started up Del Campo Nazca Saatchi & Saatchi, aiming to create a top agency worldwide. Obtaining four new awards in Cannes, Pablo already has 23 Lions. The two Clio awards in 2006 add up to the 30 already obtained. Del Campo Nazca Saatchi & Saatchi is at present #1 in Argentina and #1 in the Iberoamerican Region, according to Latinspots. It is also the most awarded agency in the whole Publicis Groupe and has achieved the Best Campaign at the competitive P&G's Brand Building Award. Pablo belongs to Bob Isherwood's Saatchi & Saatchi Worldwide Creative Board, leading the Spanish Speaking advertising for the network.

Kathy Delaney began her advertising career after completing her education at the School of Visual Arts in New York. For the past 14 years, Kathy has been at Deutsch, where she helped it grow from a small boutique of $180 million into a $ 2.5 billion marketing communications company. Her insight and passion for tapping into consumer's emotions, while simultaneously outperforming business objectives impacted clients such as Revlon, Bank of America, Tommy Hilfiger, Johnson and Johnson, Monster.com, MCI, Snapple, Pfizer, Ikea and Tanqueray. Kathy joined Deutsch in 1993 as an Associate Creative Director, was promoted to Executive Creative Director and Partner of the New York office in 1997, Executive Creative Director, Managing Partner in 2001, and Chief Creative Officer, President in 2005. Prior to Deutsch, Kathy was Associate Creative Director, VP at Chiat / Day, NY on Reebok. At Bozell, NY she worked as a Senior Art Director in the financial services, fashion and spirits categories.

Dean Di Simone has been the Creative Director and Designer on a series of award-winning branding, print, environment and interactive projects for clients such as The Eyebeam Atelier, Nike, The Sundance Channel, Converse, and MoMA. Dean continues to engage academia through teaching and has taught Advanced Digital Media at Yale University, Internet Protocols at Columbia University, and Information Culture at the University of Pennsylvania while acting as a principal and creative director of his design practice, TENDER, in New York City.

James Dive is an Art Director at the independent creative group, The Glue Society in Sydney. James has created numerous international award-winning campaigns, including a Gold Lion at Cannes, throughout his career in both London and Sydney. James most recently won the Peoples Choice Prize for the Glue Society's entrant in Sculpture by the Sea in Sydney. Currently, James is working with other company members on an upcoming TV show.

Adam Eeuwens
Co-Chair, Graphic Design

Rafael Esquer
Hybrid / Graphic Design

César Finamori
Advertising

Karin Fong
Graphic Design

Piero Frescobaldi
Hybrid / Interactive

Adam Eeuwens is editorial director of 34 Magazine, a design quarterly published from Istanbul, where he is also curator at large for the design gallery HAAZ. He is co-author of False Flat, Why Dutch Design is So Good, published by Phaidon Press in 2004. Adam is partner in Rebeca Méndez Communication Design, responsible for design strategy, research and development, copywriting and creating concepts that lead to artistic solutions and pragmatic results. Adam has almost 20 years of media industry experience, half in the United States and half in Europe, with experience as journalist, editor, publisher, event developer, strategist, copywriter and author. The red thread of his rich career is his propensity to create strategy and turn it into a story. His motto in work and life is "Think like a man of action, act like a man of thought."

A native of the Sonora desert of Mexico, Rafael Esquer has made New York City his home for a decade. As Creative Director at @radical.media, his group's work in communication design received the National Design Award in 2004 from the Cooper-Hewitt National Design Museum. Esquer now runs Alfalfa, his own design studio. Clients have included The New York Times Magazine, Nike, Björk, AIGA, Tommy Boy Records, Target, IBM, Scholastic, and MTV. The Olympic Museum and The Library of Congress Poster Collection contain some of his work. Esquer received his BFA from Art Center College of Design. He frequently serves as judge and speaker at national and international design events.

César Finamori was born and raised in São Paulo, Brazil. He started his career as an Art Director at DPZ Propaganda where he worked for 8 years. After that, he joined the creative team of AlmapBBDO, where he stayed for nine years. He has had his work recognized by several national and international award shows such as Creative Club of São Paulo, El Ojo Iberoamerica, FIAP, Cannes Festival, Clio, London Festival, NY Festival, One Show and Art Directors Club. César moved to New York in 2006 to work at BBDO NY.

Karin Fong directs and designs for film, television, and environments. Before joining Imaginary Forces in 1994, Karin studied art at Yale and worked at WGBH Boston. Her reel includes the opening sequences for Charlotte's Web, Zoom, Ray, The Cat in the Hat, and Charlie's Angels. Her work on PBS's Masterpiece Theatre earned an Emmy for title design in 2001. She has also directed commercials for Honda, Janus, Chevrolet, and Herman Miller.

Piero began his career as an Assistant Director on films and commercials in Italy. In 1996, he moved into the interactive arena, founding unit9, and relocating to London. The human dimension of interactive communication, the lack of boundaries of the internet, and the emotional awareness of active advertising, have quickly become his main passion and creative focus. He believes that great communication in all media is achieved through human environments, story telling, and dramatic rhythm. In the current crowded, hectic and loud online panorama, he is reaching for simplicity. As creative director of unit9, Piero has collaborated with agencies and brands alike on every aspect of online communication. In 2004 he was voted one of Campaign's top digital Creative directors. Awards: Cannes Lions, D&AD, One Show, LIAA, BIMA, FWA, Campain Digital, IAB, ADC*E, MSN Digital.

Mauro Gatti
Hybrid / Interactive

Anna Gerber
Graphic Design

Bryony Gomez-Palacio
Graphic Design

Folkert Gorter
Graphic Design

Tony Granger
Chair, Advertising

For over a decade Mauro Gatti has been at the forefront of new media design in Italy. Humorous, sharp and creative his work has been globally recognized. Gatti co-founded Mutado, a creative studio with offices in London and Milan in 2004. He began his career as an interactive designer in the mid-90's and became highly influential through his personal space thebrainbox.com. He has worked on projects in the advertising, new media and motion graphics fields, as well as branding and illustrations that capture the more comical side of life. He has developed work for MTV, Nike, Paramount Comedy, Nickelodeon, and Disney.

Anna Gerber is a graphic designer and writer, based in London. She is the editor and designer of All Messed Up: Unpredictable Graphics (Laurence King, 2004) and co-editor and co-designer of Influences: A Lexicon of Contemporary Graphic Design (DGV, 2006) with Anja Lutz.

For Bryony, life seems like one endless trip. Having lived in Mexico City, Atlanta, Chicago and now New York, you can usually spot her as the one with the camera and the multiple questions. Curiosity, determination, and passion are what define her work and her unique approach. Creativity and the brain being key interests, she lectures and conducts workshops on the subject around the country. She is co-founder of Under Consideration and the notorious Speak Up, The Design Encyclopedia, Brand New and most recently Quipsologies. Currently, she divides her time working for herself, pursuing her own ventures and teaching at the School of Visual Arts.

Folkert Gorter is an independent interaction designer from Amsterdam, The Netherlands, founder of Superfamous studios and co-founder of the design portal Newstoday.com. After receiving a Bachelor's of Art in Interaction Design from the Utrecht School of Art and a Master of Arts in Interactive Multimedia, he moved to New York City to work in interactive advertising. Before opening Superfamous Studios in 2004, he worked with both conceptual advertising and interior design agencies in Amsterdam. He is currently working out of Los Angeles with virtual reality filmmaker Rene Daalder on several initiatives in experimental online communities.

Tony is one of the most awarded Creative Directors in the industry. His hundreds of major awards include accolades from Cannes, New York, London, One Show, Art Directors Club and Clio (including an induction into the Hall of Fame). He has won over 46 Cannes Lions including 15 Golds. In 2006, alone he led Saatchi & Saatchi NY to the number-one-awarded U.S. agency at Cannes, the Agency of the Year at the Young Guns awards in Australia, and to the Grand Prix at the London International Awards. Additionally, in January of 2007, Saatchi & Saatchi was ranked #4 in Advertising Age's 2006 Agency A-List. He has created transformational work for some of the world's biggest and smartest marketers—BMW, P&G, Bank of America, General Mills, Ameriprise and JCPenney. But judge Tony not by the medals on his chest, but by what's inside it — a heart of great passion, compassion and a genuine love of our clients' businesses. Then look up so you don't miss the twinkle in his eye.

Christian Haas
Advertising

Jessica Helfand
Graphic Design

Rei Inamoto
Hybrid /
Chair, Interactive

Naoki Itoh
Hybrid / Interactive

Tina Johnson
Advertising

Christian Haas is a Group Creative Director at Goodby, Silverstein & Partners in San Francisco. Prior to GSP, he spent 7 years at Organic as VP Managing Director in São Paulo then GCD in San Francisco. Before that, he founded vizio, a leading Brazilian interactive agency he later sold to Organic; worked as Art Director and Creative Director in traditional advertising for Bates and Denison; and as Editor at Ultima, a film production company. But his advertising career really started at age 4 when a nanny no-show forced his mom to bring him to work. That day, he watched the agency reel 26 times, like any other kid would.

Jessica Helfand is a partner, with William Drenttel, at Winterhouse, a design studio in Northwest Connecticut. Their work focuses on publishing and editorial development, film and new media, and cultural, educational and literary institutions. Helfand is a founding editor of Design Observer, the largest online forum for design criticism and commentary. Appointed in 2006 to the US Citizens Stamp Advisory Committee, she has been a contributing editor and columnist for Print, ID, and Eye magazines and has written for numerous national publications, including The Los Angeles Times Book Review, Aperture and The New Republic. She is the author of several books including Paul Rand: American Modernist (1998), Screen: Essays on Graphic Design, New Media and Visual Culture (2001), and Reinventing the Wheel (2002). Helfand received her B.A. in architectural theory and her M.F.A. in graphic design, both from Yale University, where she is currently Senior Critic in the School of Art.

Rei Inamoto is the Global Creative Director at AKQA as well as the Internet Jury Chair for the 2006 Clio Awards. At AKQA, Rei is responsible for delivering worldwide creative solutions for the agency's international clients such as Nike and Xbox. Rei most recently served as the Executive Creative Director for R/GA, responsible for winning numerous awards including Cannes Cyber Lions, One Show and Clio Awards. In 2004, Rei was named one of the Young Guns by The Art Directors Club, which annually selects the best young talents working in the design and advertising industry. In January 2006, Advertising Age's Creativity Magazine named AKQA its first-ever Interactive Agency of the Year.

Naoki Itoh, 35, was born in Shizuoka, which is famous for Japanese green tea, and grew up in Tokyo. He entered the third largest advertising agency in Japan, ADK, and worked as Sales Promotion Planner and Account Planner. In 2003, he became Creative Director. After receiving a number of awards, he joined GT, a leading Japanese creative boutique, in July 2006. Recent clients have included Nike, Microsoft and Coca-Cola. Since 2005 he has won Gold, Silver, Bronze at the Tokyo Interactive AD Awards, Asia Pacific AdFest Silver, a One Show Interactive Merit award, and was a Future Marketing Award Finalist at the LIAA. He has served on the jury of the 2006 Clios and is also a judge at the One Show Interactive 2007. Recent works include Nike NIKEiD, Nike Cosplay," and Microsoft XBOX "Interactive Wall Big Shadow."

Tina Johnson is currently at The Richards Group, in Dallas, Texas, where she has worked on Hyundai, Greyhound, Zales, Goody's Family Clothing, and new business. Before joining The Richards Group in 2003, Tina worked at Wieden + Kennedy, in both the New York and Portland offices, as a writer on Nike, Brand Jordan, ESPN, Avon, and Microsoft. Before that, Tina was fortunate enough to enjoy her youth with fun stints at Cliff Freeman, Mad Dogs & Englishmen, and Fallon. Her work has been noted by The Art Directors Club, The One Show, Communications Arts, Archive and Graphis. It's safe to say, Tina has been around the advertising block. But no place compares to home, in Plano, Texas, where she gets a kick out of raising her two girls, Hudson and Scout.

Simon Johnston
Graphic Design

Eng San Kho
Graphic Design

Nick Klinkert
Hybrid

Kevin Lee
Advertising

Robert Lindström
Hybrid / Interactive

Simon Johnston is a graphic designer and artist living in Los Angeles. Born and educated in England, he cofounded the design partnership 8vo in the mid-1980s, developing and publishing Octavo, a journal of typography. He relocated to Los Angeles in 1989, where he opened his own design studio. His recently designed publications in the art field include Photographic Memory: William Claxton; Eye to Eye: The Photographs of Graham Nash; Cotton Puffs, Q-Tips, Smoke and Mirrors: The Drawings of Ed Ruscha. He is a Professor at Art Center College of Design in Pasadena.

Eng San Kho was born in Amsterdam and spent his teenage years touring Europe as a professional skateboarder before moving to New York City to pursue design. He worked at Joost Elffers Books, Pseudo Programs, Shooting Gallery, and Hornet Inc. before establishing his own branding and creative agency in 2006. His design work has been featured in broadcast, print and interactive media for clients such as EMI, MTV, VH1, Nickelodeon, Condé Nast, and Smirnoff, among others.

After finishing the school for communications arts, Nick learned some of the tricks of the art director trade in London and his native Amsterdam. In between, he directed a music video that was shortlisted at festivals around the world and a PSA that earned him a Young Directors nomination in Cannes. In 2004, Nick moved to NY to work at BBH where he currently avoids other early evening entertainment options by working on a range of clients such as Johnnie Walker Blue Label, Levi's and Axe. Nick was fortunate enough to gather a few trophies along the way and his work has been featured in all major trade publications.

Kevin Lee started his advertising career in 1990 with agencies like the Spider Network, BBDO, and Bates in Malaysia. In 1998, Kevin undertook the assignment of Associate Creative Director for BBDO in Beijing. Two years later, he became the Creative Director for Grey Worldwide in Beijing, Shanghai and Guangzhou. In 2004 he joined JWT Shanghai as Group Creative Director. At that agency, he created the Nike "Run Free" ads, which were ranked the second most awarded print campaign in the world by the Gunn Report 2006. His awards include 2 Silver D&AD nominations, medals at the New York Art Directors Club, Cannes, Clios, Media Spikes, London International Awards, One Show, New York Festivals, Asia Pacific Advertising Festival, and China 4As Advertising Awards.

Robert Lindström started his career as an Art Director with a company called Paregos in 1998. He quickly created himself a name as a talented designer by winning the Prix D'Italia award in 1999 for Best Innovative Solution with the website of the Swedish TV-show Mosquito. Since then he founded his own interactive agency, North Kingdom, together with Roger Stighäll in 2003 and he has become one of the world's most awarded interactive designer with five Golds and one Grand Prix in Cannes. Robert lives up north in Sweden in a small town called Skellefteå where he lives and breaths design in all forms that it may come. He always works with personal design project besides his professional ones and some of these can be found in his personal online portfolio, www.designchapel.com

Dana Lixenberg
Graphic Design

Willem Henri Lucas
Graphic Design

Fran Luckin
Advertising

Anja Lutz
Graphic Design

Jason Marks
Hybrid / Interactive

Dana Lixenberg was born in Amsterdam, The Netherlands in 1964. She currently lives and works in New York City, but studied Photography at the London College of Printing and at the Gerrit Rietveld Academie in Amsterdam. In 1993 she was awarded a project grant by WVC (the Dutch Ministry of Culture) for a series of portraits at the Imperial Courts Housing Project in Los Angeles, CA. She was soon getting commissions from a wide variety of magazines such as The New York Times Magazine, The New Yorker, Newsweek, and Vibe, among others. She was the subject of a documentary titled: Dana Lixenberg, thru dutch eyes in 1999 and in 2005 she was featured in an episode of the documentary series Hollands Zicht (Dutch Vision), both for Dutch television.

Willem Henri Lucas (b. 1962) graduated from the Academy of Visual Arts in Arnhem, NL. He lectured at several art schools in the Netherlands and abroad. In 1996 he received a grant from the 'FBKVB' a Dutch fund that supports fine arts, design and architecture, to develop his own work. In 1998 he designed the 'Holiday Stamps' for the Dutch Post and Telecom Company. In both 2003 and 2004 he won a Best Book Design Award and a nomination from the Art Directors Club Netherlands. In 2005 the AIGA nominated his design for a Design | Media Arts publication. Since 2004 Lucas lives and works in Los Angeles, he is a tenure professor at UCLA and founded Willem Augustus with designer Davey Whitcraft. He worked for Ogilvy & Mather, MOCA in Los Angeles, and designed Everythinghappensatonce a publication on artist Euan Macdonald, for Verlag für moderne Kunst, Nürnberg.

After an obligatory stint at University studying such edifying subjects as literature and philosophy, Fran Luckin joined the Jupiter Drawing Room in Johannesburg in 1994. She joined TBWA Hunt Lascaris as a copywriter in 1997, and was promoted to Creative Director in 2000. She worked at TBWA for 6 years, then joined Ogilvy Johannesburg as Creative Director in 2003. Fran Luckin has won awards internationally and in South Africa, including seven D&AD Annual entries, two Gold and two Bronze Cannes Lions, 3 silver and three Bronze Clio awards, fourteen Clio shortlists, a One Show Bronze pencil, and 3 One Show merit awards, a Loerie Grand Prix and nine Loerie Golds.

Anja Lutz is a Berlin-based graphic designer. She studied at London College of Printing and the Jan van Eyck Akademie. She was Visiting Professor at the American University of Beirut and Design Fellow at Akademie Schloss Solitude. She is the initiator of the experimental publication platform shift! (www.shift.de) comprising of sixteen publications so far, that have won numerous awards and were present at various festivals and exhibitions, including the Vitra Design Museum, the Design Biennale at St. Etienne, CMYK Festival Barcelona and the upcoming Colophon2007 in Luxemburg. Anja is also co-founder and art director of The Green Box art editions (www.thegreenbox.net), a publisher of art(ist) books.

Jason Marks recently took a position at Heavy Networks as Vice President of Programming & Development, creating online video for a true veteran of the medium, Heavy.com. This new challenge came after bringing MTV.com into the content era with the groundbreaking video platform, Overdrive. Combining hit-based television programming with viral short form video and by-appointment live events, Jason was the Creative Director behind The Stew, MyVMAs, Laguna Beach: The After Show, My Movie Awards, The Woodies and TRL Behind the Scenes, to name a few. He also oversaw all custom ad creative across the site for clients like, McDonald's, Nike, Pepsi and Saturn. He acquired his digital advertising experience at R/GA, where working as a member of the Core Team, he was responsible for an impressive body of work for the Nike Brand sites, bringing home several Cubes, Pencils, Arrows, and Lions. Jason lives and works in New York City.

Andre Matarazzo
Hybrid / Interactive

Chaz Maviyane-Davies
Graphic Design

Kevin McKeon
Advertising

Rebeca Méndez
Co-Chair, Graphic Design

Niels Meulman
Graphic Design

Andre has worked with online advertising for the past 10 years in 5 different countries around the globe, learning to communicate with different audiences and having the time of his life traveling around. Last stop before heading back to Brazil in 2006 was Tokyo. Now Andre is a partner at Gringo (gringo.nu) in São Paulo, an interactive hot shop catering mostly to the international market.

Chaz Maviyane-Davies has been described by the UK's Design magazine as "the guerrilla of graphic design." For more than two decades the award-winning and controversial designer's powerful work has taken on issues of consumerism, health, nutrition, social responsibility, the environment and human rights. He has studied (MA, Central Saint Martins College of Art and Design in London) and worked in Britain, Japan, Malaysia, the US and Zimbabwe, his country of origin. From 1983 until recently he ran the renowned design studio in Harare, Zimbabwe, The Maviyane-Project. Due to adverse political conditions in his homeland, Maviyane-Davies moved to the USA in 2001, where he is currently a Professor of Design at the Massachusetts College of Art in Boston. As well as being published in numerous books, international magazines and newspapers, his work has been exhibited extensively and is included in several permanent collections at various galleries.

Since joining StrawberryFrog in March 2005, Kevin has helped the agency grow four-fold, while launching notable work for Heineken, Sam's Club, Microsoft, Unisys, Mega Bloks, and Bank of Montreal. Previously, Kevin was Executive Creative Director of BBH New York, where he spent three years building the agency into one of the most respected creative shops in the U.S., overseeing award-winning campaigns for clients such as Axe Deodorant, Rolling Stone Magazine, Johnnie Walker, and Levis. Throughout his career, Kevin has worked at the best agencies in New York, including BBDO, Scali McCabe Sloves, Ammirati & Puris, and Lowe & Partners, creating award-winning work for a broad range of brands including Virgin Atlantic, Heineken, Sony, Schweppes, Xerox, DuPont, and Mercedes.

Rebeca Méndez is a Professor at UCLA Design | Media Arts Department in Los Angeles, California. Méndez was born and raised in Mexico City and received her BFA (1984) and her MFA (1996) from Art Center College of Design in Pasadena, California. Her career extends in various areas of practice—academic, social, cultural and corporate—simultaneously. She runs Rebeca Méndez Communication Design whose collaborations include video artist Bill Viola, architect Thom Mayne of Morphosis, architect Greg Lynn, GLFORM, and film director Mike Figgis, and clients such as Caltech, Microsoft, Guggenheim, Whitney and MOCA. From 1999 to 2003 she was the Creative Director of Ogilvy & Mather Brand Integration Group, NY and Los Angeles. She lectures nationally and internationally—from Tijuana to Taipei—and her work has been the object of numerous publications and exhibitions.

Niels Meulman's initial recognition came as 'Shoe' within graffiti culture, which evolved into formal typography, graphic design and global brand communication, recently culminating in a fashion design line for the British sports brand Umbro, which includes a signature shoe design. A graffiti legend by 18, Meulman became apprentice to Dutch graphic design master Anthon Beeke. Throughout the nineties Meulman ran his design studio Caulfield & Tensing, before joining FHV / BBDO as creative director. Currently Meulman is combining graphic design, marketing, graffiti, advertising, art and calligraphy in his company Unruly.

Antonio Montero
Advertising

Bettina Olf
Advertising

Murat Patavi
Graphic Design

Vesna Petrovic
Graphic Design

Anh Tuan Pham
Hybrid / Interactive

Graduate in journalism (Universidad Complutense de Madrid). In October '84, he began working as a trainee in McCann Erickson. Then he went on to work as an Art Director in N.C.A., el Viso, and A.VA., before joining Contrapunto as a Creative Director in 1995. He currently holds the position as General Creative Director in Contrapunto. Among the prizes he has won, including graphic and TV: 20 Lions in Cannes, several Grand Prix and various Golds and Silvers at New York festivals, 2 Grand Prix and various Golds and Silvers in FIAP, 3 grand prix and around 50 Sun awards at El Sol (San Sebastián) Spanish ad festival, and various Golds, Silvers and Bronzes at: Epica, Eurobest, Ad Spot Awards, Clio Awards, One Show, Laus, etc.

After 2 years as a designer in New York, Bettina began her career as an Art Director at Springer & Jacoby, Hamburg, in 1990, creating award-winning campaigns for Mercedes Benz. In 1992 she went to Jung von Matt, helping to make it one of the best creative agencies in Germany, working on cars, lemonade, radio stations, banking, fashion and lingerie. Since January 2000, Bettina is back at Springer & Jacoby. As a Creative Director, she is responsible for clients such as Coca-Cola, Mercedes Benz, Miele, DWS and McKinsey & Company, producing TV, print and interactive campaigns. As an Art Director and as a Creative Director, Bettina has won numerous awards including Cannes Gold, Clio, OneShow, Epica, Eurobest, D&AD, ADC of Europe and German ADC Awards.

Murat Patavi established Republica Advertising Agency in the year 2000. The agency differentiates itself from large conglomerate agencies with its design-oriented approach. Republica serves large clients such as Vodafone, CNN Turk, and Samsung, as well as local brands such as Wanna, Aija Hotel, Hillside Su, Kanyon and Gilan. Under the umbrella brand of Design42Morrow, OTTTO publishing company was established in 2004 releasing 34 magazine—the first international lifestyle magazine from Turkey. Besides the several magazines, OTTTO also publishes corporate books for clients such as NOVARTIS, handling in-house content, organization and design. In 2005, Murat Patavi set out to create a curatorial collection of design and art. Featured in Wallpaper Travel Guide as one of the coolest shopping sites in Istanbul; Haaz represents 21'st century's celebrated industrial designers, as well as encouraging the younger generation of designers and artists with commissioned installations and exhibitions.

Vesna studied at the University of Belgrade, Serbia, where she received a B.A. in Architecture and Design. In 2004, with Marci Boudreau, Vesna formed Picnic Design, to focus on design for art organizations, small businesses and creative companies. Their studio is experienced at print and exhibition design and enjoys creating unique materials and spaces. She teaches design classes at UCLA and is a board member of the American Institute of Graphic Arts Cross Cultural Design. Her work has been included in several exhibitions and has been published in the U.S. as well as abroad.

Anh Tuan founded For Office Use Only (FOUO) in 2001, where he leads the concept development, design and execution for all studio projects. A graduate in English Literature from UC Berkeley, Anh Tuan has taught interactive design at the Parsons School of Design, guest lectured at The University of Delaware, North Carolina State University, and the AIA New York. Mr. Pham's portfolio includes projects for MoMA, AIGA, MTV, Marc Jacobs, and Sony. He has been profiled in Print, Communication Arts, One, and Designers Workshop (Japan), and his work has been featured in books published by Taschen and Macromedia Press. He has won awards from the One Show, Art Directors Club, ID, Communication Arts, D&AD, Print, AIGA and more. In 2004, Anh Tuan was named one of 34 Art Directors Club Young Guns. In addition to his duties at FOUO, Anh Tuan is also Art Director at Hintmag.com, and a Broadcast Author at Newstoday.com. Last but not least, Anh Tuan loves pugs.

Michael Powers
Graphic Design

Michael Prieve
Advertising

Qian Qian
Hybrid / Interactive

Natalia Rojas
Hybrid / Interactive

Rose Sauquillo
Advertising

Michael Powers is a working photographer and artist hailing from Los Angeles, California. After graduating from Art Center College of Design, Michael began teaching photography and hosting art workshops and exhibitions in his studio in South Pasadena. Michael works commercially as a photographer, but also produces and shoots film and video. His clients include Buena Vista Films, Ogilvy & Mather, Motorola, IBM, MTV, U.S.C. Department of Sociology, L.A. Weekly, Los Angeles Magazine, 34 Magazine, Lucky Brand Jeans, WWD and Baseline Magazine.

Michael Prieve is the Chief Creative Officer at Doremus New York, the premier business communications agency within the Omnicom Group. With brief stops at Y&R in Southern California and FCB in San Francisco, Michael has spent most of his career at Wieden + Kennedy working in Portland, New York and Amsterdam. He graduated from The Art Center College of Design in Pasadena, California with honors. Michael has had the opportunity to work on such notable brands as Calvin Klein, Coca-Cola, Knight Capital Group, Levis Strauss & Co., Microsoft, and Nike. Michael currently lives in Manhattan with his wife, old dog and little boy.

Qian Qian is a multi-faceted designer from China, working in print, web, and motion. He graduated with a Masters degree in digital media design from the University of Edinburgh, UK, and now teaches graphic design at Missouri State University, USA. One of the "20 under 30 New Visual Artists" by Print magazine, he has worked with a wide range of clients, including Nike, Panasonic, Shiseido, Motorola, and British Council. His work has been published and exhibited internationally. In 2005, he conceived and co-curated Get It Louder, a tour design exhibition and event in China's Shenzhen, Shanghai, and Beijing.

She was born in Buenos Aires in 1976. Soon after, she moved to Bogotá, where she eventually graduated in Audiovisual Communications in the Pontificia Javeriana University. Subsequently, she obtained a postgraduate degree on Software Programming and IT in NIIT, Delhi. In 1999, she moved to Barcelona where she became Programmer and, soon after, Interactive Director of DoubleYou. Early in 2005 she founded Cuatic, an agency dedicated to the creation of interactive physical experiences oriented to communication events and advertising actions. Simultaneously, she is doing research on the areas where Programming and Graphic Design become one as artistic expression.

Rose began her career as an Art Director at MacLaren McCann, where she spent five years working with clients like Coca-Cola, Nestle, General Motors, and Johnson & Johnson. In 2001 Rose joined TAXI Toronto where she's done memorable work for MINI, Molson, Nike, and TELUS Mobility. She became Group Creative Director in 2004, overseeing TELUS Mobility and bringing fresh thinking to one of Canada's most respected brands. As a result of her success she is now Associate Creative Director at TAXI. Her work has been recognized by The One Show, Communication Arts, Art Directors Club, New York Festivals, Obies, Graphis, London International Advertising Awards, as well as the major Canadian shows. She loves the 80's, enjoys photographing her food, and has a karaoke room in her basement.

Gavin Simpson
Advertising

Kristina Slade
Advertising

Kash Sree
Advertising

Georgianna Stout
Graphic Design

Iain Tait
Hybrid / Interactive

As a bartender, Gavin found ad people much like the customers that drank till 3am. They smelled bad, were often incoherent and frequently broke. And those were just the women. But he found their stories interesting. He was also tired of the burly lesbians who kept harassing him for free drinks. So, with dreams of making it big in the industry, Gavin joined O&M Direct in '92. He then moved to Drayton Bird Partnership before working with Naga DDB, O&M KL, Y&R KL and Leo Burnett Jakarta. He then took on the role of ECD for Ogilvy Manila in July 2005. Within eight short months, O&M Manila picked up a Merit Award at the One Show, a Bronze Lion and four finalists at Cannes. Gavin has won numerous awards, including 3 Golds, 1 Silver and 1 Bronze Pencil at the One Show, 2 Silvers and 4 Bronze Clios, 1 Silver and 1 Bronze Cannes Lion, and an odd D&AD award. In 2002 and 2003, Campaign Brief ranked him as the No.1 Creative in Malaysia and No. 22 in Asia Pacific. One of his most recent ads— Land Rover "Direction"— clinched a Gold Lion at Cannes and was voted 4th Best in the World in the Gunn Report. Gavin has had experience serving on the jury at D&AD and Clio. He also has not seen the evening sun since 1985.

Kristina Slade is the writing portion of the ACD team at Ground Zero. Unable to justify another "lost" year in Boulder, CO, she moved to Atlanta and eventually graduated from Portfolio Center. After a year as the first female creative at CORE working on cars, fishing rods, guns, and the highly regarded St. Louis Post-Dispatch, she packed up her testosterone supplements and hightailed it to Los Angeles where she started her crazy-long stint of 7 years at Ground Zero. She is responsible for a large body of work that includes ESPN and the X Games, Virgin Digital, Virgin Mobile, Los Angeles Times, Lucy, and the anti-smoking effort in California. She is currently overseeing the global relaunch of Beck's Beer with her partner, Rodrigo Butori. Next to her desk is a drawer that includes awards from Cannes, Clios, D&AD, Art Directors Club, Athenas, Effies, Beldings and Andy's; in addition to numerous Awards of Excellence from Communication Arts, Graphis, and Archive. She's an occasional teacher at Art Center in Pasadena, translates Buddhist teachings into English, and is in the midst of struggling to banish the words "awesome" and "like" from her everyday conversation.

Born in Singapore, Kash moved to England at 7 months, later graduating from Kent Institute of Design with a B.A. in Graphic Communications. After 5 different six-week D&AD workshops, he was fired as a writer/art director at O&M London, followed by stints at Chiat, Singapore and O&M Madras. Later came Leo Burnett Chicago as an SVP Creative Director, BBH as Group Creative Director, and now JWT as Executive Creative Director.

Georgianna Stout is founding partner and creative director at 2x4. She leads diverse projects at 2x4 from extensive web site projects to large-scale identity and environmental graphics / wayfinding programs. She has recently completed branding, identity, retail and environmental programs for the Brooklyn Museum of Art, the Nasher Sculpture Center, The Studio Museum in Harlem and Dia:Beacon. She led the retail and packaging projects for the Vitra New York and Los Angeles headquarters and was partner-in-charge of a new product launch for Knoll Textiles. She is currently working on a network branding project with MTV. Stout has been a visiting design critic at Rhode Island School of Design and Yale University School of Art. She also collaborates with husband, designer David Weeks, in the design firm David Weeks Studio. Prior to founding 2x4, Stout worked at Bethany Johns Design producing publications and identity programs for arts organizations and other cultural institutions. Stout holds a B.F.A. from the Rhode Island School of Design.

Iain likes the Internet. He spends too much time looking at the Internet and playing with things that he finds there. He is normally very happy that his job is to help make interesting things on the Internet that other people will look at and play with too. 5 years ago he set up Poke with 5 like-minded people. They're still striving to create great online stuff. But now there's more of them. And the office is a bit bigger and nicer.

Jureeporn Thaidumrong
Advertising

Kate Tregoning
Graphic Design

Adam Tucker
Advertising

Mark Tutssel
Advertising

Alexei Tylevich
Graphic Design

Jureeporn Thaidumrong has 18 years of extensive experience in the advertising business. She is one of Thailand's and Asia's leading creatives with an impressive track record at Leo Burnett, DY&R, Results Advertising (the second agency of O&M), and Saatchi & Saatchi Bangkok. She has won awards at numerous international and regional shows, including local awards, Adman, TACT, and BAD Awards. In May 2005, she established JEH United, the only independent creative powerhouse in Thailand. In 2006, she led her creative agency to be the 18th most awarded agency in the world. Jureeporn won Creative of the Year from Media Agency of the year 2006, ranked as the No.1 Hottest Creative in Asia from Campaign Brief Asia Magazine, won the first Gold Lion for Thai Advertising History from Cannes Festival (international advertising competition) 2000, has Gold awards from Cannes Festival 2005 (for an Energy Saving Project (EPPO) TV campaign), and Gold awards from Cannes Festival 2006 for the TVC series of Smooth E "The Love Story". She has won best of films in Adfest 2006 & Best of Show in Asian Awards 2006, as well as best of show in "AWARDS" Australia for Smooth E "The Love Story" series, which marked the first time in Asia Pacific Advertising history.

Born in 1965 in England, Kate Tregoning currently lives in London with her partner and daughter. She studied graphics at Cornwall College, Kingston and Royal College of Art (MA). Her early career was in London as designer at Malcolm Garrett's Assorted Images, Nice and Imagination. In 1995, she left for New York and joined The Arnell Group. Tregoning moved west to Wieden + Kennedy as Art Director at their HQ in Portland, Oregon. Then in 1998, she had a second stint in New York to help grow Wieden's NY office. In 2000, she returned to London to set up as an independent designer on commercial and cultural projects.

Having started his career at the then, and now, unknown SMI, Adam made a lot of mistakes and learned from some of them. He then moved to FCA! (don't bother looking that one up either). Eventually, he got the call he'd been waiting for, joining DDB London in 1999. So far, he's made fewer mistakes and became Creative Director last year. Adam has won awards at all the major festivals including: One Show, D&AD, Cannes, The Clios, ADC and The Andys. DDBLondon topped the Gunn Report in 2006.

As Chief Creative Officer of Leo Burnett Worldwide, Mark Tutssel serves as the creative leader of the Leo Burnett brand, overseeing the work created by the network's 94 offices. Mark's work has garnered every major creative award in the industry, including the prestigious Cannes Grand Prix in print, and 30 Cannes Lions. In 2006, Leo Burnett Worldwide was awarded a coveted Black D&AD Pencil and 5 Yellow Pencils. Prior to joining Leo Burnett USA in 2002, Mark served as Executive Creative Director of Leo Burnett London. Under his creative leadership, the London agency experienced unprecedented success, becoming the No.1 creative agency in the United Kingdom and the most awarded creative agency in the world in 2001. During that time, both Heinz and McDonald's were named "Advertiser of the Year" in the U.K. Mark has served as Chairman of the Clio's, Andy's, D&AD, YoungGuns, Addy's, Eurobest, AWARD, and the Media Awards. He has also sat on the prestigious juries of Cannes, Art Directors Club of New York, Art Director's Club of Europe, and One Show.

Alexei is a Co-Founder and Creative Director of Logan, a design and production company based in Venice, California.

Ulises Valencia
Hybrid / Interactive

Guillermo Vega
Advertising

Jorge Verdin
Graphic Design

Erik Vervroegen
Advertising

Oliver Voss
Advertising

Ulises was born in 1975 in Torreon, a small city in northern Mexico. As a kid, he was interested in movies and media, so he graduated with a Communication Specialist bachelor's degree in 1996. After that, Ulises studied Film Language in Mexico City where he started his career as Multimedia Producer. In 1999 he moved to Saltillo, another small city in northern Mexico and with his partner Miguel Calderon started a company called Grupo W. Since then, Grupo W is positioned as the most important interactive agency in the country and the most awarded agency in festivals around the world. Ulises was also member of the interactive jury in competitions like Clio, Ojo de Iberoamerica, and FIAP.

Guillermo was appointed General Creative Director of Y&R Argentina in early 2004. He studied Graphic Design in UBA and started his ad career in Verdino Bates as Art Director, jr. Later he worked in Agulla & Baccetti and in 1997 joined Y&R. After a short time in Vega Olmos Ponce, he rejoined Y&R in 1999 as Art Director where, within a year, he was appointed Creative Director. Guillermo has been recognized with national and international awards such as: Cannes, FIAP, London Festival, New York Festival, Clio, British, One Show, El Ojo de Iberoamérica, Gramado, several Lápiz de Oro and Lapiz de Platino, among others. He has also been invited to be part of the jury in many international and regional festivals: Clio Awards, D&AD, FIAP, New York Festivals, Gramado, ACHAP, Eagle Awards, El Ojo de Iberoamérica.

Jorge Verdin was born in Los Angeles CA, and was raised in Tijuana, Mexico. He studied in the design program at San Diego City College, and received a B.A. in Graphic Design from Art Center College of Design. As a musician / producer, he is a member of the Nortec Collective with his music project Clorofila, and alongside Fritz Torres, is a member of Cha3, their ongoing design collaboration. Verdin works as an Art Director at Rubin Postear Associates in Santa Monica, CA. He has done freelance work for Razorfish, Rebeca Méndez Communication Design, Morphosis, Palm Pictures, Nacional Records, Virgin Records-Spain, Designworks USA, AOL, City Search, Ogilvy & Mather, Sci-Fi Channel, Go2Net, Art Center College of Design and others. As a musician, Verdin has performed with the Nortec Collective in the US, Mexico, South America, Europe and Japan, at festivals and venues as varied as nightclubs, art galleries, wrestling arenas, The Hollywood Bowl, and 100 capacity joints in desert towns. Last year, he was nominated for 2 Latin Grammys: Best Cover Design for his work on Nortec's "Tijuana sessions Vol. 3", and a group nomination for Best Alternative Album. Despite these achievements, he doesn't plan to quit his day job anytime soon.

Erik Vervroegen began his career as an Art Director in Belgium. Having been crowned Best Belgian Creative for several consecutive years, he decided to leave this environment, which had become too comfortable for him. Thoroughly convinced that discomfort encourages creativity, he threw himself into conquering South Africa. One year working at TBWA / HUNT LASCARIS was sufficient to propel him to the position of highest ranked creative in the country. Erik decided to follow Tony Granger to Bozell NY as Creative Director and helped to make Bozell one of the best creative agencies in the US by achieving 3rd place for "Agency of the Year" at the Cannes Awards in 2002. In January 2002, Erik Vervroegen became Executive Creative Director at TBWA / Paris. And in September 2003, President and Executive Creative Director. Erik himself has been voted 4 years running Best Creative Director in France. In 2005, the agency won 15 Cannes Lions, including the Press Grand Prix and was voted Agency of the Year for the 3rd year running. In 2006, after winning 15 Clios and its Grand Prix, TBWA / Paris was voted Agency of the Year at the Cannes Awards for an incredible 4th time.

Oliver Voss is a member of the board at Jung von Matt working on international clients like MINI Cooper, eBay and Europe's biggest tour operator, TUI. Being one of Germany's most awarded creatives he's listed third in the worldwide ranking in copywriters of Archive magazine. Oliver is also president of Miami Ad School Europe in Hamburg.

Jörg Waldschütz
Hybrid / Interactive

Ben Walker
Advertising

Jan Wilker
Graphic Design

Yanyan Yang
Hybrid / Interactive

David Yu
Hybrid / Interactive

Jörg Waldschütz has been working at NEUE DIGITALE, Frankfurt (Germany) since 2005 as Senior Art Director, where he is responsible primarily for Adidas. Before joining NEUE DIGITALE, Jörg Waldschütz worked as an Art Director at Scholz & Volkmer, Wiesbaden (Germany) where he was responsible for projects for Mercedes-Benz, ThyssenKrupp and Vogue.com. He has also worked as a freelance designer for various agencies such as Büro X, Hamburg, Ogilvy & Mather and Saatchi & Saatchi Healthcare, Frankfurt, and Neville Brody / Research Studios, London. He has won numerous national and international awards (among them Gold at the ADC Germany, Golden Cyberlion in Cannes, Grand Prix at Cresta Awards & Eurobest Awards, Grand Award at New York Festivals and Silver Clio Awards & Andy Awards) for his work and has recently been a member of the jury at The One Show in New York. Since 2006, Jörg Waldschütz also holds a lectureship position at Hochschule für Gestaltung in Karlsruhe.

Ben made so many bad McDonald's and Kellogg's ads that Burnett's fired him. He resurfaced at TBWA and now finds himself a Creative Director at Wieden + Kennedy London. He works mostly on Honda, Lurpak and Visit Wales with his partner of 17 years Mat. (By Partner he means work colleague, not spouse. Just to be clear.) They have won numerous awards which they use to spell out rude words like 'poo' (a Campaign Press Silver and two Creative Circle Golds). They won a Grandy once, but somebody stole the ring…didn't get their thieving hands on the money though.

A couple of years ago, Jan ran his own pathetic little design studio back in his homeland Germany. Then, in very late 2000, he and Icelander Hjalti Karlsson founded karlssonwilker inc., a design studio located in the heart of Manhattan. The two of them (plus one intern) are working on all sorts of projects and from time to time, there are parties on their backyard rooftop. Their work has appeared in various design publications and magazines and they have received numerous awards, because their parents are extremely rich and thus gave them the best design education available. A book on their studio, tellmewhy, that chronicles their first 24 months in business, was published by Princeton Architectural Press in 2003. Since then, nothing really changed. They continue to work with an eclectic list of clients, including A, the B, C, D, E, the F Club, G, H mag, I, J, and K.

Yanyan Yang is one of the most seasoned interactive creatives in Mainland China. After graduating from the Tsinghua Academy of Fine Arts in 1996, she soon found her passion for interactive design; her first job as an Art Director for an interactive design company was as early as 1996. In 1998 Yanyan started her career with Ogilvy & Mather advertising as Offline Art Director on the IBM account. When in the year 2000 Ogilvy started its interactive unit, Yanyan was the first to volunteer. Except for a recent short break with FCBi, she has been with Ogilvy for almost 6 years, now in the position as Interactive Creative Director for OgilvyOne Beijing. Over the past years Yanyan has worked on a number of different accounts, such as Audi, China Mobile, Motorola, IBM, Unilever and Bank of China J&J. Yanyan's sense for branding, her skills as art director and her passion for innovation has earned her respect with clients and colleagues, and brought her accolades at many local, regional and international award shows, including medals at DM, Asia, AdFest, Cannes and New York Festivals.

David Yu is a graphic designer working primarily in interactive design. Graduating with a Computer Science degree in 1995 from the University of British Columbia in Vancouver, he went on to study multimedia in 1996. Later that same year, he moved to New York to work for AGENCY.COM as a Junior Designer. David went on to work as Senior Designer for Nettmedia, building sites for such clients as BMG Entertainment and David Bowie. In 2000 David co-founded a small design studio called The Office for Fun and Profit, and was a guest speaker at the IdN Fresh Conference in Hong Kong. That same year David exhibited poster designs at the Nisen Exhibition in Tokyo and Osaka. In 2002 David became Art Director of Online Marketing at Rockstar Games, working on such titles as Grand Theft Auto, Max Payne and Midnight Club. In 2003 David moved from New York to Hong Kong, where he is currently freelancing. Past and current clients include The Body Shop Hong Kong, Lee Jeans Asia, Universal Music Hong Kong, Nokia Hong Kong, McDonald's China, Eric So, and Brothersfree, among others.

HYBRID /
ADC LXXXV

THE JUDGE
AWARDED 1
4 SILVER CUBES /
2 DISTINCTIVE MERIT
WINNERS /
5 MERIT WINNERS IN
THIS CATEGORY

GOLD CUBE /

Infect Truth / Merit / see page 39

Living Video / Merit / see page 40

Nike Cosplay / Silver / see page 32

Milk Aliens Campaign / Gold / see page 24

I think we've found good quality players in this factory.

ADC LXXXVI

Hybrid
Multi-channel / Campaign
Multiple Winner
see page 214

Silver
HP Hands

28

HP HANDS
Art Director
Pete Conolly, Stephen
Goldblatt
Copywriter
Mike McKay, Steve
Simpson, John Matejczyk
Creative Director
Rich Silverstein,
Steve Simpson
Other
Associate Creative
Director: Mike McKay,
Stephen Goldblatt
Agency
Goodby, Silverstein &
Partners
Client
Hewlett-Packard
Country
United States

HP launched "The computer
is personal again" campaign
to remind people their PC
was one of the most personal things they own, not merely a commodity. To shift this
perception, the campaign
reveals the personal con-
tents of the most interesting
and creative people in the
world. "The computer is personal again" campaign was
launched globally with a 60
second commercial, print
and online. Also, a media
"roadblock" was implement-
ed for the launch television
spot, ensuring it would be
seen on dozens of networks
at exactly the same time. The
campaign was also launched
in outdoor mediums around
the world. Since the cam-
paign was launched last
year, HP surpassed Dell in
global PC sales for the first
time in 10 years.

*
Hybrid
Multi-Channel / Campaign
Silver
HP Hands
+
Graphic Design
Television & Cinema Design
Art Direction / Campaign
Distinctive Merit
HP Hands

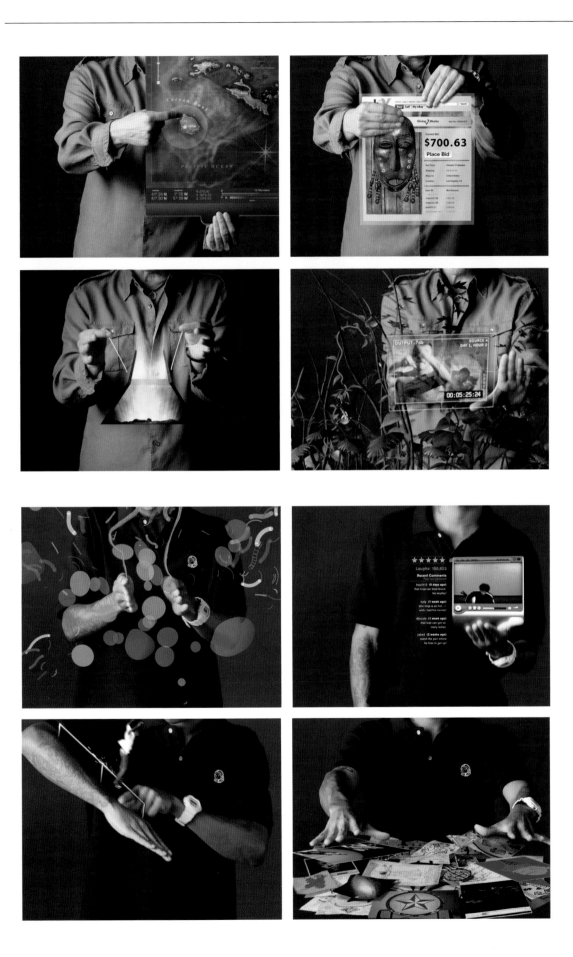

ADC LXXXVI

Hybrid
Other Professional / Single
Multiple Winner
see page 336

Silver
Nike+

30

NIKE+
Copywriter
Josh Bletterman,
Alison Hess
Creative Director
Kris Kiger, Nick Law,
Richard Ting, Gui Borchert,
Natalie Lam, Jill Nussbaum,
Michael Spiegel
Designer
Jeff Baxter, Wade Convay,
Gary Van Dzura, Ed Kim,
Michael Reger, Elena
Sakevich, Claudia Bernett,
Joe Tobens
Producer
Matt Howell, Brock Busby,
Daniel Jurow, James Kuo,
David Ross
Other
Technology Lead: Nick
Coronges, Technical
Director: Sean Lyons,
Programmer: Aaron
Ambrose, Noel Billig,
Matthias Hader, Asako
Kohno, William Lee, Michael
Mosley, Michael Piccuirro,
Geoffrey Roth, Ben
Sosinski, John Tubert, Stan
Wiechers, Quality
Assurance: Nauman Hafiz,
Michele Roman, August
Yang, Animator: Mark
Voelpel, Kiril Yeretsky
Agency
R/GA
Client
Nike
Country
United States

ADC LXXXVI

Hybrid
Multi-Channel /
Campaign

Silver
Nike Cosplay

32

NIKE COSPLAY

Art Director
Naoki Ito

Copywriter
Naoki Ito

Creative Director
Naoki Ito

Designer
Saiko Kamikanda

Director
Kan Eguchi

Producer
Shunsuke Kakinami, Takeshi
Fukuda, Yasutoshi Hosoike

Production Company
TYO, Root Communications

Other
Senior Creative Director:
Tatsuro Sato, Client
Supervisor: Mitsuhiro
Minowa, Technical Director:
Tohru Terashima

Agency
GT

Client
Nike Japan

Country
Japan

NIKEiD is an online service
for choosing the color of
every part of your shoe to
create a shoe unique to you.
However, the awareness of
NIKEiD was extremely low.
Starting with YouTube-
exclusive commercials, we
link up with reality in a new
viral campaign, "The Net
meets Reality"...A massive
blow to the lack of individuality in Japan.

ADC LXXXVI

Hybrid
Multi-Channel /
Campaign

Distinctive Merit
The City is Your Stadium

34

**THE CITY IS
YOUR STADIUM**
Art Director
Forsman & Bodenfors
Copywriter
Forsman & Bodenfors
Designer
Forsman & Bodenfors
Production Company
B-Reel
Agency
Forsman & Bodenfors
Client
Stadium
Country
Sweden

Stadium is one of Sweden's leading sports retail chains. Our objective was to emphasize the Stadium brand as a credible sports company with the most trendy, sporty and professional dealers on the market. The assignment was to realize Stadium's vision: to inspire and activate everyone to a healthy and active life. A second aspect was to get Stadium's target group accustomed to the fact that the web—in addition to the shops—is prominent channel for Stadium. We prepared a communicative platform The City Is Your Stadium with a brand-new concept for Stadium that stood out from that of the competition. The first campaign went under the theme Running and was aimed at inspiring people to test how easy and fun it is to be active. We designed a unique track for 33 different Swedish cities. The outdoor areas were physically used as signposts. All stations lead into the shop or to the campaign site (thecityisyourstadium.com). Maps over the 33 tracks were published on the campaign site alongside tips on suitable clothing for the day's local weather conditions.

TATE TRACKS
Art Director
Juan Cabral
Copywriter
Juan Cabral
Creative Director
Juan Cabral
Designer
Hugh Tarpey
Photographer
Jeremy Murch
Producer Art Buyer
Susie Morley & Sarah
Kavanagh
Other
Executive Creative Director:
Richard Flintham,
Production Manager:
Arjun Singh
Agency
Fallon London
Client
Tate Tracks
Country
United Kingdom

The brief was to bring 16 to 24 year olds to Tate Modern. That's how we created Tate Tracks: an experiment between art and music. We invited several music artists to walk around the Tate Modern to find a piece of work that would inspire them to write a music track. Chemical Brothers, Graham Coxon from Blur, Klaxons, Union of Knives, Roll Deep and many others came along. Each one of them chose an art piece that they felt inspired by. After recording the track in the studio, we released the song exclusively inside Tate Modern. We placed listening posts in front of the artworks, so people could listen to the tracks in the same place where they were originated.

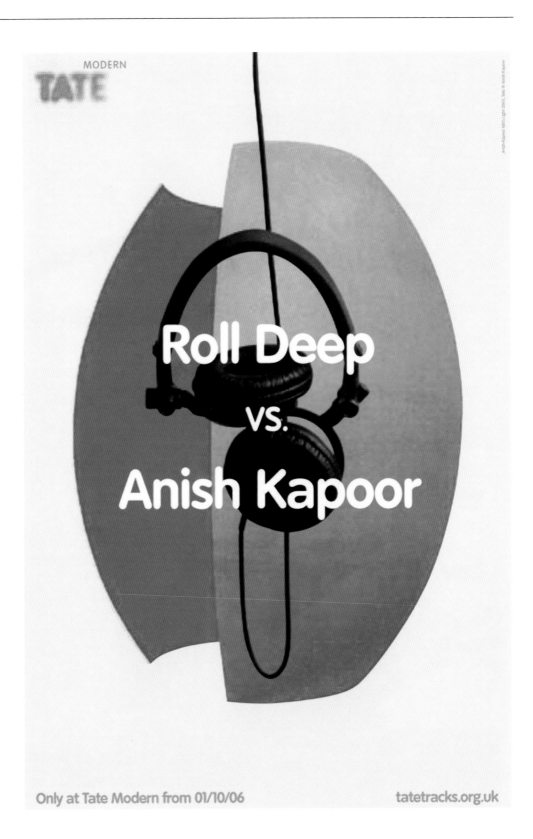

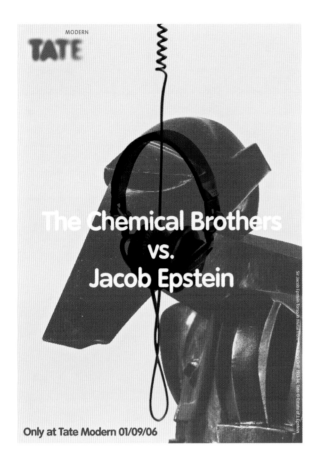

Tate Tracks

The Chemical Brothers vs. Jacob Epstein

This is the first in a series of original music tracks written about Tate Modern artworks.

Tate invited The Chemical Brothers to walk around the gallery and find a work of art that would inspire them to write a track.

In the end, it was Jacob Epstein's Torso in Metal from 'The Rock Drill' 1913-14 which grabbed their attention because it "just seemed so techno". They wanted to "capture the latent feeling of force that the figure has". This is the result.

There'll be a new original track original appearing in the gallery on the first day of every month. To find out what's coming up, visit www.tatetracks.org.uk

The Chemical Brothers – The Rock Drill
(p) 2006 Virgin Records Ltd
5 min 12 secs
Written by Rowlands / Simons
Published by Universal Music Publishing Limited

ADC LXXXVI

Hybrid
Multi-Channel /
Campaign

Merit
Das Taxi

38

DAS TAXI

Art Director
Bertrand Kirschenhofer,
Tim Schierwater
Copywriter
Ingmar Bartels,
Sebastian Behrendt
Creative Director
Lars Ruehmann, Ingo Fritz
Designer
Christoph Bielefeldt,
Stephanie Schneider,
Barbara Schirner
Other
Das Taxi: Christiane Moje
Nolte, Jo Ferschen, Ralf
Elfering, Anne Regine-Rach
Agency
Nordpol Hamburg Agentur
fuer Kommunikation GmbH
Client
Das Taxi
Country
Germany

Das Taxi attracts attention
with its own interpretation
of public transport insignia.
In subway and railway stations hangs a special map
next to the official plan of
the Hamburg passenger
transport authority. Every
street in Hamburg can be
found on the billboard. A
matching timetable booklet
is distributed to waiting
passengers and sent to all
relevant key customers. The
detailed timetable booklet
for Das Taxi is all in red, just
like the official public transport guide. Times, accurate
to the minute, services and
booking options are shown
for each and every street in
postcode region 20. The
Internet presence
(www.das-taxi.org) is also
modeled on the public
transport site.

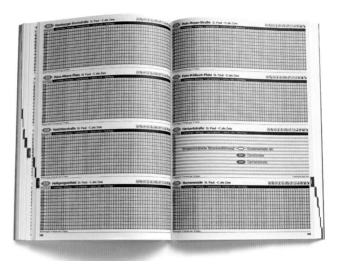

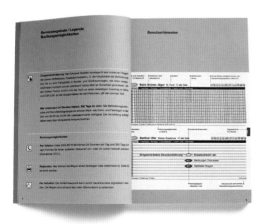

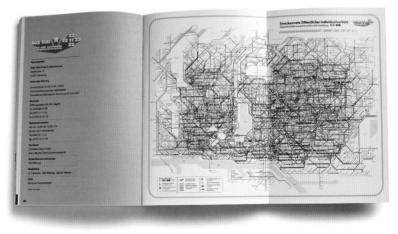

ADC LXXXVI

Hybrid
Viral Campaign, Non-Profit /
Campaign
Multiple Winner
see page 65

Merit
Infect Truth

39

INFECT TRUTH

Art Director
Meghan Siegal, Gabe
Jeffrey, Tim Mahoney,
Pamela Coatti , Adam
Larson, Kevin Grady,
Lee Einhorn, Mike Costello,
Rob Kottkamp, Jason
Ambrose, Doug Pedersen,
Keith Scott

Copywriter
Roger Baldacci, John
Kearse, Pete Harvey, Marc
Einhorn, Will Chambliss,
Matt Ledoux, Jake Mikosh,
Dustin Ballard, Mike
Howard, Guy Rooke,
Yutaka Tsujino

Creative Director
Pete Favat, Alex Bogusky,
John Kearse, Tom Adams,
Meghan Siegal

Designer
Web Designers: Meghan
Siegal, Ryan Habbyshaw,
Gabe Jeffrey, Max
Pfenninghaus, Cuban
Council

Director
Nicolai Fuglsig

Editor
Tom Scherma, Lawrence
Young

Producer
Sarah Spitz, Mary
Donington, Cindy Perez,
Sheri Radel, Barry
Frechette, Paul Fortuin,
Zach Jagentenfl, Kate
Sutherland, Bart Smith,
Dane Gorman

Production Company
MJZ, Bart Radio

Other
Cinematographer:
Joaquin Baca-Asay

Agency
Arnold Worldwide

Client
American Legacy
Foundation

Country
United States

Truth is about spreading
info to teenagers, so they
can make informed deci-
sions about smoking.
"Infect truth" helps those
kids take what they've
learned and pass it on in
rebellious ways. Knowledge
is contagious. Infect truth.

LIVING VIDEO

Art Director
Nina Zimmermann
Copywriter
Sebastian Oehme
Creative Director
Lorenz Ritter, Sven Klohk,
Ulrich Zuenkeler
Producer
Finn Gnoycke
Agency
Kolle Rebbe Werbeagentur
GmbH
Client
Google Germany GmbH
Country
Germany

At Google video, users can
find all sorts of films. That's
the message Google want-
ed to promote – with innovative advertising in
German cities like Berlin
and Hamburg. We therefore
had to teach billboards how
to display moving images.
How? By designing and
constructing special, large-
format frames with a win-
dowpane in the middle, to
resemble the Google Video
screen. Looking through the
frame turned everyday
street scenes into films. The
search terms in the dialog
box matched the location
and some of the possible
situations the billboard
would show, for example
"group of tourists" in front
of Berlin's landmark
Brandenburg Gate. The surroundings simply provided
the films in real time. Any
film you can imagine.

INCOGNITO DESIGN EXHIBITION

Art Director
Susanne Backer
Creative Director
Matthias Richter
Director
Susanne Backer
Producer
Syneo
Production Company
Tecnostand
Agency
Syneo
Client
Persol
Country
Italy

Incognito was an interactive exhibition about Persol, a premium Italian eyewear brand. The exhibition, "Persol Incognito," was part of a strategic activity to rejuvenate the brand. This event was set up at the Triennale, Milan's most prestigious art and design Museum. Incognito represented a milestone for Persol in experiential communication, and is now traveling around the world as a modular exhibition to support the new campaign.
After receiving a movie ticket, the visitor enters the exhibition space by passing through a "paparazzi wall," as a tribute to Persol's ongoing love story with the movie world. Triggering a motion sensor, each visitor finds himself unexpectedly immersed in a flashbulb thunderstorm, making him feel the spirit of a red carpet scenario. In the main space of the exhibition the visitor is immersed in a multimedia and multi-sensory experience that changes its atmosphere, light and sound scheme every four minutes — an exhibition which reveals its content in four acts. Each act gives the visitor the option to explore the Persol brand differently, according to the themes cinema, craftsmanship and production, the new collection, and the iconic model 649.

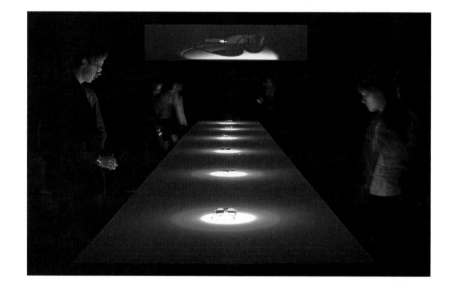

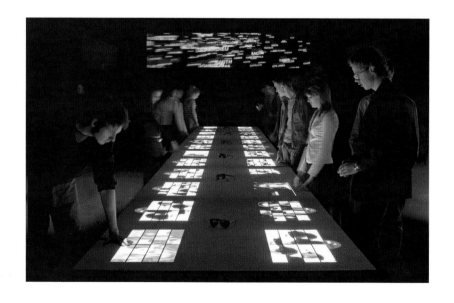

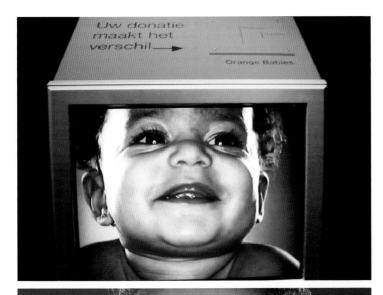

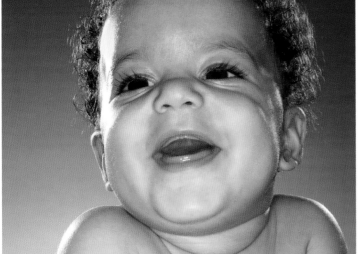

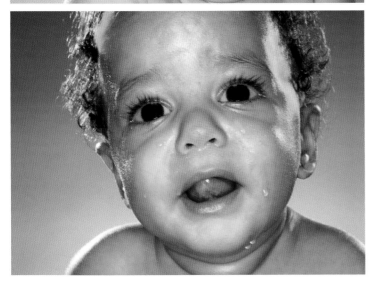

DONATION TV

<u>Art Director</u>
Deborah Bosboom
<u>Copywriter</u>
Tim den Heijer, Maxim van Wijk
<u>Creative Director</u>
Carl Le Blond
<u>Other</u>
Model maker: Jaap Hoogerdijk, Photographer: Jonathan Weyland
<u>Agency</u>
Ogilvy Groep Nederland
<u>Client</u>
Orange Babies
<u>Country</u>
Netherlands

The Orange Babies Foundation raised funds for babies in Africa infected with HIV during the Millionaire's Fair in Amsterdam. They took an unconventional approach. The stand featured a screen with a crying baby on it. But whenever a visitor would put in some coins or notes, the baby would stop crying and start smiling. Everything was focused on the motto: "Your donation makes the difference." Visitors approaching the stand also received the following message via Bluetooth: "Do you hear a baby crying? Let her smile again. Orange Babies."

ADVERTISING /
ADC <u>LXXXVI</u>

THE JUDGES HAVE AWARDED 6 GOLD CUBES / 12 SILVER CUBES / 10 DISTINCTIVE MERIT WINNERS / 94 MERIT WINNERS IN THIS CATEGORY.

Beard / Gold / see page 46

Paint / Silver / see page 56

The Love Story Series / Gold / see page 48

Trade / Gold / see page 47

Head / Silver / see page 62

Beautiful Day / Merit / see page 78

Tate Collections / Gold / see page 50

Sundial / Silver / see page 64

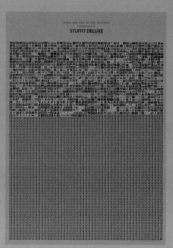

Compress Everything / Distinctive Merit / see page 74

The Wrong Working Environment Campaign / Merit / see page 136

Shapes / Merit / see page 137

BEARD, TRADE, LEAK
Art Director
Craig Allen (Beard), Scott Vitrone (Trade, Leak)
Copywriter
Eric Kallman (Beard), Ian Reichenthal (Trade, Leak)
Creative Director
Gerry Graf, Ian Reichenthal, Scott Vitrone
Director
Tom Kuntz
Editor
Gavin Cutler
Producer
Lora Schulson
Production
Company MJZ
Agency
TBWA\Chiat\Day
Client
Skittles
Country
United States

"**Beard**" A man with a long beard is sitting at a desk being interviewed for a job by a woman. There is a jar of Skittles on the woman's desk. Throughout the spot the man's beard is picking up Skittles one at a time and feeding them to the man. The woman is looking over the man's resume. **WOMAN: Good…… Good……You're in Mansfield?** MAN: Uh huh. **W: I have a cousin from Mansfield.** M: That's nice. The man's beard continues to feed the man Skittles one at a time. **W: Your resume looks good, but we're looking for someone with more experience.** The man's beard then feeds the woman a Skittle and begins gently caressing her cheek. M: Experience…ha ha ha…ah, funny. The man's beard then picks up another skittles and flips it into the man's mouth. Cut to Skittles end treatment. *Super/AVO: Share the rainbow. Taste the rainbow.*

*
Advertising
Television & Cinema
Commercials TV: 30 Seconds /
Single
Gold
Beard
+
Advertising
Television & Cinema
Commercials TV: 30 Seconds /
Single
Gold
Trade
+
Advertising
Television & Cinema
Commercials TV: Spots of
Varying Length (one
Campaign Per Entry) /
Campaign
Gold
Beard, Trade, Leak

"Trade" Open on a guy at his friend's backyard. The guy is holding a bag of Skittles. His friend is holding a rabbit that is singing in an operatic voice. **RABBIT: Yaaaaaa yaaaaa yaaaaaaaaaaaa….** The friend trades the rabbit for the guy's Skittles. Cut to the guy at home that night. It's dark. The rabbit is in a cage nearby, singing at the top of its lungs. The guy looks miserable. **R: Yaaaaaa yaaaaaa yaaaaaaaaaaaa….** He realizes he's made a bad trade. Cut to the guy running through the rain, carrying the singing rabbit. He arrives at his friend's house. The guy looks in through the window of his friend's house and sees his friend eating and enjoying the bag of Skittles in front of a fire. The guy looks inside at his friend. Then down at the wet, annoying rabbit. **R: Yaaaaaa yaaaaaa yaaaaaaaaaaaa….**The guy realizes even more so that he's made a bad trade. The rabbit stops singing for a moment and bites the guy's hand. Then runs away. **R: (Getting quieter as it runs off into the distance) Yaaaaaa yaaaaaa yaaaaaaaaaaaa….** Cut to Skittles end treatment. *Super/AVO: Treasure the rainbow. Taste the rainbow.*

"Leak" Open on a homeowner and a contractor standing in a suburban house. There's a rainbow-colored stain on the ceiling, and one-by-one, Skittles drip from it. The contractor studies the situation. He reaches out his hand and catches one of the falling Skittles. He tastes it. **CONTRACTOR: Oh yeah. You got yourself a Skittles leak.** HOMEOWNER: Can you fix it? **C: Sure.** The contractor bends down and reaches into a satchel. He pulls out two small handles and a drill. He quickly drills the two handles into the ceiling, next to one another. Then, he reaches into his satchel and pulls out a small man. He lifts up the small man, and the small man grabs onto the handles and hangs from the ceiling. When Skittles drip from the ceiling, the small man catches them in his mouth and swallows them. **H: That's how you fix it? C: That's how we fix it.** SMALL MAN: That's it. The contractor and the small man laugh. Cut to Skittles end treatment. *Super/AVO: Catch the rainbow. Taste the rainbow.*

ADC LXXXVI

Advertising
Television & Cinema
Commercials Online
Commercial / Single

Gold
The Love Story Series

48

**THE LOVE
STORY SERIES**

Art Director
Jureeporn Thaidumrong
Copywriter
Jureeporn Thaidumrong
Creative Director
Jureeporn Thaidumrong
Director
Thanonchai Sornsrivichai
Editor
Manop Boonvipas
Producer
Angsana Promprasert
Production
Company Phenomena
Agency
Jeh United Ltd.
Client
SmoothE Co.,Ltd.
Country
Thailand

We adapted the idea from
a classic Thai selling
method—free outdoor
cinema that sells a product
during a show. So we created "The Love Story" series
of 4 episodes that appeal to
a younger age group and
sell the product, and also
poke fun on a conventional
"beauty" commercial.

Smooth E, babyface foam. Non-Ionic, Soap free.

He would do anything for the one he loves.

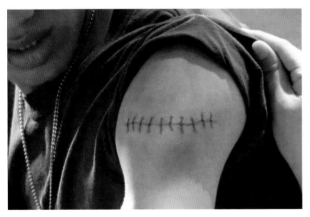

But don't forget Smooth E...

happiness with brightened face and love.

ADC LXXXVI
    Advertising
Advertising Posters &
Billboards Public Service /
Non-Profit / Educational
    Gold
Tate Collections
    50

TATE COLLECTIONS
Art Director
Juan Cabral
Copywriter
Juan Cabral
Creative Director
Richard Flintham
Producer
Print Production: Arjun
Singh
Other
Typographer / Designer:
Ginny Carrel, Account
Supervisor: Chris Kay
Agency
Fallon London
Client
Tate Britain
Country
United Kingdom

The idea was to change
the perception of Tate
Britain and invite people to
experience the Gallery in
their own terms. We generated 20 different 'tours'
("I'm Hungover," "I'm happi-
ly depressed," "I Like yellow," etc). At the same time
we made different posters
to promote this idea. Each
poster suggested different
moods and worked as an
invitation to the museum.
The posters were made to
work as cross-tracks so
people could read in train
platforms and experience a
journey in their heads.

The **I HAVE A BIG MEETING** Collection

Meetings, meetings, meetings... all of them important, all of them crucial. How crazy is today's world? Anyway, if you need a hand with a meeting, this Tate Britain Collection is designed to help you look good and ooze confidence. Lesson number one: important matters should be treated as small matters. In Room 6, *Harvest Home* by John Linnell should help you achieve this state of mind. You can almost breathe the fresh air from a stunning golden afternoon. Fill your lungs with its greatness, and always remember to make yourself bigger before entering a room. Now it's time to take a look at a champion. *Teucer* by Sir Hamo Thornycroft, near the Millbank entrance, portrays one of the heroes of Homer's Trojan War. This monumental bronze archer teaches us to never lose focus on what we're aiming for. Now we need to work on your look. Eyes are the most powerful weapons in meetings. Stare at the portrait of *Queen Elizabeth I* in Room 2. Study her eyes and her pose because she's the model to follow. Don't even dare leave the room until you've nailed that look. Finally, spend some time in front of *The Battle of Camperdown* by Philip De Loutherbourg. This breathtaking sea battle dominates Room 9 completely. Meetings are often a lot like this, but take heart from the fact that this painting still depicts the precise moment of victory. So off you pop bravery's the name of the game, and remember, for maximum effect, we suggest you experience this Collection twenty-four hours prior to your meeting.

Create your own Collection

Admission Free   ⊖ Pimlico
www.tate.org.uk   🚢 Millbank Pier

British Art Displays 1500 – 2006
Supported by BP

BRITAIN
TATE

The **I'M HUNGOVER** Collection

OK. Right now you're in a very particular emotional state. We understand, so we've put together a mini Collection for you with lots of stops for a sit down. Firstly, we need to run a check on you. Are we talking about a *Cholmondeley Ladies* hangover or a *Heads of Six of Hogarth's Servants* hangover? A *Cholmondeley Ladies* hangover is fine as it is a portrait of identical twins and means you are just seeing double. The other is slightly more serious as Hogarth painted six portraits swirling around on a single canvas, and if this is what your head feels like then you're in trouble. If you are feeling some guilt, a visit to the Vatican might help redeem your soul. Have a look at Richard Wilson's picture of the Vatican in Room 6, showing a splendid morning view from a hill above the Tiber. (Stand still until you see just one Vatican). Now, let's ease your headache. What you need is a strong dose of the *The Plains of Heaven* by John Martin in Room 9. This hypnotizing image oozes tranquillity and harmony, whilst the blissful landscape represents salvation. You should be feeling better now. Just to make sure that the symptoms are completely gone, we need to run another quick check. The painting of *The Cock Tavern* in Room 7 is a good test as it portrays a classic English country pub. If you can bear to stare at it for a decent amount. of time, it means you're cured. Don't get any ideas about going out again though; it's an eight o'clock bedtime for you tonight.

Create your own Collection

Admission Free   ⊖ Pimlico
www.tate.org.uk   ⚓ Millbank Pier

British Art Displays 1500 – 2006
Supported by BP

BRITAIN

TATE

The **I'VE JUST SPLIT UP** Collection

We know how it feels. You don't even want to wake up in the morning. Your confidence has taken a bit of a knock and we understand. So much so we've prepared a little Collection to cheer you up. Especially, since you have a little more time on your hands now. (Sorry). Ready to feel better? First, stand in front of the Pre-Raphaelite masterpiece *Ophelia from Hamlet* by Millais. See? Someone else went through that too. Her loneliness should make you feel... less lonely, strangely enough. Maybe it's not the end of the world for you. Actually, you should look at the monumental *The Last Judgement* by John Martin in Room 9. Now, that is the end of the world, quite literally. This painting will help you put things in perspective, so no more sobbing, alright? Now we should talk about your future. Think about it, you're facing a moment of endless possibilities, a bit like Simon Patterson's contemporary work *The Great Bear* in Room 26. (You know, the one with the underground map.) It means that anything can happen. So comb your hair because you never know who's around. Now, you're ready for a Turner Stand in front of *Sunrise, with a Boat between Headlands*. Its highlights represent the idea of a bright new beginning. Everything will be okay. And remember, we're always here for you (10.00 – 17.50 daily).

Create your own Collection

Admission Free   ⊖ Pimlico
www.tate.org.uk   ⚓ Millbank Pier

British Art Displays 1500 – 2006
Supported by BP

BRITAIN

TATE

ICONS (1)

Art Director
Philip Bonnery

Copywriter
Brian Ahern

Creative Director
Tony Granger, Jan Jacobs,
Leo Premutico

Agency
Saatchi & Saatchi

Client
42 Below Vodka

Country
United States

*
Advertising
Advertising Posters &
Billboards Wild Postings /
Campaign
Gold
Icons (1)
+
Advertising
Print Advertising Newspaper,
Consumer, Less Than a Full
Page / Single
Merit
Transvestite
+
Advertising
Print Advertising Magazine,
Consumer, Less Than a Full
Page / Campaign
Merit
Icons (1)
+
Advertising
Print Advertising Magazine,
Consumer, Less Than a Full
Page / Single
Merit
Government Eavesdropping
+
Advertising
Print Advertising Magazine,
Consumer, Less Than a Full
Page / Single
Merit
Bareback Mountain
+
Advertising
Print Advertising Magazine,
Consumer, Less Than a Full
Page / Single
Merit
Wedding
+
Advertising
Advertising Posters &
Billboards Wild Postings /
Single
Merit
Bareback
Mountain Advertising Posters
& Billboards Wild Postings /
Single
+
Advertising
Print Advertising Magazine,
Consumer, Less Than a Full
Page / Single
Merit
Sheep
+
Advertising
Advertising Magazine,
Consumer, Less Than a Full
Page / Single
Merit
Transvestite

+
Advertising
Advertising Posters &
Billboards Promotional /
Single
Merit
Flight Attendant
+
Advertising
Advertising Posters &
Billboards Promotional /
Single
Merit
Government Eavesdropping
+
Advertising
Advertising Posters &
Billboards Promotional /
Single
Merit
Sheep
+
Advertising
Advertising Posters &
Billboards Promotional /
Single
Merit
Transvestite
+
Advertising
Advertising Posters &
Billboards Wild Postings /
Single
Merit
Flight Attendant
+
Advertising
Advertising Posters &
Billboards Wild Postings /
Single
Merit
Government Eavesdropping
+
Advertising
Advertising Posters &
Billboards Wild Postings /
Single
Merit
Office Party Blackout
+
Advertising
Advertising Posters &
Billboards Wild Postings /
Single
Merit
President Bush
+
Advertising
Advertising Posters &
Billboards Wild Postings /
Single
Merit
Sheep
+
Advertising
Advertising Posters &
Billboards Wild Postings /
Single
Merit
Sheep
+
Advertising
Advertising Posters &
Billboards Wild Postings /
Single
Merit
Transvestite
+
Advertising
Advertising Posters &
Billboards Wild Postings /
Single
Merit
Do it Yourself

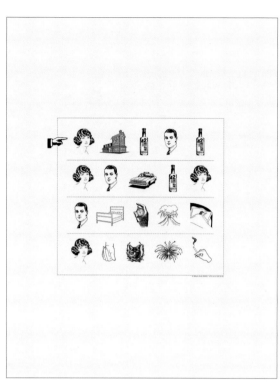

ADC LXXXVI

Advertising
Advertising Posters &
Billboards Wild Postings /
Campaign

Gold
Icons (1)

53

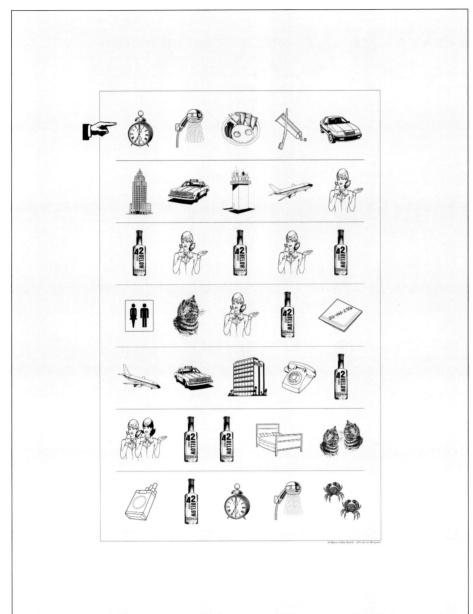

**HEART-TO-HEART,
FEVER, VIDEOGAME,
GRACE, DINNER**

Art Director
Jeff Anderson
Copywriter
Isaac Silverglate
Creative Director
Gerry Graf, Ian Reichenthal,
Scott Vitrone
Director
Martin Granger
Editor
Tom Scherma
Producer
Lora Schulson
Production Company
Moxie Pictures
Agency
TBWA\Chiat\Day
Client
Combos
Country
United States

*
Advertising
Television & Cinema
Commercials TV:
30 Seconds / Campaign
Silver
Heart to Heart, Fever,
Videogame
+
Advertising
Television & Cinema Crafts
Copywriting / Campaign
Silver
Heart to Heart, Fever,
Videogame
+
Advertising
Television & Cinema
Commercials TV:
30 Seconds / Single
Distinctive Merit
Fever
+
Advertising
Television & Cinema
Commercials TV:
30 Seconds / Single
Distinctive Merit
Video Game
+
Advertising
Television & Cinema
Commercials TV:
30 Seconds / Single
Distinctive Merit
Grace
+
Advertising
Television & Cinema
Commercials TV:
Under 30 Seconds / Single
Merit
Dinner
+
Advertising
Television & Cinema
Commercials TV:
30 Seconds / Single
Merit
Heart to Heart

"Heart-To-Heart" A very manly-looking mother (Man Mom) stands in the kitchen eating Cheddar Cheese Pretzel Combos. Her grown-up son walks up to her—he looks upset. **SON: Got a sec, mom? MAN MOM: Yeah. S: (Heartfelt) There's some stuff going on at work. All the guys think that I'm never going to make anything of myself. I feel like they're all better than me… Maybe I should just quit.** He waits for his mom's response. MM: (Holding a Combos and studying it) How do you think they get the cheese inside that little pretzel? …I'm going to lay down. Man Mom leaves the room. Cut to Combos end treatment. *VO: Combos. What your mom would feed you if your mom were a man.*

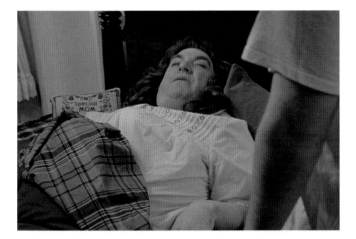

"**Fever**" An adult son walks into his mother's room at night. The mother is a very manly-looking woman: a Man Mom. The son turns the light on and she wakes up. The son is drenched in sweat. **SON: Mom? MAN MOM: What's your problem? S: (Sniffles) I think I have a fever.** Man Mom puts her hand against his forehead. **MM: You're just hungry. Here...** Man Mom takes an open bag of Pizzeria Pretzel Combos off the nightstand and gives them to her son. **MM:...these have pizza stuff in 'em.** The son eats a few Combos. Man Mom turns back over in bed. **MM: Hit the lights on your way out.** The son walks out and hits the lights. **MM: Love ya!** Cut to Combos end treatment. *VO: Combos. What your mom would feed you if your mom were a man.*

"**Video Game**" A very manly-looking mother (Man Mom) sits with her grown up son playing a video game. Her other son sits nearby, watching and eating Combos. Man Mom is viciously beating her son at the game. There's a bag of Pizzeria Pretzel Combos on the table in front of them. *SFX: Video game punches.* Mom wins and tosses down her controller. The son reaches for the bag of Combos on the table. Man Mom pushes the bag away from him, and takes some Combos herself. **MAN MOM: These are for winners.** Man Mom eats the Combos in front of her son. Cut to Combos end treatment. *VO: Combos. What your mom would feed you if your mom were a man.*

PAINT

Art Director
Juan Cabral, Richard
Flintham, Jonathan Glazer

Copywriter
Juan Cabral, Richard
Flintham, Jonathan Glazer

Creative Director
Juan Cabral

Director
Jonathan Glazer

Editor
Paul Watts

Producer
Kirsty Burns, Nicky Barnes

Production Company
Academy

Other
Executive Creative Director:
Richard Flintham

Agency
Fallon London

Client
Sony Bravia

Country
United Kingdom

· Toryglen, Glasgow 2006
· 70,000 litres of paint
· 1700 detonators
· 622 bottle bombs
· 455 mortars
· 330 meters of steel pipe
· 57 km of copper wire
· Colour like no other

ADC LXXXVI

Advertising
Television & Cinema
Commercials TV: Over 30
Seconds / Single

Silver
I Feel Pretty

58

I FEEL PRETTY

Art Director
Mira Kaddoura

Copywriter
Sheena Brady

Creative Director
Steve Luker, Alberto Ponte

Director
Ivan Zacharias

Producer
Robyn Boardman

Production Company
Smuggler

Editor
Filip Malasek

Agency
Wieden+Kennedy

Client
Nike

Country
United States

The spot is about the duality of Maria being pretty and a kick ass athlete.

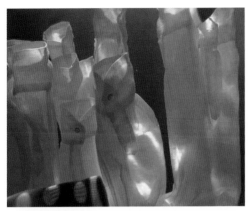

UNDERWATER WORLD
Art Director
Antonio Cortesi
Copywriter
Francesco Simonetti
Creative Director
Enrico Dorizza
Director
Dario Piana
Editor
Michele Mortara
Producer
Agency Producer:
Renato Lamberti
Production Company
Film Master
Other
CDP Producer: Karim
Bartoletti
Agency
Leo Burnett Co S.r.l.
Client
Indesit Company
Country
Italy

Advertising
Television & Cinema Crafts
Art Direction / Single
Silver
Underwater World
+
Advertising
Television & Cinema Crafts
Special Effects / Single
Distinctive Merit
Underwater World
+
Advertising
Television & Cinema
Commercials TV: Over 30
Seconds / Single
Merit
Underwater World

REAL MEN OF GENIUS:
MR. REALLY LOUD
CELL PHONE GUY,
MR. REALLY BIG GOLF
CLUB MAKER,
MR. HAIR
GEL OVER GEL-ER,
MR. HOT DOG EATING
CONTEST
CONTESTANT,
MR. ENORMOUS SUV
DRIVER,
MR. HOLIDAY GIFT
RE-GIFTER,
MR. PROFESSIONAL
SPORTS LEG CRAMP
RUBBER OUTER

Copywriter
Aaron Pendleton, Jeb
Quaid

Creative Director
Group CD: Mark Gross,
Associate CD: Chuck
Rachford, Chris Roe

Editor
Audio Engineer:
Dave Gerbosi

Producer
Senior Producer:
Will St. Clair

Production Company
Chicago Recording
Company

Other
Composer: Sandy Torano
(Scandal Music)

Agency
DDB Chicago

Client
Anheuser-Busch

Country
United States

"Mr. Really Loud Cell Phone Guy" ANNCR: Bud Light presents… Real Men of Genius. SINGER: Real Men of Genius! A: Today we salute you, Mr. Really Loud Cell Phone Talker Guy! S: Mr. Really Loud Cell Phone Talker Guy! A: Ignoring the latest advances of cell phone technology, you bark into your phone as if you were communicating with two cans and a string. S: You're breaking up now! A: Discussing your cousin's intestinal problems during a quiet dinner party? Unacceptable. Discussing them on a cell phone during a quiet dinner party? Perfectly acceptable. S: Can you keep a secret?! A: Nothing screams "I'm important" more than a man who screams "I'm important" into his cell phone. S: Did I mention I'm important? A: So crack open a nice cold Bud Light oh Duke of the Decibel. Because when we need a friend, you're the one we call. S: Mr. Really Loud Cell Phone Talker Guy! A: Bud Light Beer, Anheuser-Busch, St. Louis, Missouri.

"Mr. Really Big Golf Club Maker" ANNCR: Bud Light presents… Real Men of Genius. SINGER: Real Men of Genius! A: Today we salute you, Mr. Really Big Golf Club Maker. SINGER: Mr. Really Big Golf Club Maker! A: Shanks, duffs, banana-balls and worm-burners… We can't break a hundred… and we're pretty sure it's the equipment's fault. S: Stupid, stupid clubs! A: Forget flash-in-the-pan trends like 'lessons' and 'practice'. You gave golfers what we really need: a sweet spot the size of a compact car. S: Sweet like candy! A: Thanks to you, we're no longer slicing the ball 200 yards into the woods, we're slicing it 300 yards into the woods. SINGERS: Baaaaaalll! A: So crack open an ice cold Bud Light, oh titan of the Titanium. We still can't hit the side of a barn. But thanks to you, we can swing one. S: Mr. Really Big Golf Club Maker! A: Bud Light Beer, Anheuser-Busch, St. Louis Missouri.

"Mr. Hair Gel Over Gel-er" ANNCR: Bud Light presents Real Men of Genius. SINGER: Real Men of Genius! A: Today we salute you, Mr. Hair Gel Over Gel-er SINGER: Mr. Hair Gel Over Gel-er! A: Less ambitious men stop with two in one shampoo. But you put in countless hours, tireless dedication, and a five-gallon drum of industrial adhesive. S: Sticky goo! A: Like a lacquered hedgehog or oily porcupine, what woman wouldn't want to run her fingers through your razor-sharp stalagmites of hair? S: Or is it stalactites? A: Wind, water, stray bullets… even repeated hammer blows… Nothing can muss your immovable mane. S: I got a hair helmet! A: So crack open an ice-cold Bud Light Oh Master of the Moose. And while you're at it, crack open another bucket of goo. S: Mr. Hair Gel Over Gel-er! A: Bud Light Beer, Anheuser Busch St. Louis Missouri.

"Mr. Hot Dog Eating Contest Contestant" ANNCR: Bud Light presents Real Men of Genius SINGER: Real Men of Genius. A: Today we salute you Mr. Hot Dog Eating Contest Contestant. S: Mr. Hot Dog Eating Contest Contestant. A: What does it take to eat two dozen hot dogs in twelve minutes? Determination, fortitude, and a complete disregard for what they actually put in a hot dog. S: Open wide! A: How many times have we said: Sure one hot dog is nice, but forty-seven more would really hit the spot? S: Get me to a bathroom! A: What's for desert? Nine pounds of antacids, one bleeding ulcer, and seven hours of routine angioplasty. S: My left arm feels tingly! A: So crack open an ice-cold Bud Light oh Diplomat of the Dog. Because our appetite for you will never be satisfied. S: Mr. Hot Dog Eating Contest Contestant. A: Bud Light Beer, Anheuser Busch St. Louis Missouri.

"Mr. Enormous SUV Driver" ANNCR: Bud Light presents Real Men of Genius SINGER: Real Men of Genius. A: Today we salute you, Mr. Enormous SUV Driver. S: Mr. Enormous SUV Driver! A: Your mammoth machine strikes the perfect balance between the towing capacity of a tractor-trailer, and the sleek styling...of a tractor-trailer. S: Keep on truckin'! ANNCR: Lesser men might say a 26-cylinder engine is overkill. But some day they'll have to tow a cruise ship into dry dock... and that's when they'll come crying to you. S: I got the towing package! A: You've got a tough choice to make—fill up the tank, or relieve the national debt. SINGERS: Fill 'er up! ANNCR: So truck on home and grab a Bud Light, Mr. Enormous SUV Guy. If you're going to compensate for something small, go really, really big. S: Mr. Enormous SUV Driver! A: Bud Light Beer, Anheuser Busch St. Louis Missouri.

"Mr. Professional Sports Leg Cramp Rubber Outer" ANNCR: Bud Light presents Real Men of Genius SINGER: Real Men of Genius. A: Today we salute you Mr. Professional Sports Leg Cramp Rubber Outer... S: Mr. Professional Sports Leg Cramp Rubber Outer ... A: Most men dream of one day playing in front of 60,000 fans. Your dream: giving another man a tender thigh massage in front of 60,000 fans. S: Look at me! A: When you snap on the surgical gloves and start rubbing, you tell the world: this is the part of my job my parents don't tell their friends about. S: Utterly embarrassed! A: Deep thigh bruises, no problem. But if someone has a groin pull? Well, he'll have to take that into his own hands. SINGERS: Rub, rub rub it out! A: So crack open an ice cold Bud Light, oh Healer of the Hamstring, because you'll never rub us the wrong way. S: Mr. Professional Sports Leg Cramp Rubber Outer... A: Bud Light Beer, Anheuser-Busch, St. Louis, Missouri.

Advertising
Radio Advertising Over 30 Seconds / Single
Silver
Genius /Mr. Really Loud Cell Phone Guy
+
Advertising
Radio Advertising Over 30 Seconds / Single
Silver
Genius/Mr. Really Big Golf Club Maker
+
Advertising
Radio Advertising Over 30 Seconds / Single
Silver
Genius/Mr. Hair Gel Over Gel-er
+
Advertising
Radio Advertising Over 30 Seconds / Campaign
Silver
Genius / Cell Phone, Golf Club, Hot Dog
+
Advertising
Radio Advertising Over 30 Seconds / Single
Merit
Genius / Mr. Hot Dog Eating Contest Contestant
+
Advertising
Radio Advertising Over 30 Seconds / Single
Merit
Genius / Mr. Enormous SUV Driver
+
Advertising
Radio Advertising Over 30 Seconds / Single
Merit
Genius / Mr. Holiday Gift Re-Gifter
+
Advertising
Radio Advertising Over 30 Seconds / Single
Merit
Genius / Mr. Professional Sports Leg Cramp Rubber Outer

HEAD
Art Director
Sebastien Vacherot,
Jessica Gerard-Huet,
Loic Cardon, Ingrid Varetz,
Gregory Barry
Copywriter
Sebastien Vacherot,
Jessica Gerard-Huet,
Loic Cardon, Ingrid Varetz,
Gregory Barry
Creative Director
Erik Vervroegen
Photographer
Yann Robert
Other
3D: Baptiste Masse
Agency
TBWA \ Paris
Client
Sony Playstation
Country
France

*
Advertising
Print Advertising Magazine,
Consumer,
Spread / Single
Silver
Head
+
Advertising
Advertising Posters &
Billboards Point-of-Purchase /
Single
Silver
Head

ADC LXXXVI

Advertising
Advertising Posters &
Billboards Outdoor/
Billboard / Single

Silver
Sundial

64

SUNDIAL

Art Director
Vince Cook

Copywriter
Gary Fox-Robertson

Creative Director
Mark Tutssel, John
Montgomery

Other
Chief Creative Officer:
John Condon

Agency
Leo Burnett

Client
McDonald's

Country
United States

To showcase the
McDonald's breakfast
menu throughout different
times of the morning, an
accurate working sundial
was designed.

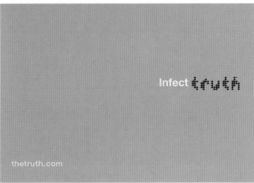

SINGING COWBOY

Art Director
Adam Larson, Kevin Grady
Copywriter
Roger Baldacci, John
Kearse
Creative Director
Pete Favat, Alex Bogusky,
John Kearse, Tom Adams
Director
Nicolai Fuglsig
Editor
Lawrence Young
Producer
Sarah Spitz, Mary
Donington, Kate Sutherland
Production Company
MJZ
Agency
Arnold Worldwide
Client
American Legacy
Foundation
Country
United States

"Singing Cowboy" VIDEO: We open on a NY city street. We see a man dressed as a cowboy riding a horse. He is followed by a man pulling a donkey. They both stop near a busy intersection and sit down at a campfire. AUDIO: *Car horns honking. Horse hooves on pavement.* VIDEO: The sidekick strums the guitar to get people's attention. The singing cowboy removes the red bandanna around his throat to reveal a small hole in his neck. He has had a laryngectomy. He begins to sing through the hole in his neck. The cowboy sings while the sidekick plays guitar. The lyrics appear as supers at the bottom of the screen. An asterisk bounces on every word as it's sung. **AUDIO: You don't always die from tobacco. Sometimes you just lose a lung. Oh, you don't always die from tobacco. Sometimes they just snip out your tongue. And you won't sing worth a heck, With a big hole in your neck Cuz you don't always die from tobacco Cuz you don't always die from tobacco.** VIDEO: We cut to shot of an orange sign that's slung over the donkey. It reads: over 8.5 million Americans live with tobacco related illnesses. We see people's reactions to the song and the sign. Asterisks appear over a crowd shot of people's heads. AUDIO: *(COWBOY) Yippee Kai-o!* ART CARD: **Knowledge is contagious.* ART CARD: *Infect truth.*

ADC LXXXVI

Advertising
Television & Cinema
Commercials TV: Over 30
Seconds / Single

Distinctive Merit
Endure

66

ENDURE
Art Director
Paulo Martins
Copywriter
Oliver Frank
Creative Director
Alvaro Sotomayor, Mark
Hunter
Director
Lance Acord, Joaquin
Baca-Asay
Editor
Adam Pertofsky
Producer
Lalou Dammond
Production Company
Park Pictures
Other
Agency Producer:
Elissa Singstock,
Veronika Kaufmann
Agency
Wieden+Kennedy
Amsterdam
Client
Nike
Country
Netherlands

Endure portrays athletes
overcoming both the mental
and physical pain of sport.
Moments many athletes
endure in order to reach the
high levels of excellence
and success within their
sports. Ending with the ultimate payoff of Nike Air
cushioning, helping to soft-
en the physical impact on
your body, a little. The aim
was to reintroduce the performance benefits of Air to
athletes: Air is an invitation
for us to perform longer,
harder, faster, higher.

A LITTLE LESS HURT

HAPPINESS FACTORY

Creative Director
Rick Condos, Hunter
Hindman
Designer
Todd Mueller,
Kylie Matulick, Ben Chan
Director
Todd Mueller,
Kylie Matulick
Producer
Boo Wong
Production Company
PSYOP
Other
Executive Producer: Justin
Booth Clibborn, Lead 3D
Artist: Joe Burrascano,
Animation Director: Kevin
Estey, Technical Director:
Josh Harvey, 3D Team: Kyle
Mohr, Miles Southan, Boris
Ustaev, Dan Vislocky, Chris
Bach, Clay Budin, David
Chontos, Tom Cushwa, Josh
Frankel, Jonathan Garin,
Scott Hubbard, Jaye Kim,
Joon Lee, Paul Liaw, Joerg
Liebold, David Lobser,
Dylan Maxwell, Naomi
Nishimura, Ylli Orana, Matte
Painter: Dylan Cole, Lead
Flame Artist: Eben Mears,
Editor: Cass Vanini
Agency
Wieden+Kennedy
Amsterdam, PSYOP
Client
The Coca-Cola Company
Country
United States

Coke and Wieden+Kennedy
Amsterdam asked PSYOP
to imagine the world inside
an average Coke vending
machine. We created a mag-
ical land where deliciously
twisted creatures labor to
fulfill their destinies by
infusing joy into each bottle
of Coke. The tiny denizens
of the Happiness Factory
craft and launch a Coke
whenever currency is insert-
ed. The challenge was to
deliver on "Happiness" with
both character designs and
storytelling whilst never
making it saccharine.

*
Advertising
Television & Cinema Crafts
Animation / Single
Distinctive Merit
Happiness Factory
+
Advertising
Television & Cinema
Commercials TV: Over 30
Seconds / Single
Merit
Happiness Factory

ADC LXXXVI

Advertising
Television & Cinema
Commercials TV: Public
Service / Non-Profit / Single

Distinctive Merit
No Spot Film Festival

70

**NO SPOT
FILM FESTIVAL**
Art Director
Jaclyn Rink
Copywriter
Chris Soskin, Chip Rich,
Stephen Lundberg, Raj
Kamble
Chief Creative Officer
Mark Wnek
Executive Creative Director
Fernanda Romano, Peter
Rosch, John Hobbs
Director
Randy Krallman
Editor
PS 260
Producer
Sara Ryniec
Production Company
Smuggler
Agency
Lowe New York
Client
Creativity Magazine
Country
United States

**COMBOS:
DOUG, GROWTH
SPURT, WRESTLING,
FRANCE**
Producer
Lilian Lopez
Art Director
Jeff Anderson
Copywriter
Isaac Silverglate
Creative Director
Gerry Graf,
Ian Reichenthal,
Scott Vitrone
Agency
TBWA\Chiat\Day
Client
Combos
Country
United States

"Growth Spurt" *Jingle: Dresses like a lady; looks like a man. Always eating Combos with her big man-hands. It's Man Mom! SFX: A sensitive piano solo.* **MOM: Like all mothers, I'm also a teacher. Like one time my son asked: "Mom, may I have some Pizzeria Pretzel Combos?" So I threw a garbage can at him. Then I sat on him and I told him: "If you want crunchy pizza-filled pretzels, use proper grammar: It's can I, not may I. This isn't France."** *VO: Combos. What your mom would feed you if your mom were a man.*

"France" *Jingle: Dresses like a lady; looks like a man. Always eating Combos with her big man-hands. It's Man Mom! SFX: A sensitive piano solo* **MOM: Like all mothers, I'm also a teacher. Like one time my son asked: "Mom, may I have some Pizzeria Pretzel Combos?" So I threw a garbage can at him. Then I sat on him and I told him: "If you want crunchy pizza-filled pretzels, use proper grammar: It's can I, not may I. This isn't France."** *VO: Combos. What your mom would feed you if your mom were a man.*

*
Advertising
Radio 30 Seconds or Less /
Single
Merit
Growth Sport
+
Advertising
Radio 30 Seconds or Less /
Single
Merit
Doug
+
Advertising
Radio 30 Seconds or Less /
Single
Merit
Wrestling
+
Advertising
Radio 30 Seconds or Less /
Campaign
Merit
Growth Spurt, Doug, France

"Doug" *Jingle: Dresses like a lady; looks like a man. Always eating Combos with her big man-hands. It's Man Mom! SFX: A sensitive piano solo.* **MOM: As far as moms go, I'm a softy. I got this pet name for my oldest son: I call him Combos, because just like Cheddar Cheese Pretzel Combos are full of creamy-tasting cheddar cheese, my baby is special on the inside. (Dismissive) I couldn't think of anything for my other son, so I call him Doug.** *VO: Combos. What your mom would feed you if your mom were a man.*

"Wrestling" *Jingle: Dresses like a lady; looks like a man. Always eating Combos with her big man-hands. It's Man Mom! SFX: a sensitive piano solo.* **MOM: Moms like me know: Big boys need plenty of crunchy pretzels and pizza-stuff. On Saturday I gave my son Pizzeria Pretzel Combos, and then he went and won that wrestling championship down at the community center. Sure, he gouged his opponent's eyes out, but whatever; he's a champion.** *VO: Combos. What your mom would feed you if your mom were a man.*

**COMPRESS
EVERYTHING:
CHINA, DIVORCE,
TOURIST PHOTOS**
Art Director
Menno Kluin
Copywriter
Icaro Doria
Creative Director
Tony Granger, Jan Jacobs,
Leo Premutico
Agency
Saatchi & Saatchi
Client
Allume Systems/StuffIT
Deluxe
Country
United States

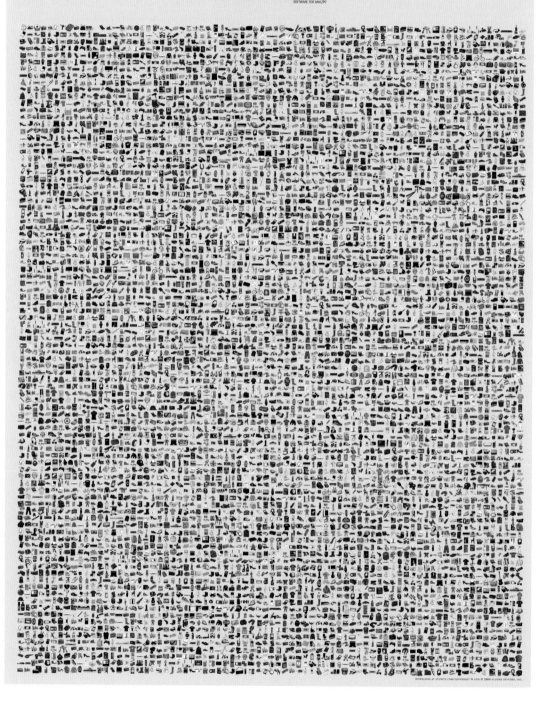

Advertising
Print Magazine, Consumer,
Full Page / Campaign
Distinctive Merit
Compress Everything
+
Advertising
Print Magazine, Consumer,
Full Page / Single
Merit
China
+
Advertising
Print Magazine, Consumer,
Full Page / Single
Merit
Divorce
+
Advertising
Posters & Billboards
Wild Postings / Single
Merit
China
+
Advertising
Posters & Billboards
Wild Postings / Campaign
Merit
Compress Everything

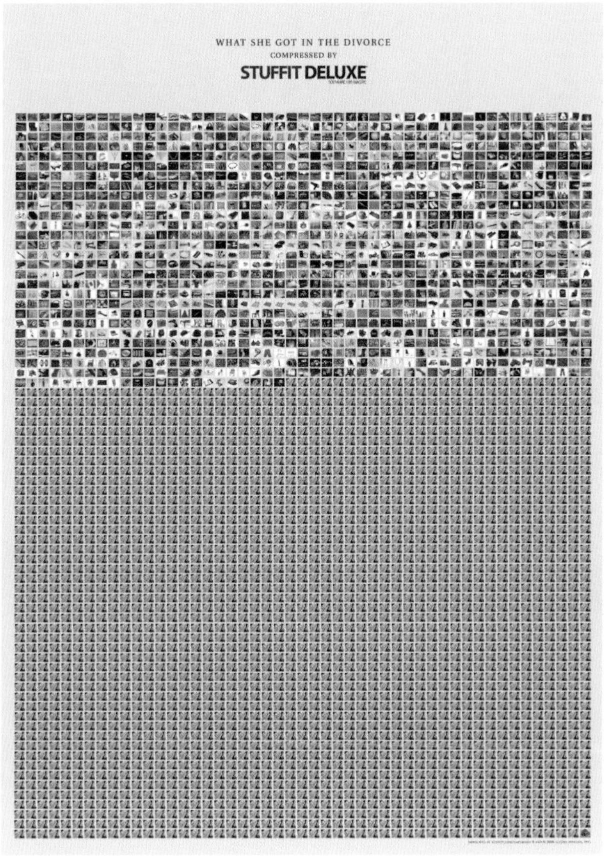

WHAT SHE GOT IN THE DIVORCE
COMPRESSED BY
STUFFIT DELUXE

A JAPANESE TOURIST'S NEW YORK PHOTOS
COMPRESSED BY
STUFFIT DELUXE

**HALF & HALF,
FRUIT PANTS, SLAP**

Art Director
Matt Miller, Noel Haan
Copywriter
Megan Sovern,
G. Andrew Meyer
Creative Director
Noel Haan,
G. Andrew Meyer
Producer
Eric Faber, David Zander,
Jeff Scruton
Director
Tom Kuntz
Editor
Matt Wood
Production Company
MJZ Los Angeles
Other
Chief Creative Officer:
John Condon
Agency
Leo Burnett
Client
Altoids
Country
United States

The Altoids Sours
Challenge swept the nation
in 2006. Contestants were
encouraged with dances,
questions and the occasional
slap. Eventually everyone
agreed Altoids Sours are
the best!

Advertising
Television & Cinema
Commercials TV: 30 Seconds
/ Single
Merit
Half & Half
+
Advertising
Television & Cinema
Commercials TV: Over 30
Seconds / Single
Merit
Fruit Pants
+
Advertising
Television & Cinema
Commercials TV: Under 30
Seconds / Single
Merit
Slap

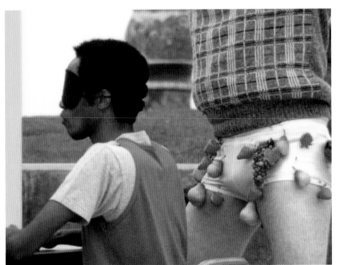

ADC LXXXVI

Advertising
Television & Cinema
Commercials TV: Under 30
Seconds / Single

Merit
Beautiful Day

78

BEAUTIFUL DAY
Art Director
Robin Heisey
Copywriter
Chris Taciuk
Creative Director
Joe Piccolo
Director
Chris Sargeant
Editor
Pete McCauley
Producer
Judy Hamilton
Production Company
Untitled
Agency
DraftFCB Toronto
Client
World Wildlife Foundation
Country
Canada

ADC LXXXVI

Advertising
Television & Cinema
Commercials TV: 30 Seconds /
Single

Merit
Bud Light "Pick Up Game"

80

**BUD LIGHT
"PICK UP GAME"**
Director
Craig Gillespie
Producer
David Zander, Lisa Rich
Production Company
MJZ
Creative Director
Mark Gross, Dan Fietsam
Editor
David Brixton
Other
Agency Producer: Brian
Smego
Agency
MJZ
Client
Bud Light
Country
United States

©2006 Anheuser Busch, Inc., Bud Light® Beer, St. Louis, MO

ADC LXXXVI

Advertising
Television & Cinema
Commercials TV: 30 Seconds /
Single

Merit
Dribbling Machine

82

DRIBBLING MACHINE
Copywriter
Ludwig Berndl (DDB Berlin)
Creative Director
Amir Kassaei (DDB Berlin)
Director
Sebastian Strasser
Editor
Nils Landmark
Producer
Marion Lange (DDB Berlin)
Production Company
Radical.Media Berlin
Other
Executive Producer:
Christiane Lochte
Agency
Radical Media
Client
Volkswagen AG
Country
United States

ADC LXXXVI

Advertising
Television & Cinema
Commercials TV: 30 Seconds /
Single

Merit
Tide

84

TIDE
<u>Art Director</u>
ACD Dino Spadavecchia
<u>Copywriter</u>
Greg Farley
<u>Executive Creative Director</u>
Harvey Marco
<u>Creative Director</u>
Steve Chavez
<u>Director</u>
Baker Smith
<u>Editor</u>
Paul Martinez
<u>Producer</u>
Mala Vasan, Agency
Producer: Richard Bendetti
<u>Production Company</u>
Harvest Films
<u>Other</u>
Account Executive:
Marisstella Marinkovic
<u>Agency</u>
Saatchi & Saatchi Los
Angeles
<u>Client</u>
Toyota Motor Sales,
USA, Inc.
<u>Country</u>
United States

Toyota's unbreakable
Tacoma campaign has
quickly established its
tough brand image with
consumers. To keep it fresh,
Toyota changed the tone
from a gasp to a long
uncomfortable shudder by
giving the consumer a
voyeuristic front seat to a
violent, sustained beating.
The result leaves no doubt
in anyone's mind that the
Tacoma is uncannily hard to
damage.

"Toyota Tacoma—Tide" Rocky coastline, as captured on a streaming surf camera. *Audio: (Ambient ocean noise)* A tacoma parks on the beach and the driver paddles off into the ocean in a kayak. The tide rises and the heavy oncoming waves capture the truck, tossing it about and beating it violently on the rocks. *Audio: (Sounds of scraping metal and heavy impacts)* The tide recedes, leaving the undamaged truck in precisely the same place it started.

ADC LXXXVI

Advertising
Television & Cinema
Commercials TV: 30 Seconds /
Single

Merit
Good Morning

86

GOOD MORNING
Art Director
Stuart Jennings
Copywriter
Greg Kalleres
Creative Director
Todd Waterbury, Kevin
Proudfoot
Director
Randy Krallman
Editor
Jun Diaz
Producer Agency
Head of Production: Gary
Krieg, Spot Producer:
Temma Shoaf
Production Company
Smuggler
Other
Associate Creative
Directors: Paul Renner,
Derek Barnes
Agency
Wieden+Kennedy New York
Client
ESPN
Country
United States

Our business goal was to
increase consumer aware-
ness that Monday Night
Football was moving to
ESPN for the 2006 season,
after spending its entire 35-
year history on broadcast
television. We met this goal
by engaging fans in a dialogue about what football
means to them on a daily
basis, and how their football
week culminates in the ultimate stage that is Monday
Night. Is It Monday Yet?

ADC LXXXVI

Advertising
Television & Cinema
Commercials TV: 30 Seconds /
Single

Merit
Endzone Options

88

ENDZONE OPTIONS

Art Director
Stuart Jennings

Copywriter
Brant Mau

Creative Director
Todd Waterbury, Kevin
Proudfoot

Director
David Shane

Editor
Jun Diaz

Producer
Agency Head of
Production: Gary Krieg,
Spot Producer: Temma
Shoaf

Production Company
Hungry Man

Other
Associate Creative
Directors: Paul Renner,
Derek Barnes

Agency
Wieden+Kennedy
New York

Client
ESPN

Country
United States

ESPN is the epicenter of a
fan's sports universe. "This
is SportsCenter" gives
viewers an inside peek into
the daily lives of the
SportsCenter anchors and
all things ESPN. In "End
Zone Options" Chad
Johnson asks for some help
from the anchors in coming
up with new touchdown
dances.

MAC VS. PC
Art Director
Scott Trattner
Copywriter
Jason Sperling, Barton
Copley
Creative Director
Eric Grunbaum
Executive Creative Director
Duncan Milner
Associate Creative
Director
Scott Trattner, Jason
Sperling, Barton Copley
Editor
Lucas Eskin, Val Thrasher,
Mad River Post
Senior Producer
Mike Refuerzo
Producer
Anne Oburgh
Assistant Producer
Hank Zakroff
Production Company
Epoch Films

Hello, I'm a PC, and I hate
this campaign. Is hate too
strong a word? Sorry, but
why would I like a campaign
that consistently points out
my flaws and imperfections,
that attempts to color me as
boring and bureaucratic,
and makes Mac seem so
smart and talented? Of
course, I realize Apple was
simply attempting to "educate the masses" by pointing out Mac's strengths and
my so-called weaknesses
(at least people write viruses for me!) through dozens
of light-hearted debates.
But come on. Who ever
heard of a computer com-
mercial set against a white
backdrop? Where are we
supposed to be—heaven? I
don't think so. Heaven is
glorious place where nothing ever depreciates, the
profit margins never shrink
and the angelic sound of fax
machines establishing connections fills the air. Memo
to the folks at Apple: No
one cares. Especially me.
Warmest regards, PC.

"Out of the Box":30 Visual: Open on PC and Mac, white backdrop.
They're both sitting inside opened boxes. PC is making circles with his
arms. **MAC: (stretching, yawning) Hello, I'm a Mac.** PC: (Intensely
stretching, knee bends with arms out) And I'm a PC. **MAC: Ready to
get started?** PC: (Cocky, touching fingers to toes, knees and shoul-
ders, knees to chest) Not quite, got a lot to do. What's your 'big'
plan? **MAC: I might make a home movie, create a website, try out
my built-in camera…I can do it all right out of the box. What about
you?** Visual: As Mac talks, PC stretching slows to a stop. PC: (Gloating,
but starting to second guess himself) First, I am going to download
some drivers, then I'm going to erase the trial software that came on
my hard drive…then I have a lot of manuals to read… **MAC: You
know it sounds like you gotta do a lot of stuff to do before you do
any stuff. I'm just gonna get started cause I'm kind of excited. Let
me know when you're ready.** PC: Actually, the rest of me is in some
other boxes. So, I'll catch up with you later. *Title: Mac.*

"**Better Results**" :30 Visual: Open on two men standing side-by-side. One is the PC guy. One is the Mac guy. **MAC: Hello, I'm a Mac.** PC: I'm a PC. (to Mac) You know, I actually just finished a home movie. **MAC: That's so funny. I just finished my own home movie. I did it on iMovie. It was really easy.** PC: Well I doubt it's as excellent as mine, but I would be happy to take a look. **MAC: Yeah, that would be great.** PC: Roll it. Visual: A Mac home movie, in the form of Giselle Bundchen, walks up and stands next to Mac. **MAC MOVIE:** Hi. I'm a Mac home movie. **MAC: It looks really professional, right?** PC: (Looking Mac Movie over, amazed) Well, great. Bye. **MAC: Wait, what about yours? Can we see yours?** PC: (Nervous, fumbling for words) Ummmm. **MAC MOVIE: Please?** PC: Okay, sure. Visual: PC relinquishes. A shlubby Paul Giamatti type walks up and stands next to PC. He's dressed in drag and wearing a wig. He smiles. Cut to PC looking embarrassed. PC MOVIE: What's up, PC home movie. *Title: Mac PC. VO: Work in progress.*

ADC LXXXVI

Advertising
Television & Cinema
Commercials TV: Over 30
Seconds / Single

Merit
How to Make a Boring TVC

92

HOW TO MAKE A BORING TVC

Art Director
Yoshimitsu Sawamoto,
Sohei Okano

Copywriter
Yoshimitsu Sawamoto,
Sohei Okano

Creative Director
Ichiro Kinosita, Yoshimitsu
Sawamoto

Director
Gen Sekiguchi

Producer
Toru Igarashi, Kumiko
Kitamura, Kazuto Nakamura

Production Company
Aoi Advertising Promotion
Inc.

Other
Agency: Dentsu Inc.,
Agency Producer: Natsuo
Ishikawa, Photographer:
Makoto Shiguma, Lighting
Director: Akihiro Nomoto,
Account Executive:
Shuji Nezu

Agency
Dentsu Inc. Tokyo

Client
The National Association of
Commercial Broadcasters
in Japan (NAB)

Country
Japan

In Japan, over the past
few years, more and more
people own digital video
recorders, or DVRs.
People use the DVR skip
button to skip TV commer-
cials. The Association of
Broadcasters in Japan
believes one reason may
be that more and more TV
commercials are rushed
onto the airwaves, resulting
lower quality TV commer-
cials. A unique campaign
called "Good TVC Wanted"
was launched. This new
campaign has affected
viewers, the television
industry, the TV commercial
industry, and the clients,
becoming a social phenom-
enon gaining wide media
coverage.

"How to make a boring TVC" TV COMMERCIAL NA:
With satisfying taste. KING DOG Now on Sale! CLIENT:
Not enough IMPACT! A TVC needs to have an
IMPACT... ADVERTISING AGENCY A: ...is what the
president said. ADVERTISING AGENCY B: IMPACT?!
AD AGENCY A: I'm sorry but just fix it! TV
COMMERCIAL NA: With super exploding taste! KING
DOG Now on Sale! VIEWER (MAN): That hair style
makes me feel too hot. AD AGENCY A:...is what a con-
sumer said. AD AGENCY B:Too hot?! ADVERTISING
AGENCY A: Anyway just fix it. TV COMMERCIAL NA:
With high flying taste. KING DOG Now on Sale!
VIEWER (WOMAN): It's sexist, women eat hot dogs too!

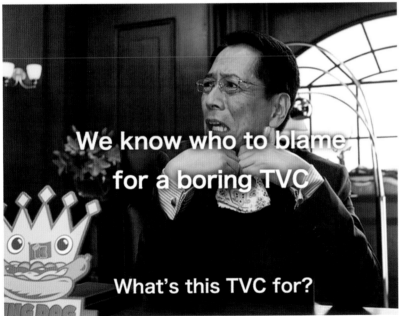

TV COMMERCIAL NA: With a taste for love. KING
DOG Now on Sale! VIEWER (GIRL): It should be cuter!
TV COMMERCIAL NA: The super cute taste. KING
DOG Now on Sale! AD AGENCY A: Still too hot?
AD AGENCY C: Or that bears don't eat hot dogs!
AD AGENCY D: Or maybe a heart warming story.
AD AGENCY A: With an environmentally message, too.
TV COMMERCIAL NA: With the most impressive taste.
An environmentally friendly taste!! KING SALMON Now
on Sale! CLIENT: This is so good! What's this TVC for?
*Super: We know who to blame for a boring TVC. Good
TVC* Wanted. Association of Broadcasters in Japan.

ADC LXXXVI

Advertising
Television & Cinema
Commercials TV: Over 30
Seconds / Single

Merit
Breast Exam

94

BREAST EXAM
Art Director
Mariana O'Kelly
Copywriter
Gary du Toit
Creative Director
Mike Schalit, Julian Watt
Producer
Sandra Gomes
Production Company
Luma
Director
Gerhard Painter
Other
Chris Wieffering, Donnie
Steyn
Agency
NetWork BBDO
Client
Virgin Atlantic
Country
South Africa

This ad flighted during
International Breast Cancer
Awareness Month. The ad
takes the form of an animated instructional video, in
which a topless woman
shows viewers how to per-
form a breast self-exam.
Once the exam is completed
we reveal that the woman
has been sitting in a Virgin
Upper Class Suite all along.
This illustrates the extreme
privacy offered by the Suite.

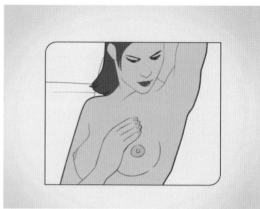
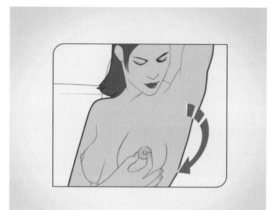

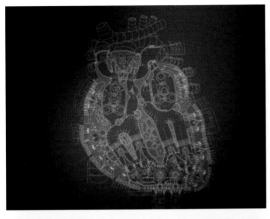
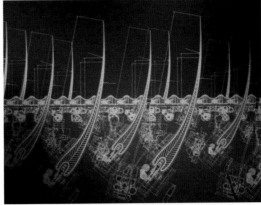

EMOTIONS
Art Director
Jaume Badia
Copywriter
Alfredo Binefa
Creative Director
Alberto Astorga
Director
David Ruiz
Production Company
Ruiz + Company
Agency
DDB Espana
Client
V.A.E.S.A. / Audi
Country
Spain

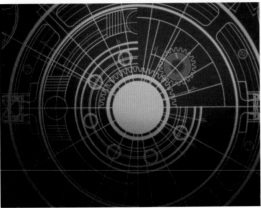

The commercial shows several human
emotions expressed as if they were a
technical drawing. We see an accelerat-
ed heartbeat, hairs that stand on end
and finally a tear falling. Then we see a
packshot of the Audi RS4. *Super: New
Audi RS4 V8 420 CV Quattro.
Designed to thrill.*

**COME HOME TO THE
SIMPSONS**

<u>Art Director</u>
Nik Stewart
<u>Copywriter</u>
Jonny Parker
<u>Creative Director</u>
Richard Holman
<u>Director</u>
Chris Palmer
<u>Editor</u>
Jonny Scarlett
(The Quarry)
<u>Producer</u>
Audrey Hawkins
<u>Production Company</u>
Gorgeous Enterprises
<u>Other</u>
Flame Artist: Tom Sparks
(Alteration Services),
Sound: Scramble, Director
of Photography: Ian Foster
<u>Agency</u>
Devilfish
<u>Client</u>
Sky One
<u>Country</u>
United Kingdom

Sky One has been the home
of The Simpsons in the UK
for the past two decades.
As well as re-affirming the
channel as the home of the
show we also were asked to
create a loveable and entertaining brand film to
enhance viewers' relationship with the channel. We
came up with disconcert-
ingly simple idea of showing an archetypical British
family—who bear an uncan-
ny resemblance to the
show's characters—rushing
home to watch the show in
the way that The Simpsons
themselves do in the title
sequence. Springfield
becomes Sheffield. An
exhaustive casting process
and intense location scout-
ing brought us cast and
locations which bear a
strong resemblance to the
original, whilst being
authentically British.

Advertising
Television & Cinema
Commercials TV: Over 30
Seconds / Single
Merit
Come Home to the Simpsons
+
Advertising
Television & Cinema
Commercials Online
Commercial / Single
Merit
Come Home to the Simpsons

ADC LXXXVI

Advertising
Television & Cinema
Commercials TV: Over 30
Seconds / Single

Merit
Wes Anderson

98

WES ANDERSON
Art Director
David Lloyd
Copywriter
Dan Kroeger
Creative Director
Chris Mitton, Terry Finley,
David Apicella
Director
Wes Anderson
Editor
Vincent Marchand
Producer
Alice Mintzer
Production Company
Moxie Pictures
Agency
Ogilvy & Mather
Client
American Express
Country
United States

The Wes Anderson
American Express
Commercial was one of two
spots within the "My Life,
My Card" campaign called
The Directors Series.
We collaborated with select
writer/directors to create
short films where they could
tell their own somewhat fic-
tionalized story. We chose
Wes because we admire
his work, and because he
fits well with the American
Express brand. He is
uncompromising, self-
directed, and utterly unique.

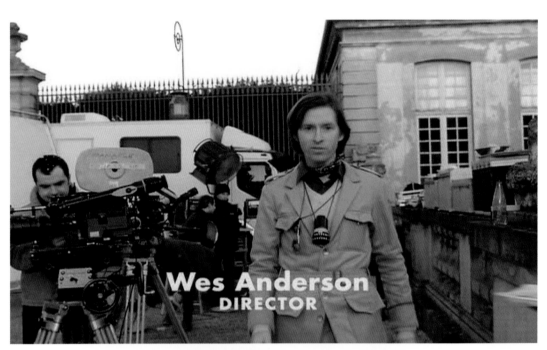

Idea: Set on the grounds of a chateau in the French countryside, Wes Anderson, in the character of a big action movie director, attempts to simultaneously direct an international blockbuster and make an American Express commercial. As Wes briskly walks across the set, and attempts to explain his movie-making process to the camera, he is continually bombarded by members of his crew, with requests ranging from the typical to the ridiculous. He never actually gets to clearly explain anything about his process to us, but the chaos of the world in which he works says it all. **WES ANDERSON: My life is about telling stories. My card is American Express.** *Graphic: Wes Anderson's signature writes itself across the American Express Card's signature strip.*

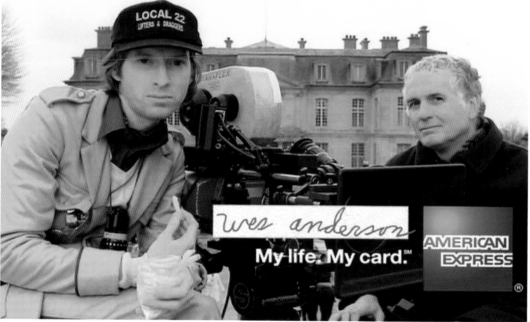

**THE DAY I WENT
TO WORK**
Art Director
Will Bate
Copywriter
Curtis Brittles
Creative Director
Graham Fink
Director
Vince Squibb
Editor
Jonnie Scarlet
Producer
Spencer Dodd
Production Company
Gorgeous Enterprises
Agency
Gorgeous Enterprises
Client
Transport For London
Country
United Kingdom

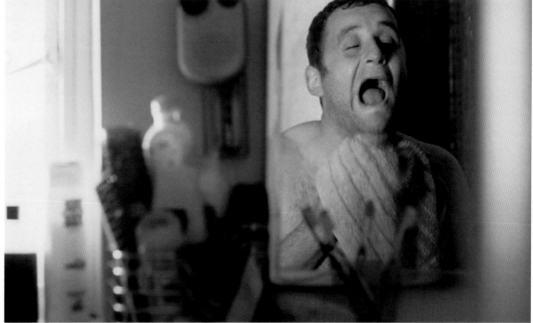

Advertising
Television & Cinema
Commercials TV: Public
Service / Non-Profit /
Single
Merit
The Day I Went to Work
+
Advertising
Television & Cinema
Commercials TV: Over
30 sections
Merit
The Day I Went to Work

+10 CAMPAIGN

Art Director
Chris Landy, Andy Fackrell,
Bertrand Fleuret,
Dario Nucci

Copywriter
Lee Hempstock,
Richard Bullock,
Andy Fackrell

Creative Director
Executive Creative Director:
Andy Fackrell

Designer
Julian Wade

Director
Ivan Zacharias,
James Brown

Producer
Executive Producer: Cedric
Gairard, Agency Producers:
Claire Finn, Cat Reynolds,
Agency Production
Assistant: Sarah Billens

Production Company
Stink, London

Other
Media Company: Carat

Agency
180 Amsterdam

Client
Adidas International

Country
Netherlands

Brazil vs Argentina:
Brazilian superstar Kaka is
struggling to find ten
Brazilians for his upcoming
match against Argentinean
Riquelme. He calls his old
coach Visolli who scours
the streets, beaches and
favelas of Sao Paulo to find
four young men to fly to
Milan. Riquelme lands in
Milan with his brother, and
has three hours to find nine
more for the "international"
game later that evening.
Their first stop, the
Argentine Embassy, is
closed, but he strikes it
lucky; spotting an Argentine
Steakhouse full of willing
employees. The campaign
has been made to celebrate
the FIFA World Cup 2006.

*
Advertising
Television & Cinema
Commercials TV: Spots of
Varying Length / Campaign
Merit
Recruitment Films
+
Advertising
Television & Cinema
Commercials TV: Over 30
Seconds / Single
Merit
Equipo

LITTLE RICHARD
Art Director
Adam Stockton
Copywriter
Bob Meagher
Creative Director
Steve Bassett
Director
Chris Smith
Editor
Spotwelders
Producer
Holly Flaisher
Production Company
Smuggler
Agency
The Martin Agency
Client
GEICO
Country
United States

Open on woman in a living room sitting next to Little Richard. *SUPER: Denise Bazik, Real Person. SUPER: Little Richard, Celebrity. VO: Denise Bazik is a real GEICO customer, not a paid celebrity. So to help tell her story we hired a celebrity.* **DENISE: It was Thanksgiving night when I accidentally hit a deer.** RICHARD: (Whooooo) Lookout! Lookout! **DENISE: I called GEICO expecting to get a recording, but someone was there to help me.** RICHARD: Help me. Somebody help me. **DENISE: GEICO got my claim in the works right away. And I was actually able to enjoy my Thanksgiving.** RICHARD: Mashed potatoes. Gravy. And cranberry sauce. (Whooooo). *Cut to logo. VO: GEICO. Real service. Real savings.*

ADC LXXXVI

Advertising
Television & Cinema
Commercials TV: Public
Service / Non-Profit /
Campaign

Merit
Sweet Smokes / Joggers /
Anonymous / Mattress

104

**SWEET SMOKES /
JOGGERS
ANONYMOUS /
MATTRESS**

Art Director
Mike Costello, John Parker
Copywriter
Marc Einhorn, Evan Fry
Creative Director
Pete Favat, Alex Bogusky,
John Kearse, Tom Adams
Director
Eddy Moretti
Editor
Lawrence Young, Aaron
Langley
Producer
Rupert Samuel, Chris
Kyriakos, Emily Moore,
Katie Porter, Shane Smith,
Jim Czarnecki, Monica
Hampton, Ben Dietz
Production Company
VICE Films
Other
Director of Photography:
Geoff O'Connor
Agency
Arnold Worldwide
Client
American Legacy
Foundation
Country
United States

The tobacco industry
makes a product that kills
about 1,200 people every
day. What's crazier than
that? Well, for starters,
they've been manufacturing
this product for over a hundred years now. And they
continue to do so even
after the landmark Master
Settlement Agreement
forced them to pony up the
largest monetary settlement
in history. It seems ridiculous, right? Well, it is. And
in defending their business,
the tobacco industry says
the darnedest things. Things
that make you want to ask
"whudafxup?" And through
the investigative work of our
man-on-the-scene, Derrick,
that's what this campaign
aims to find out.

"Sweet Smokes" *TITLE SEQUENCE: Truth Presents. TITLE SEQUENCE: Whudafxup with Sweet Smokes?* Open on our Whudafxup filmmaker making a "lemonade-style-stand" in a garage. The stand reads "Twista Lime," "Midnight Berry," and "Mocha Taboo." See our filmmaker painting the sign. **FILMMAKER: You know that tobacco companies these days are making cigarettes with flavors like Mocha Taboo and Midnight Berry and Twista Lime. They say they're for adults. Now I'm no expert... but let's see some reactions.** Cut to the filmmaker who's now set up in a park with his stand. We watch as kid after kid approaches. the filmmaker has to turn them away because they're not adults. **FILMMAKER: Get your flavors here. These are adult flavors, sorry. Twista Lime. You guys shouldn't actually be even looking at these. Alright, you guys gotta get out of here. Go on. I'm so sick of people thinking these are for kids. It's ridiculous.** As more and more kids are turned away. **FILM-MAKER: Mocha Taboo. This is for adults. I shouldn't be showing you this.** TEEN 1: This is like gum. **FILMMAKER: Are you serious? Can I get some ID? Do you have ID?** See more and more of this turning away kids who are interested in these flavors as we hear his voiceover. *FILMMAK-ER VO: So just who does the tobacco industry REALLY think these fla-vors are for? Well considering in 1972, an internal tobacco document stated 'it's a well-known fact that teenagers like sweet products.' Kind of makes you think...* Cut to the Whudafxup? slate. Clap to black.

"Joggers Anonymous" Open on our Whudafxup filmmaker jogging on the street. *TITLE SEQUENCE: Truth Presents.* He jogs up into an addiction treatment center. *TITLE SEQUENCE: Whudafxup with Jogging?* He approaches the receptionist. **FILMMAKER: Hello.** RECEPTIONIST: How ya'll doing today? **FILMMAKER: Good. How are you doing?** RECEPTIONIST: Pretty good and you? **FILMMAKER: Good. Good. You treat addictions here?** RECEPTIONIST: Yes sir. **FILMMAKER: Do you treat jogging addictions?** RECEPTIONIST: No, indeed. **FILMMAKER (as he exits the center): Have a good day.** Cut to the filmmaker going into a different treatment center. RECEPTIONIST 2: M&Ms and jogging? **FILMMAKER: Joggings and M&Ms. I'm assuming you treat that kind of thing?** RECEPTIONIST 2: No, not here. Cut to filmmaker jogging in the street. *FILMMAKER VO: At a 1997 deposition, a tobacco-industry scientist compared the addictiveness of cigarettes to M&M's and jogging.* Cut to our filmmaker approaching another treatment center. **FILMMAKER: So I can't get any help at all for this?** RECEPTIONIST 3: Jogging? **FILMMAKER: Yes.** RECEPTIONIST 3: No. RECEPTIONIST 4: For M&Ms and jogging? Cut to the filmmaker trying other centers and getting turned away more and more. RECEPTIONIST 5: No. RECEPTIONIST 6: No. RECEPTIONIST 7: No. RECEPTIONIST 8: No. **FILMMAKER: Cigarette addiction comparable to jogging and M&Ms?** Cut to Whudafxup? slate. Clap to black.

ADC LXXXVI

Advertising
TV & Cinema Commercials:
Over 30 Seconds / Single
Multiple Winner
see page 363

Merit
Guinness—Hands

106

GUINNESS—HANDS
Art Director
Michael Durban
Copywriter
Tony Strong
Creative Director
Paul Brazier
Director
Michael Schlingmann
Producer
Matt Saxton
Production Company
Uli Meyer Animation
Agency
Abbott Mead Vickers BBDO
Client
DIAGEO
Country
United Kingdom

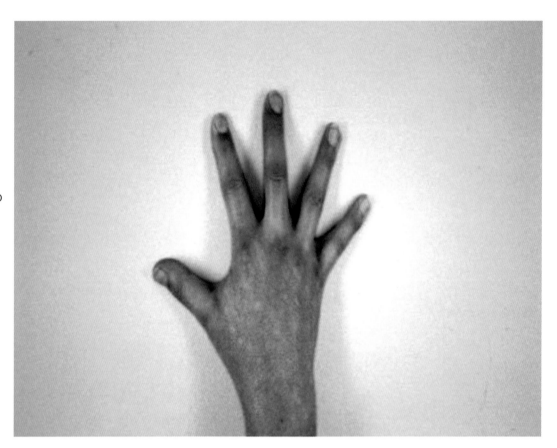

"Hands" Two hands are resting on a surface, doing nothing, waiting. The owner of the hands starts to twiddle his thumbs. Then he drums his fingers. His fingers start to go all over the place. The thumbs come right off and on again. The hands flip back to front, and swivel: the fingers bend as if rubber….. It's remarkable how many different twisty things a pair of waiting hands can do with their fingers. So what are these hands waiting for so eagerly? Finally we see their reward—a perfect pint of Guinness... *Good Things Come To Those Who Wait.*

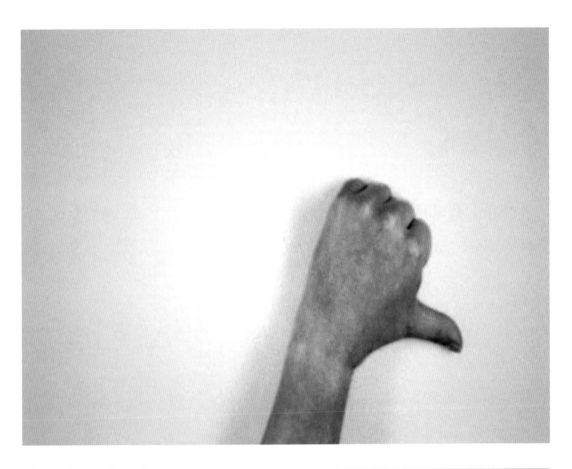

ADC LXXXVI

Advertising
Television & Cinema Crafts
Copywriting / Single

Merit
Biathlon

108

BIATHLON
Art Director
Rèmy Tricot
Copywriter
Olivier Couradjut
Creative Director
Stèphane Xiberras
Production Company
Hamster, Spy Films
Director
Trevor Cornish
Agency
BETC Euro RSCG
Client
13EME RUE
Country
France

ADC LXXXVI   **Advertising**   **Merit**   110
Television & Cinema Crafts   Bedroom
Copywriting / Single

BEDROOM
Associate
Creative Director
Richard Ardito,
Grant Smith
Executive Creative Director
Eric Silver
Director
Daniel Kleinman
Editor
Gary Knight (Final Cut)
Producer
Ed Zazzera
Production Company
Kleinman Productions
Other
Chief Creative Officers:
David Lubars, Bill Bruce
Agency
BBDO New York
Client
G4
Country
United States

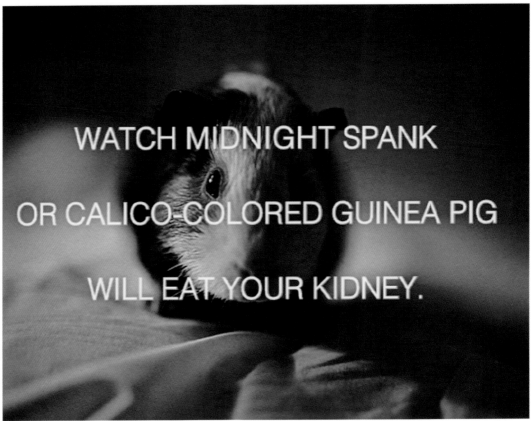

SCARY TALE

Art Director
Ron Brown, Niall Downing,
Helen Downing

Copywriter
Tony Strong

Creative Director
Paul Brazier

Director
Niall Downing, Helen
Downing

Producer
Nick Crabb

Production Company
2AM Films

Agency
Abbott Mead Vickers BBDO

Client
Anorexia

Country
United Kingdom

"Scary Tale" We open on close up's of young girl's hands cutting pictures out of a magazine. *Girl VO: When I grow up I'm going to cheat and lie to my friends, to my parents but most of all to myself.* Next we cut to a black screen, text appears: *Instructions for anorexics…* We cut to a slow tracking shot observing a girl aged 15 walking past a group of boys, also in uniform. The boys are joking around. She glances at them and clearly feels uncomfortable. She puts her head down slightly letting her hair drop as if she wants to be invisible. *Girl VO: Eat naked in front of the mirror so you're not tempted to eat too much.* We sharp cut to an extreme close-up of food on a plate being scraped aside. Cut to a family kitchen. Lunch is being served. We see our girl make an excuse and start to walk out. *Girl VO: Say you are going to eat at a friend's house and instead go for a walk… or leave dirty plates out so that your mum will think you've eaten.* Sharp cut to an extreme close up of a girls mouth spitting after being sick. SFX amplify the images. Cut to a teenage girl's bedroom. There are 4 girls, including our girl. They are having fun and showing off clothes and phones. We can only see our girl in the reflection of her mirror. She looks removed from the scene. *Girl VO: Do your aerobics until you want to faint. Keep your hair in good*

condition so no one will suspect anything. Sharp cut to an extreme close-up of skin stretched tight over a hip bone. Cut to the hallway in the house. our girl is putting on her coat. She slips quietly out the door so no-one will hear her. The girl's mother enters the frame looking, helpless to stop her daughter. *Girl VO: Take cold baths to make your metabolism work harder.* Cut to close ups of a naked figure curled up in a ball. Cut to the girl taking a freezing cold bath. Cut to a female adult hand. It starts to lose its grip of the child's hand which is pulling away. *Girl VO: Being thin and not eating are signs of true will power and success… You can never be too thin.* The hands separate and the child's hand falls away. Cut to a black screen with title.

**MONDAY NIGHT
FOOTBALL**

<u>Art Director</u>
Stuart Jennings

<u>Copywriter</u>
Greg Kalleres

<u>Creative Director</u>
Todd Waterbury, Kevin
Proudfoot

<u>Director</u>
Randy Krallman

<u>Editor</u>
Jun Diaz

<u>Producer</u>
Agency Head of
Production: Gary Krieg,
Spot Producer: Temma
Shoaf

<u>Production Company</u>
Smuggler

<u>Other</u>
Associate Creative
Directors: Paul Renner,
Derek Barnes

<u>Agency</u>
Wieden+Kennedy
New York

<u>Client</u>
ESPN

<u>Country</u>
United States

Our business goal was to
increase consumer aware-
ness that Monday Night
Football was moving to
ESPN for the 2006 season,
after spending its entire 35-
year history on broadcast
television. We met this goal
by engaging fans in a dialogue about what football
means to them on a daily
basis, and how their football
week culminates in the ultimate stage that is Monday
Night. Is It Monday Yet?

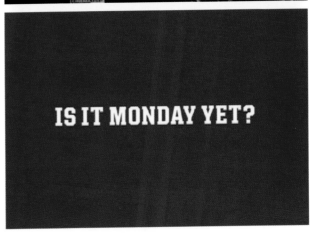

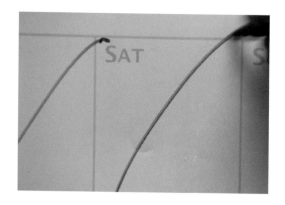

IS IT MONDAY YET?

IS IT MONDAY YET?

ADC LXXXVI

Advertising
Television & Cinema Crafts
Music / Sound Design /
Single

Merit
Defy

116

DEFY
Art Director
Paulo Martins
Copywriter
Oliver Frank
Creative Director
Mark Hunter, Alvaro
Sotomayer
Director
Joaquin Baca-Asay
Editor
Adam Pertofsky
Producer
Elissa Singstock, Veronika
Kaufmann
Production Company
Park Pictures
Other
Music: Human
Agency
Human Worldwide
Client
Nike
Country
United States

**RAILCYCLE,
BARRIERCYCLE**

Art Director
Pipat Uraporn, Sompat
Trisadikun

Copywriter
Noranit Yasopa

Creative Director
Keeratie Chaimoungkalo,
Sompat Trisadikun

Photographer
Chup Nokkeaw

Producer
Sarawut Lertkittipaporn

Production Company
Zone Retouch

Agency
Leo Burnett Bangkok

Agency
Leo Burnett

Client
Clima Co., Ltd.

Country
United States

Leaving bicycles in public
areas isn't always safe.
Safety precautions are
needed, especially now
when people are encour-
aged to ride bicycles
instead of driving their
cars. The challenge was to
make consumers trust in
the quality of this brand.

*
Advertising
Print Newspaper, Consumer,
Full Page / Single
Merit
Barriercycle
+
Advertising
Print Newspaper, Consumer,
Full Page / Single
Merit
Railcycle

ADC LXXXVI

Advertising
Print Magazine, Consumer,
Less Than a Full Page / Single

Merit
Bottles

120

BOTTLES
Art Director
Mark Voehringer
Copywriter
Jake Benjamin
Creative Director
Tony Granger, Jan Jacobs,
Leo Premutico
Designer
Kevin Li
Other
Digital Artist: Yan
Apostolides
Agency
Saatchi & Saatchi
Client
Procter & Gamble, Tide
Coldwater
Country
United States

ADC LXXXVI

Advertising
Print Magazine, Consumer,
Less Than a Full Page /
Campaign

Merit
Dreamscapes

122

DREAMSCAPES
Art Director
Danielle Thornton
Copywriter
Josh Schildkraut
Creative Director
Tony Granger, Jan Jacobs,
Leo Premutico
Illustrator
Helene Builly, Tomi
Lahesmaki, Dylan Nelson,
Alessandro Bavari
Other
Digital Artist: Aaron Padin
Agency
Saatchi & Saatchi
Client
Procter & Gamble,
Folgers Coffee
Country
United States

ADC LXXXVI   **Advertising**   **Merit**   124
Print Magazine, Consumer,   Initiation
Full Page / Campaign

INITIATION

Art Director
Jeremy Smallwood,
Julie Scelzo Fitzpatrick
Copywriter
Pam Mufson,
Desmond LaVelle
Creative Director
Noel Haan, G. Andrew
Meyer
Photographer
Tony D'Orio
Other
Chief Creative Officer:
John Condon
Agency
Leo Burnett
Client
William Wrigley Jr.
Company
Country
United States

The young have been taught
to be wary of all things
curious. Be it drugs, sex or
the mysterious production
of hair, they will eventually
have to experience such
things for themselves.
Altoids are no different. In
order to initiate this new
generation of users, it was
necessary to convince them
to embrace their curiosities.
The Altoids "Initiation"
campaign challenges the
audience to set aside their
fears and take the next step
into adulthood.

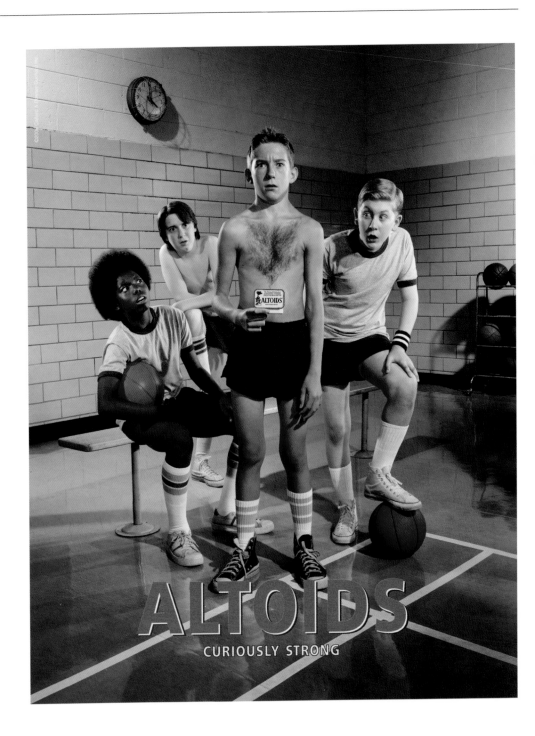

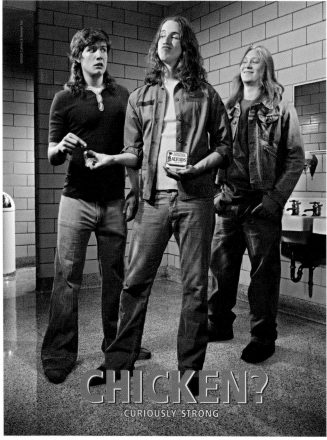

BALLOON, MOTH, ICE
Art Director
Emer Stamp, Ben Tollet
Copywriter
Ben Tollet, Emer Stamp
Creative Director
Adam Tucker
Designer
Peter Mould
Photographer
Dimitri Daniloff
Agency
DDB London
Client
Harvey Nichols
Country
United Kingdom

ADC LXXXVI

Advertising
Print Magazine, Trade, Less
Than a Full Page / Single

Merit
Coupons

128

$1.25 extra

Bring this coupon and pay an extra $1.25 on your next Stella Artois.

1 1004623 2384623 0

No valid with any other offers.
Excludes tax and other charges.
Valid at participating locations only.
Expires 11/30/2005.

STELLA ARTOIS

Reassuringly expensive.

$4.00 reg. $2.75

Bring this coupon and pay an extra $1.25 on your next Stella Artois.

1 1004623 2384623 0

No valid with any other offers.
Excludes tax and other charges.
Valid at participating locations only.
Expires 11/30/2005.

STELLA ARTOIS

Reassuringly expensive.

20% more

Bring this coupon and pay an extra $1.25 on your next Stella Artois.

1 1004623 2384623 0

No valid with any other offers.
Excludes tax and other charges.
Valid at participating locations only.
Expires 11/30/2005.

STELLA ARTOIS

Reassuringly expensive.

ADC LXXXVI

Advertising
Print Magazine, Trade,
Full Page / Single

Merit
Buttons

129

BUTTONS
Art Director
Andrea Jaimes, Mariana
Orozco, Christian Rio de la
Loza
Copywriter
Diana Vazquez, Christian
Rio de la Loza
Creative Director
Jose Montalvo, Diana
Vazquez
Photographer
Enrique Segarra
Producer
Mariana Orozco, Andrea
Jaimes
Agency
Leo Burnett Mexico
Client
Procter & Gamble
Country
Mexico

RISKS

<u>Art Director</u>
Martin Darfeuille

<u>Copywriter</u>
Edouard Perarnaud

<u>Creative Director</u>
Alexandre Hervè, Sylvain Thirache

<u>Photographer</u>
Jean Yves Lemoigne

<u>Other</u>
Art Buyer: Sophie Megrous, Strategic Planner: Martine Corbusie

<u>Agency</u>
DDB Paris

<u>Client</u>
Volkswagen Commercial Vehicles

<u>Country</u>
France

Volkswagen Utility Vehicles have very high level of safety equipment, which is pretty unique in their category. We hence decided to focus on this point, in order to create an original and innovative speech. The aim of the campaign was to emphasize security at work, showing that not choosing a Volkswagen van is as stupid as taking unnecessary risks.

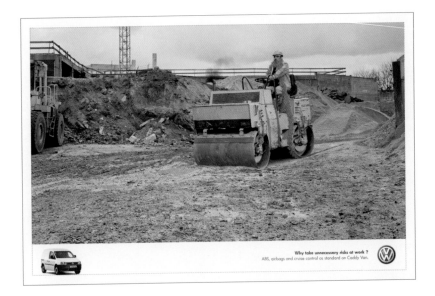

ADC LXXXVI

Advertising
Posters & Billboards
Promotional / Single

Merit
Fresco

131

adidas

adidas Fresco

TASK: The agency was briefed to show that adidas partners with the best football players on this planet.

IDEA: Football stars like Beckham, Zidane, Raul, Messi, Kaka or Ballack are considered to be real football gods by their fans. We simply elevated them where they belong anyway – into football heaven. We created the world's largest football fresco in the main lobby of the Cologne central train station, which happens to be right next to the stunning Cologne Cathedral.

RESULTS: 8.5 million people saw the fresco live and millions saw it across all media. Five minutes after revealing the fresco it already was on national TV. During the full course of the FIFA World Cup™ 2006 the fresco was part of global press coverage. The results by far exceeded the expectations of the client with a PR value generated by this single installation of approximately 8–10 million euros.

FRESCO
Art Director
Boris Schwiedrzik
Copywriter
Helge Blöck
Creative Director
Kurt Georg Dieckert, Stefan Schmidt
Producer
Katrin Dettmann
Illustrator
Felix Reidenbach
Production Company
Methodik Management & Partner
Project Manager
Sirrka Koster
Management Supervisor
Bela Ziemann
Account Manager
Falk Lungwitz
Media Agency
Carat
Strategic Planner
Moritz Kiechle
Art Buyer
Martina Kersten
Agency
TBWA \ Germany
Client
Adidas AG
Country
Germany

Football stars like Beckham, Zidane, Raul, Messi, Kaka or Ballack are considered to be real football gods by their fans. We simply elevated them where they belong anyway—into football heaven. We created the world´s largest football fresco in the main lobby of the Cologne central train station, which happens to be right next to the stunning Cologne Cathedral.

ADC LXXXVI

Advertising
Posters & Billboards Public
Service / Non-Profit /
Educational / Campaign

Merit
Painted Walls Campaign

132

**PAINTED WALLS
CAMPAIGN**
Art Director
Ingrid Varetz
Copywriter
Veronique Sels
Creative Director
Erik Vervroegen
Agency
TBWA \ Paris
Client
Aides
Country
France

NOT HERE BUT NOW

Copywriter
Pius Walker

Creative Director
Pius Walker

Designer
Marianne Friedli, Florian
Froehlich, Carolina Gurtner

Photo Editor
Renè Weber, Goran Basic

Photographer
Federico Naef

Other
Head of Marketing:
Daniel Meienberger

Agency
Walker

Client
Amnesty International

Country
Switzerland

This campaign was
designed to make people in
Switzerland aware of human
rights abuse and to awaken
the public interest in
Amnesty International's
mission. The poster cam-
paign entitled "It's not happening here, but it's happening now" puts real examples
of the worldwide human
rights abuse directly in front
of our eyes. Two worlds col-
lide on 200 individual
posters, each single one
meticulously matched to
its specific surroundings.
The brutal scenes from
Guantanamo for instance
suddenly take place in the
middle of Zurich. The campaign generated resounding
echoes. With only 200
posters in Switzerland,
Amnesty International saw
a twenty-fold increase in
visits to its webpage.

*
Advertising
Posters & Billboards
Public Service / Non-Profit /
Educational / Campaign
Merit
Not Here but Now
+
Advertising
Posters & Billboards
Public Service / Non-Profit /
Educational / Single
Merit
Not Here but Now
+
Advertising
Posters & Billboards
Public Service / Non-Profit /
Educational / Single
Merit
Not Here but Now,
Liberia-Winterhur

ADC LXXXVI

Advertising
Posters & Billboards
Outdoor / Billboard /
Campaign

Merit
The Wrong Working
Environmwent Campaign

136

THE WRONG WORKING ENVIRONMENT CAMPAIGN

<u>Art Director</u>
David Fischer

<u>Copywriter</u>
Daniel Boedeker,
Axel Tischer

<u>Creative Director</u>
Matthias Spaetgens,
Jan Leube

<u>Producer</u>
Sören Gessat

<u>Other</u>
Photographer: Hans Starck
Graphic: Robert Bilz,
Steffen Kreft, Tabea
Rauscher

<u>Agency</u>
Scholz & Friends Berlin
GmbH

<u>Client</u>
Jobsintown.de

<u>Country</u>
Germany

The task was to increase the brand awareness of Jobsintown.de, by exactly targeting people who are dissatisfied with their actual job, people who already thought of changing their job and, even more important, people who have good reasons to do so but somehow haven't thought about it yet. We reached this goal by providing a surprising insight into petrol pumps and washing machines of laundromats. Full-sized posters on the side walls of these service machines show people working under hair-raising conditions instead of the expected machinery. With this unusual positioning and interactive use of media we reveal how terrible it could be to have the wrong job in a striking way. To reach the target group exactly, we situated the machines where we could reach commuters on their way from or to work—on highly frequented gas stations and laundromats.

ADC LXXXVI

Advertising
Advertising Posters &
Billboards Outdoor /
Billboard / Campaign

Merit
Shapes

137

SHAMES

Art Director
Boris Schwiedrzik

Copywriter
Helge Blöck

Creative Director
Kurt Georg Dieckert, Stefan
Schmidt

Designer
Arnaud Loix Van Hooff

Producer
Katrin Dettmann

Illustrator
Jutta Kuss

Project Manager
Sirrka Koster

Management Supervisor
Bela Ziemann

Strategic Planner
Moritz Kiechle

Agency
TBWA \ Germany

Client
Adidas AG

Country
Germany

We showed in a very simple
way that stars like Ballack,
Zidane, Kahn or Beckham
are part of the team.
In this execution of the adidas' +10 idea, it's the team
that literally makes the star.

ADC LXXXVI

Advertising
Posters & Billboards
Outdoor / Billboard /
Single

Merit
Bird Seed

138

BIRD SEED

Art Director
João Roque

Copywriter
Miguel Gonçalves

Creative Director
Fernando Bellotti

Designer Photographer
Máquina Invisivel

Agency
Leo Burnett Publicidade,
LDA

Agency
Leo Burnett

Client
Friskies

Country
United States

To generate brand aware-
ness, we created huge
"Friskies Packages" on
small billboards strategical-
ly located in the cities main
squares where people are
known for feeding birds.
The packages had a deposit
full of bird food on top,
not visible from the street,
which attracted birds to
the billboards. Significant
word-of-mouth communica-
tion was generated and
the boards became a popu-
lar attraction with locals
and tourists.

ADC LXXXVI

Advertising
Posters & Billboards
Outdoor / Billboard /
Campaign

Merit
Kid's Headache

139

KID'S HEADACHE
Art Director
Hernán Cerdeiro
Copywriter
Ariel Serkin, Juan Frontini
Creative Director
Guillermo Vega (DGC),
Juan Frontini
Producer
Fernando Costanza, Daniel
Romanos
Agency
Young & Rubicam Buenos
Aires
Client
Bayer
Country
Argentina

QUOTES:
DON'T KNOW WHY,
I HAVE MY ID,
THANK YOU OFFICER

<u>Art Director</u>
Menno Kluin

<u>Copywriter</u>
Icaro Doria

<u>Creative Director</u>
Tony Granger,
Beverly Okada, Jan Jacobs,
Leo Premutico

<u>Agency</u>
Saatchi & Saatchi

<u>Client</u>
Procter & Gamble,
Olay Total Effects

<u>Country</u>
United States

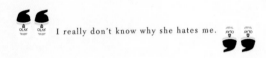

I really don't know why she hates me.

 Just a second, I have my ID here somewhere.

*
Advertising
Posters & Billboards
Transit / Campaign
Merit
Quotes
+
Advertising
Posters & Billboards
Outdoor / Billboard / Single
Merit
Don't Know Why
+
Advertising
Posters & Billboards
Outdoor / Billboard / Single
Merit
I Have My ID

 I get that a lot.

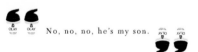 No, no, no, he's my son.

 No, seriously, I'm 47.

**BBC VOTING:
IMMINENT /
PREVENTABLE,
BEFRIEND/ BEWARE**

<u>Art Director</u>
Jamie Overkamp, Jerome
Marucci

<u>Copywriter</u>
Adam Kanzer, Ari Weiss

<u>Creative Director</u>
Executive Creative Director:
Eric Silver, Creative
Directors: Jerome Marucci,
Ari Weiss

<u>Other</u>
Chief Creative Officers:
David Lubars, Bill Bruce

<u>Agency</u>
BBDO New York

<u>Client</u>
BBC World

<u>Country</u>
United States

*
Advertising
Posters & Billboards
Electronic Billboard / Single
Merit
BBC Voting Imminent /
Preventable
+
Advertising
Posters & Billboards
Electronic Billboard / Single
Merit
BBC Voting: Befriend /
Beware
+
Advertising
Posters & Billboards
Electronic Billboard /
Campaign
Merit
BBC Voting Electronic
Billboard Campaign

ADC LXXXVI

Advertising
Guerrilla / Unconventional /
Campaign

Merit
Restart

144

RESTART

Art Director
Helena Sidova

Copywriter
Iva Bizova

Creative Director
Tomas Kopecny

Designer
Pavel Bures

Director
Julius Sevcik

Producer
Karla Stojakova

Production Company
Axman production

Agency
Publicis Prague, s.r.o.

Client
Axman Production

Country
Czech Republic

The campaign brings out
a connection between the
movie and the real life in
the city of Prague. The main
hero, Sylva, finds herself
in a relationship crisis with
a boyfriend, Martin. She
leaves messages on
Polaroids, Post-its, and
transparents. She leaves
signs all around Prague.
The primary communication
objective was grabbing the
interest of young people and
the demanding target group.
We wanted to inspire peo-
ple and wake up the interest
of people in the movie and
the story. The marketing target was to attract at least
10,000 viewers to come to
the cinema. This target was
achieved at 153 percent.
This is a campaign for a
graduate movie, so we
decided to go for a guerilla
marketing campaign, with a
minimum budget narrowed
to $12,000.

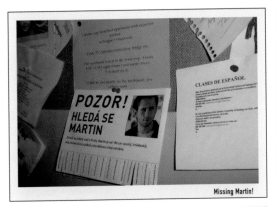

Missing Martin!

Martin, I did not mean it! Sylva

Martin, I regret it! Sylva

Martin, damn it, pick up the phone! Sylva

Martin, I'm sorry! Sylva

Martin, I'm afraid I fucked it up! Sylva

Martin, don't be crazy! Sylva

Martin, don't be crazy! Sylva

ADC LXXXVI

Advertising
Guerrilla / Unconventional /
Single

Merit
Landmines

145

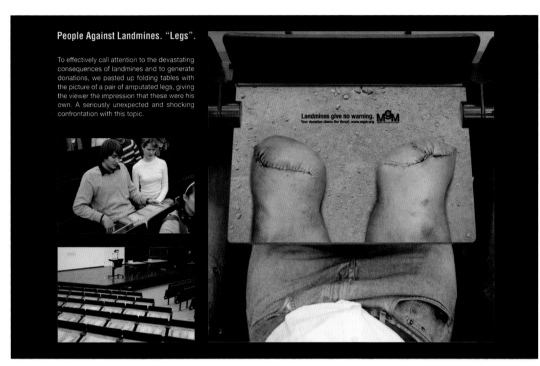

People Against Landmines. "Legs".

To effectively call attention to the devastating consequences of landmines and to generate donations, we pasted up folding tables with the picture of a pair of amputated legs, giving the viewer the impression that these were his own. A seriously unexpected and shocking confrontation with this topic.

LANDMINES
Art Director
Damjan Pita
Copywriter
Henning Robert
Creative Director
Goetz Ulmer, Daniel
Frericks, Oliver Voss
Designer
Damjan Pita
Agency
Jung von Matt AG
Client
MGM—people against land-
mines
Country
Germany

PHOTOGRAPHY /
C LXXXVI

THE JUDGES HAVE AWARDED / 2 DISTINCTIVE MERIT WINNERS /
15 MERIT WINNERS IN THIS CATEGORY.

Honda Skyline / Merit / see page 178

Heroines & Heroes: Hope, HIV and Africa / Merit / see page 154

Churches / Merit / see page 168

Pictures of the Year / Merit / see page 158

The Damage Done / Merit / see page 162

Beyond the Pale / Merit / see page 150

Ricefields / Merit / see page 172

On Location / Merit / see page 156

Fat Factors / Merit / see page 164

Great Performers / Distinctive Merit / see page 148

ADC LXXXVI

Photography
Magazine Editorial /
Campaign

Distinctive Merit
Great Performers

148

GRET PERFORMERS
Art Director
Arem Duplessis
Creative Director
Janet Froelich
Designer
Cathy Gilmore-Barnes
Editor
Gerry Marzorati
Photo Editor
Kathy Ryan, Kira Pollack
Photographer
Inez van Lamsweerde,
Vinoodh Matadin
Publisher
The New York Times
Agency
The New York Times
Magazine
Client
The New York Times
Magazine
Country
United States

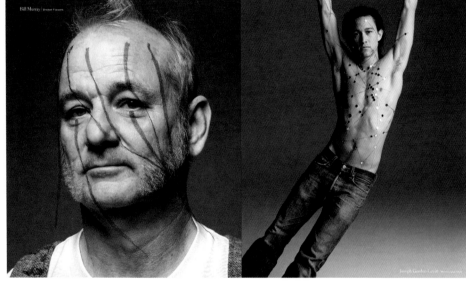

ADC LXXXVI

Photography
Magazine Editorial /
Campaign

Merit
Beyond the Pale

150

BEYOND THE PALE

Art Director
David Sebbah, Christopher
Martinez

Creative Director
Janet Froelich

Designer
Christopher Martinez

Editor
Stefano Tonchi

Photographer
Adam Fuss

Publisher
The New York Times

Producer
Anne Christenson

Fashion Editor
Anne Christensen

Agency
T: The New York Times Style
Magazine

Client
The New York Times
Magazine

Country
United States

In these photograms, created by the artist Adam Fuss
with the fashion editor Anne
Christenson, the dresses of
the season are given an
aura of sweetness and time-
less melancholia. Fuss
takes the pictures without a
camera, using light and
light-sensitive paper.

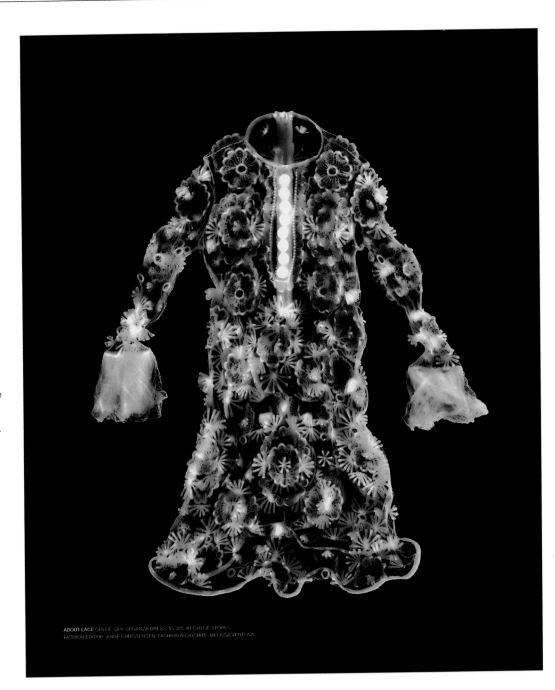

ABOUT LACE CHLOÉ SILK ORGANZA DRESS, $5,320, AT CHLOÉ STORES.
FASHION EDITOR: ANNE CHRISTENSEN. FASHION ASSOCIATE: MELISSA VENTOSA

FRILL SEEKING FENDI COTTON SHIRT, $1,170, AND SKIRT, $863, AT FENDI STORES.

PRETTY BABY CALVIN KLEIN COLLECTION COTTON DRESS, $3,615, AT CALVIN KLEIN, 654 MADISON AVENUE.

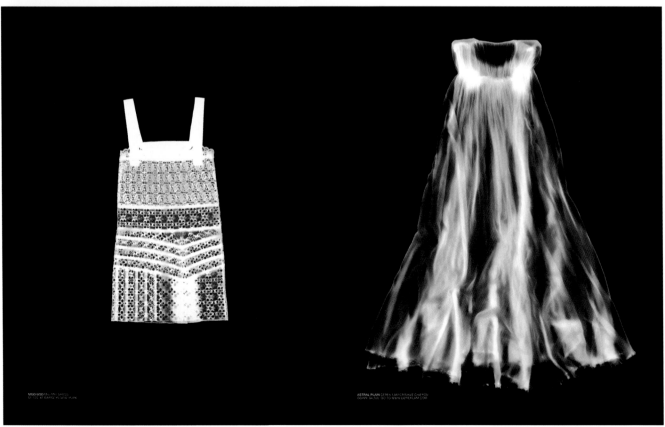

MOD ROD KNITTED DRESS, $1,135, AT BARNEYS NEW YORK.

ASTRAL PLAIN DEREK LAM CRINKLE CHIFFON GOWN, $4,500, GO TO WWW.DEREKLAM.COM.

ADC LXXXVI   **Photography**   **Merit**   152
Magazine Editorial /   DJ Living Rooms
Campaign

DJ LIVING ROOMS

Photo Editor
Heiko Hoffmann

Photographer
Ragnar Schmuck

Production Company
Groove Magazin

Publisher
Alex Lacher

Designer
Stefanie Baumgartner

Editor
Heiko Hoffmann

Agency
Ragnar Schmuck

Client
Groove

Country
Germany

The work is part of a long
term project, which is still
running. A second part of
the series is going to be
published this summer.
It´s a look behind the
scenes where you can
easily recognize who must
have been there, since style
is an aspect in both music
and living.

ADC LXXXVI

Photography
Public Service / Non-Profit /
Single

Merit
Heroines & Heroes: Hope,
HIV and Africa

154

HEROINES & HEROES: HOPE, HIV AND AFRICA

<u>Copywriter</u>
Sylvia Palombi

<u>Designer</u>
Daniela Meda

<u>Director</u>
Filomena Moscatelli

<u>Editor</u>
Charles Gute

<u>Photographer</u>
Steve Simon

<u>Producer</u>
Francesca Sorace

<u>Publisher</u>
Giuseppe Liverani-Charta

<u>Production Company</u>
Printed in Italy by Tipografia
Rumor s.r.l. Vicenza

<u>Other</u>
Barbara Bonacina, Lucas
Robinson

<u>Agency</u>
stevesimonphoto.com

<u>Client</u>
Charta

<u>Country</u>
United States

This book was inspired by
photographs taken for
several NGO's, including
CARE, World Vision,
Save The Children and
PhotoSensitive. I went back
on my own to Africa to fin-
ish the work in 2006, after
meeting with Giuseppe
Liverani of Charta, who
wanted to publish this work
as a book. There is a call-to-
action section in the back
of the book for people who
may be inspired by what
they see, to get involved.
All Royalties go to AIDS
Charities. I wanted to show
some of the positive steps
being taken in the fight, as
well as the harsh reality. The
AIDS Pandemic Worldwide
is a big problem for us all,
and I wanted to add my
voice to the issue to promote awareness, and
encourage people to help,
even if it is in some small
way. It is a reminder: where
love and determination
exist, there is hope.

ON LOCATION
Art Director
Brian Anstey
Creative Director
Geraldine Hessler
Photo Editor
Richard Maltz
Photographer
Henrik Knudsen
Photo Director
Fiona McDonagh
Agency
Henrik Knudsen
Photography
Client
Entertainment Weekly
Country
United Kingdom

ADC LXXXVI

Photography
Magazine Editorial /
Campaign

Merit
Pictures of the Year

158

PICTURES OF THE YEAR

Art Director
Arthur Hochstein
Deputy Art Director
Cynthia A. Hoffman
Director of Photography
Michele Stephenson
Picture Editor
MaryAnne Golon
Associate Picture Editor
Crary Pullen
Photographer
Ghaith Abdul-Ahad (Getty
Images), Shaul Schwarz
(Getty Images), Christopher
Morris (VII), Anthony Suau,
Lauren Greenfield (VII)
Publisher
TIME Inc.
Agency
TIME Magazine
Client
TIME Magazine
Country
United States

BRIGHT YOUNG
THINGS

Teens take a party bus
to the senior prom of
California's Newport
Harbor High—the school
that inspired the Fox TV
show *The OC*

Photograph by
Lauren Greenfield—VII

ADC LXXXVI   **Photography**   **Merit**   160
Magazine Editorial /   America's Divide
Campaign

AMERICA'S DIVIDE

Art Director
Leah Purcell

Creative Director
Lynn Staley

Director of Photography
Simon Barnett

Photo Editor
Michelle Molloy

Photographer
James Whitlow Delano

Agency
Newsweek

Client
James Whitlow Delano
(Newsweek)

Country
United States

**INSIDE BUSH
COUNTRY**
Art Director
Arthur Hochstein
Deputy Art Director
Cynthia A. Hoffman
Director of Photography
Michele Stephenson
Picture Editor
MaryAnne Golon
Photographer
Christopher Morris (VII)
Publisher
TIME Inc.
Agency
TIME Magazine
Client
TIME Magazine
Country
United States

For the past five years, photojournalist Christopher Morris has traveled around the country with George W. Bush, taking pictures for TIME. In *My America*, Morris presents not just what he saw of the President but also what he saw when he turned the lens away from him—"a nation," he says, "trying to find its identity in the war on terror," looking for a place to put its faith. In this world, audiences mimic congregations (mouths agape, eyes moist), soldiers look young and fresh, untouched by battle, and everyone's clothes fit perfectly. Morris, who spent most of the past 20 years covering wars, often has just seconds to compose pictures before the presidential entourage whisks him along. Much of the time, the scene is chaotic, but Morris' photographs never are. Even as commotion surrounds him, he walks away with pictures that are quiet, calm and at times quite sobering. —*By Barbara Kiviat*

From My America by Christopher Morris,
Steidl Publishers © October 2006

WASHINGTON
Morris frequently crops out heads to force the viewer's eye to a telling detail elsewhere. In the picture on the previous pages, the President waits to address a group of insurance agents last year. Sometimes introductions run long. When that happens, the President tends to grow impatient. In this picture his fingers fidget as he waits to take the mike.

TAMPA,
FLORIDA
His Secret Service retinue is a constant part of the President's immediate environment. Morris was drawn to the crystal blue eyes of the agent pictured above, who stood guard in an airplane hangar in 2004 as the President addressed military staff members and their families. The flag hanging above the agent's head capped the composition.

PHILADELPHIA
In the picture at top right, taken at the 2004 Army-Navy football game, the focus is on the implacable blank screen that is the Army cadet's tunic. With its upright black trim, the uniform imposes a "uniformity" that the cadet's gently canted head belies.

SAGINAW,
MICHIGAN
On his travels with the President, Morris finds that when Bush takes the stage, supporters often react with devoted attentiveness. Eyes well with tears, and mouths drop open. The bright lipstick of the young woman at right, who is attending a 2004 campaign speech, drew Morris in. "It's almost like people can't believe that they're there," says Morris, "right in front of the President, listening to him speak."

ADC LXXXVI   **Photography**   **Merit**   162
Magazine Editorial /   The Damage Done
Campaign

THE DAMAGE DONE
Art Director
Arthur Hochstein
Deputy Art Director
Cynthia A. Hoffman
Director of Photography
Michele Stephenson
Picture Editor
MaryAnne Golon
Associate Picture Editor
Alice Gabriner
Publisher
TIME Inc.
Photographer
Gamma: Frederic Lafargue
(New York Times); Redux:
Tyler Hicks; Getty Images:
Shaul Schwarz
Agency
TIME Magazine
Client
TIME Magazine
Country
United States

SHATTERED
After three straight
days of Israeli rocket
attacks, stillness
falls on ruined
apartment buildings
in the Dahiya, a
suburb of Beirut
Photograph by
Frederic Lafargue—
Gamma

"I got my family
out on the first day of the strikes, but I
stayed. I thought it was wrong to leave
because if we all left, it would be like
surrendering to Israel."
—AHMAD HAMMOUD, 40,
taxi driver and Dahiya resident

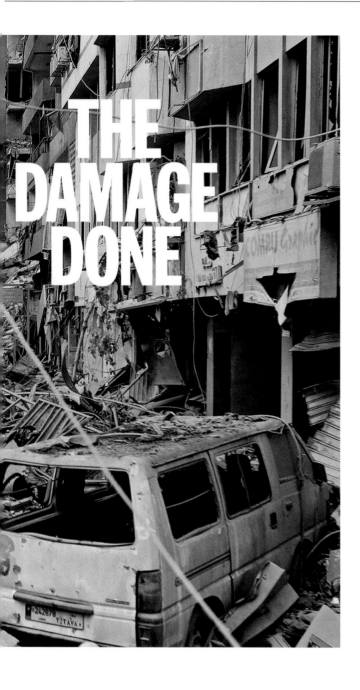

THE DAMAGE DONE

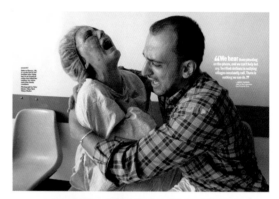

ADC LXXXVI

Photography
Magazine Editorial /
Campaign

Merit
Fat Factors

164

FAT FACTORS
<u>Art Director</u>
Arem Duplessis
<u>Creative Director</u>
Janet Froelich
<u>Designer</u>
Jeff Glendenning
<u>Editor</u>
Gerry Marzorati
<u>Photo Editor</u>
Kathy Ryan
<u>Photographer</u>
Gary Schneider
<u>Publisher</u>
The New York Times
<u>Agency</u>
New York Times Magazine
<u>Client</u>
The New York Times
Magazine
<u>Country</u>
United States

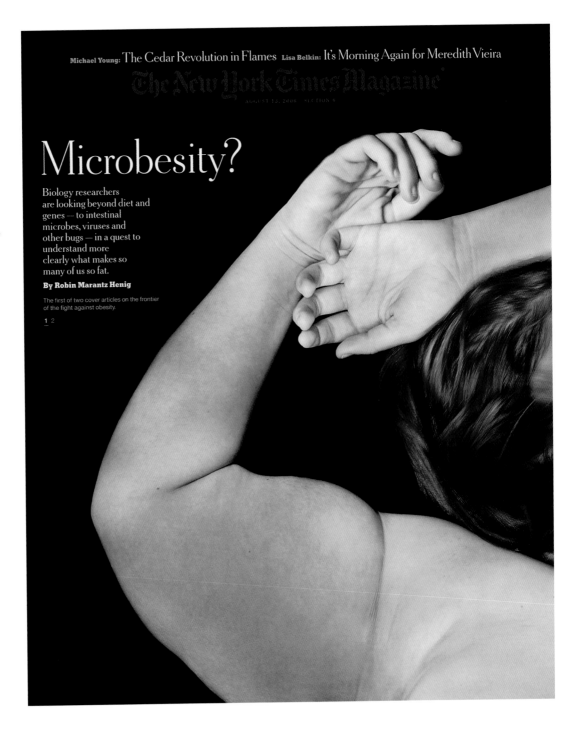

Michael Young: The Cedar Revolution in Flames   Lisa Belkin: It's Morning Again for Meredith Vieira

The New York Times Magazine

AUGUST 13, 2006 · SECTION 6

Microbesity?

Biology researchers
are looking beyond diet and
genes — to intestinal
microbes, viruses and
other bugs — in a quest to
understand more
clearly what makes so
many of us so fat.

By Robin Marantz Henig

The first of two cover articles on the frontier
of the fight against obesity.

<u>1</u> 2

FAT
FACTORS

IT'S CLEAR THAT DIET
AND GENES CONTRIBUTE
TO HOW FAT YOU ARE.

BUT A NEW WAVE OF
SCIENTIFIC RESEARCH
SUGGESTS THAT,

FOR SOME PEOPLE,

THERE MIGHT BE A
THIRD FACTOR —
MICROORGANISMS.

By Robin Marantz Henig

PHOTOGRAPHS BY
GARY SCHNEIDER

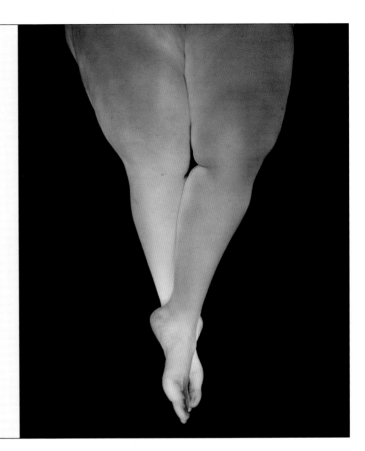

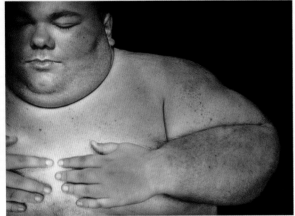

The New York Times Magazine

The Fat Virus What if obesity, long seen as a personal failing, turns out to come from a bug that you can catch?
Photograph by Gary Schneider for The New York Times. (Page 28)

Back Story 8.13.06

"When I first read about this research, I thought how nice it would be if it were really so simple," says Robin Marantz Henig, a contributing writer for the magazine, who wrote this week's cover article about obesity. "We're full of moral judgments about people who are fat. We think being overweight is about laziness and gluttony." It is too early to say what role microbes and viruses and other bugs might play in obesity, but it may be that obesity is about more than diet and exercise. Henig herself is slender, but she was a chubby teenager and sensitive to the discrimination that fat people face. "This research is a reason we should be more tolerant and forgiving about why people are so fat," she says. Next week, the magazine looks at a macro-cause of obesity — school lunches — and the efforts of one Florida school district to combat it. And next month, on Sept. 17 to be exact, we'll resume our Sunday Serial, with a criminal thriller by Michael Connelly.

Cover Story

On the cover: Photograph by Gary Schneider for The New York Times.

6

Continued on Page 8

ADC LXXXVI

Photography
Magazine Editorial /
Campaign

Merit
Behind Closed Doors

166

**BEHIND CLOSED
DOORS**
Art Director
Arem Duplessis
Creative Director
Janet Froelich
Designer
Arem Duplessis
Editor
Gerry Marzorati
Photo Editor
Kathy Ryan
Photographer
Taryn Simon
Publisher
The New York Times
Agency
New York Times Magazine
Client
The New York Times
Magazine
Country
United States

In her new body of work
entitled "An American
Index of the Hidden and
Unfamiliar", photographer
Taryn Simon captures a
sense of what we don't
allow one another to see.
From a Contraband Room in
Kennedy International
Airport to a white tiger
named Kenny who suffers
from mental retardation due
to inbreeding. This body of
work allows entry into a
world few knew existed.

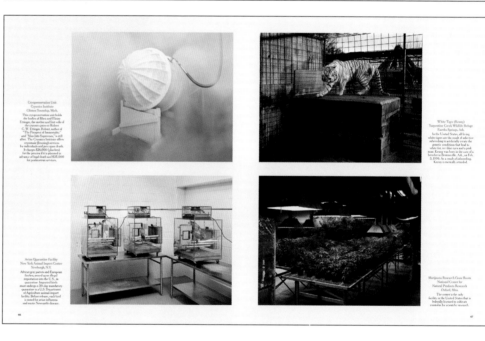

Hibernating Black Bear and Cubs
Bear Den
Monongahela National Forest, W. Va.
The American black bears in the photograph are part
of the West Virginia Division of Natural Resources Black
Bear Research and Monitoring Project. Researchers
monitor the health and development of mother (sow) and
cubs through their hibernation from approximately
mid-December to early April. Sows both give birth and
nurse the cubs while in their winter dens.

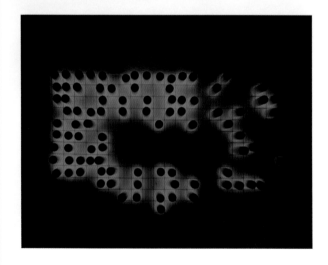

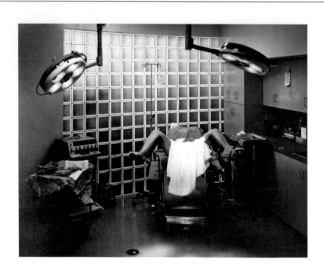

Waste Encapsulation and Storage Facility, Cherenkov Radiation
Hanford Site, U.S. Department of Energy
Benton County, Wash.

Submerged in a pool of water at the Hanford Site are 1,936 stainless-steel
nuclear-waste capsules. The pool serves as a shield against radiation; anyone standing
within one foot from an unshielded capsule would receive a lethal dose of radiation
in less than 10 seconds. The blue glow is created by the Cherenkov effect, which
describes the electromagnetic radiation emitted when a charged particle, giving off
energy, moves faster than light through a transparent medium.

Hymenoplasty
Cosmetic Surgery, Professional Association
Fort Lauderdale, Fla.

The hidden patient in this photograph is a 21-year-old Arab woman
living in the United States. In order to adhere to cultural and familial expectations
regarding her virginity, she had her hymen reconstructed.

ADC LXXXVI

Photography
Magazine Editorial /
Campaign

Merit
Churches

168

CHURCHES

<u>Photographer</u>
Christoph Morlinghaus
<u>Publisher</u>
Federico Pepe, Pierpaolo
Ferrari
<u>Creative Director</u>
Federico Pepe, Pierpaolo
Ferrari
<u>Agency</u>
The Morlinghaus
<u>Client</u>
Le Dictateur Magazine
<u>Country</u>
United States

The selected images are
part of an art project on
ecclesiastical architecture
of significant 20th century
architects. They were shot
with an 8x10 large format
camera, using only available
light. The project is ongoing
and will include a book and
exhibitions.

ADC LXXXVI

Photography
Book (Commercially
Published Volumes Only) /
Single

Merit
Perfect Intimacy

170

PERFECT INTIMACY
<u>Art Director</u>
Mine Suda
<u>Designer</u>
Lili Almog, Mine Suda
<u>Photographer</u>
Lili Almog
<u>Publisher</u>
powerHouse Books
<u>Photo Editor</u>
Lili Almog
<u>Agency</u>
powerHouse Books
<u>Client</u>
Lili Almog
<u>Country</u>
United States

RICEFIELDS
<u>Photographer</u>
Christian Schmidt
<u>Art Director</u>
Christian Schmidt
<u>Agency</u>
Christian Schmidt
Photodesign
<u>Client</u>
Christian Schmidt
Photography
<u>Country</u>
Germany

ADC LXXXVI

Photography
Magazine Advertisement /
Single

Merit
Honda Skyline

173

HONDA SKYLINE
Art Director
Jennifer Young
Photographer
Michael Schnabel
Production Company
Loni Weholt
Art Producer
Annie Ross
Retoucher
Etizy Digital
Agency
Michael Schnabel
Client
Honda Acura
Country
Germany

This image is an excerpt of
an ongoing series of
Schnabels painterly land-
scapes, exploring new
approaches to this classic
genre.

**ANY OLD CLOTHES
WILL DO**

<u>Art Director</u>
Yvonne Hall

<u>Copywriter</u>
Angela Collins

<u>Creative Director</u>
Vanessa Pearson

<u>Photographer</u>
Clive Stewart

<u>Agency</u>
Lobedu Leo Burnett

<u>Client</u>
Salvation Army

<u>Country</u>
United States

Any old clothes will do. You
wouldn't be caught dead in
them but, for a homeless
person, they could mean the
difference between life and
death. Please donate your
unwanted clothes to the
homeless this winter.

ADC LXXXVI

Photography
Newspaper Advertisement /
Campaign

Merit
Airmail

175

AIRMAIL

<u>Art Director</u>
Andreas Jeutter
<u>Copywriter</u>
Paul Fleig
<u>Creative Director</u>
Joachim Silber, Paul Fleig
<u>Designer</u>
Dominic Stuebler, Mario
Loncar
<u>Photo Editor</u>
Joerg Macha
<u>Photographer</u>
Peter Schumacher, Thomas
Baumann
<u>Other</u>
Account Supervisor: Frank
Lotze, Frauke Schmidt, Nina
Weinmann
<u>Agency</u>
Jung von Matt AG
<u>Client</u>
DHL
<u>Country</u>
Germany

ILLUSTRATION /
ADC <u>LXXXVI</u>

THE JUDGES HAVE AWARDED 1 SILVER CUBE / 10 MERIT WINNERS IN THIS CATEGORY.

Might is Wrong / Merit / see page 182

Hugo Boss "Fantasy Tree" / Merit / see page 183

Filling / Merit / see page 189

Kamasutra / Merit / see page 188

Waiting for the Pandemic / Merit / see page 190

The Pop-up Book of Celebrity Meltdowns / Merit / see page 184

Bottles / Merit / see page 186

Cyberneologoliferation / Merit / see page 180

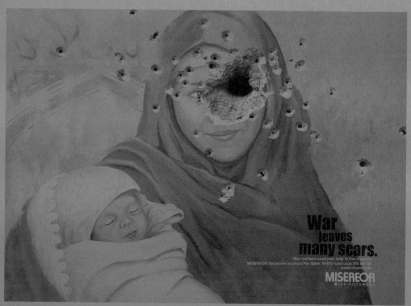

War Orphans / Merit / see page 192

Taking the Least of You / Merit / see page 181

TANGO XMAS CARD

Art Director
Dana Robertson

Creative Director
Dana Robertson

Illustrator
Paul Davis

Copywriter
Dana Robertson, Paul Davis

Other
Artwork & Production:
Spencer Forster, Carolyn
Lindsey

Agency
Tango

Client
Tango Design

Country
United Kingdom

A thought provoking
Christmas gift from Tango
in the form of a large format
booklet that contrasts some
pretty bleak observations
about Christmas with some
rather jolly Christmas
imagery. The juxtaposition
of harsh truths and
Christmas wrapping paper
produces a wry and knowing
smile rather than a belly
laugh but acts as a com-
mentary on the commercial-
ism of Christmas itself.
Questioning why we give,
what we give and who
benefits with some rather
telling illustrations of consumerism makes for an
interesting and certainly
different approach to the
corporate Christmas card.

ADC LXXXVI

Illustration
Magazine Editorial /
Campaign

Merit
Cyberneologoliferation

180

**CYBER-
NEOLOGOLIFERATION**

<u>Art Director</u>
Arem Duplessis

<u>Creative Director</u>
Janet Froelich

<u>Designer</u>
Gail Bichler

<u>Editor</u>
Gerry Marzorati

<u>Illustrator</u>
Sam Winston

<u>Publisher</u>
The New York Times

<u>Agency</u>
New York Times Magazine

<u>Client</u>
The New York Times
Magazine

<u>Country</u>
United States

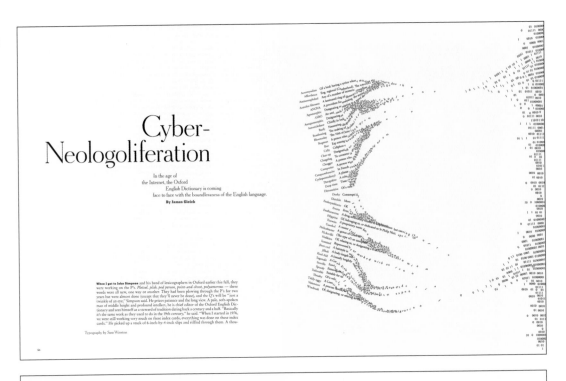

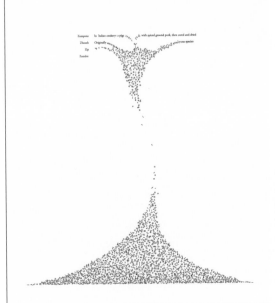

ADC LXXXVI

Illustration
Magazine Editorial /
Campaign

Merit
Taking the Least of You

181

The New York Times Magazine

APRIL 16, 2006 / SECTION 6

Body-Stuff Politics

Those blood and tissue samples you routinely give — where are they?
Who owns them? What are they being used for? And how come you don't know? **By Rebecca Skloot**

Also: Strawberry Saroyan on Flacks for Jesus

TAKING THE LEAST OF YOU

Art Director
Arem Duplessis
Creative Director
Janet Froelich
Designer
Jeff Glendenning
Editor
Gerry Marzorati
Illustrator
Marcel Dzama
Publisher
The New York Times
Agency
New York Times Magazine
Client
The New York Times
Magazine
Country
United States

"Body-Stuff Politics" uncovers what really happens to your donations of blood and tissue. We chose Marcel Dzama, an artist well known for his visual articulation of the strange and surreal to illustrate the piece. In the end, Marcel discovered the answer: little bats and bears are the culprits.

ADC LXXXVI

Illustration
Magazine Editorial /
Campaign

Merit
Might is Wrong

182

MIGHT IS WRONG

Creative Director
Antonio De Luca

Designer
Antonio De Luca

Editor
Ken Alexander

Illustrator
Rinzen

Publisher
The Walrus Foundation

Art Director
Antonio De Luca

Agency
The Walrus Magazine

Client
The Walrus Magazine

Country
Canada

ADC LXXXVI

Illustration
Corporate / Institutional
(Annual Reports, Brochures,
Etc.) / Single

Merit
Hugo Boss "Fantasy Tree"

183

**HUGO BOSS
"FANTASY TREE"**
Creative Director
Martin Grothmaak,
Projekttriangle
Illustrator
Franz-Georg Staemmele,
Projekttriangle
Production Company
Weskstätten
(Silkscreenprinting)
Agency
Projekttriangle
Informationdesign
Client
Hugo Boss AG
Country
Germany

A hand drawn illustration (6
meters high) for Shanghai
based Hugo Boss Orange
Concept Store. After scan-
ning the illustration it had
been silkscreened inside a
wooden walk-through box.
Additionally we made ten
large wooden stamps of
beautiful German birds.
These stamps were hand-
printed directly on the box
surface.

ADC LXXXVI

Illustration
Book (Commercially
Published Volumes Only) /
Single

Merit
The Pop-Up Book of Celebrity
Meltdowns

184

**THE POP-UP BOOK OF
CELEBRITY
MELTDOWNS**

Copywriter
Heather Havrilesky

Designer
Paul Kepple (Headcase
Design)

Editor
Megan Worman (Melcher
Media Inc.)

Illustrator
Mick Coulas (Coulas &
Lourdes Inc.)

Publisher
Melcher Media Inc.

Creative Director
Charles Melcher (Melcher
Media Inc.)

Other
Paper Engineer:
Bruce Foster

Agency
Mick Coulas, Coulas &
Lourdes Inc.

Client
Melcher Media Inc.

Country
Canada

The Pop-Up Book of
Celebrity Meltdowns took
our illustration studio 5
months to complete - per-
haps I am the slowest
paparazzo in the world!
"Everything about the book
was to play off of our love of
tabloid journalism," Charles
Melcher said to CNN. I think
the biggest thrill was to see
our book reviewed on CNN
by Jeanne Moos. In the segment, Jeanne comments
"Celebs like baby dangler,
Michael Jackson, may be
embarrassed by their meltdowns, but the pop-ups are
engineered with pride."
One unusual challenge in
the process of creating the
illustrations for a pop-up
book was to fit them to the
very cool pop-up engineering by Bruce Foster, making
the exaggerated, but realis-
tically rendered celebrities
move in a comic fashion
when "popped".

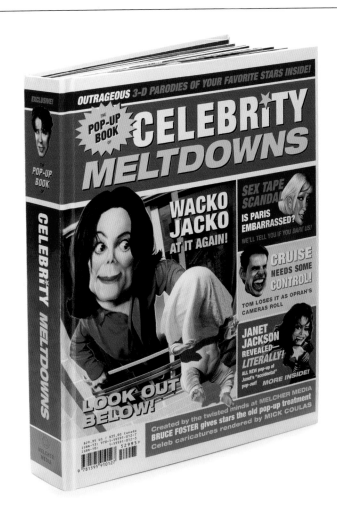

BOTTLES
Art Director
Carl Broadhurst, Lovisa
Almgren-Falken
Copywriter
Diccon Driver, Peter Reid,
Alan Wilson
Creative Director
Ed Morris
Producer
Gary Wallis
Illustrator
Aesthetic Apparatus
Agency
Lowe London
Client
Inbev UK
Country
United Kingdom

A poster to promote
Stella's six-hundred-
year-old heritage.

ADC LXXXVI

Illustration
Magazine Advertisement /
Campaign

Merit
Kamasutra

188

KAMASUTRA
Art Director
Jan Kromka
Copywriter
Sandra Illes
Creative Director
Tim Jacobs, Thomas
Schwarz
Illustrator
Peter Klanke
Photo Editor
Peter Klanke
Other
Chief Creative Officer: Amir
Kassaei; Executive Creative
Officer: Eric Schoeffler;
Account Director: Marion
Tobor, Ute Brando
Agency
DDB Germany
Client
Beate Uhse AG
Country
Germany

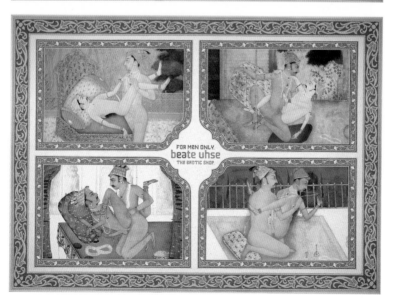

ADC LXXXVI

Illustration
Poster or Billboard
Advertisement / Campaign

Merit
Filling

189

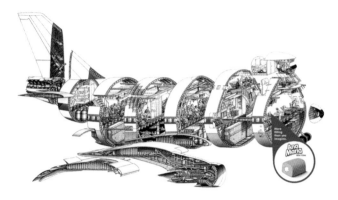

FILLING
Art Director
Fernando Reis
Copywriter
Marcelo Padoca
Creative Director
Adriana Cury, Danilo
Janjácomo, Danilo Martins
Illustrator
Stephen Biesty
Producer
Ricardo Ramos
Agency
McCann Erickson Brazil
Client
Bimbo
Country
Brazil

The perception consumers
had about Ana Maria's mini
cakes was that they were
tasty, but had little filling. In
truth this was an incorrect
perception, and it was precisely our task to show that
in that dough there was
much more filling than people imagined.

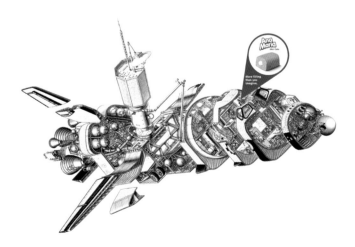

ADC LXXXVI

Illustration
Photo Illustration / Campaign

Merit
Waiting for the Pandemic

190

WAITING FOR THE PANDEMIC

Art Director
Antonio De Luca

Creative Director
Antonio De Luca

Designer
Antonio De Luca

Editor
Ken Alexander

Illustrator
Tamara Shopsin

Photo Editor
Natalie Matutschovsky

Photographer
Jason Fulford

Publisher
The Walrus Foundation

Agency
The Walrus Magazine

Client
The Walrus Magazine

Country
Canada

These cards / illustrations
were produced (silk
screened) and then pho-
tographed.

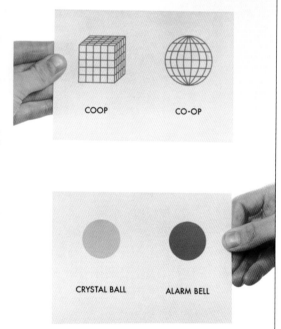

WAR ORPHANS
Art Director
Maik Beimdiek
Copywriter
David Leinweber
Creative Director
Sven Klohk, Lorenz Ritter
Illustrator
Eva Salzmann
Other
Retouching: Kathrin Meske,
Account Manager:
Alexander Duve
Agency
Kolle Rebbe Werbeagentur
GmbH
Client
Bischoefliches Hilfswerk
Misereore.V.
Country
Germany

Misereor wants to raise
awareness about the topic
of war orphans by means of
intelligent—as well as
shocking—treatment of the
subject. The viewer should
feel moved and encouraged
to become interested in the
Misereor website and
maybe also to make a donation. In a very graphic way,
the ads show just how war
can destroy whole families.

GRAPHIC DESIGN /

AFTER XVI

After Neoconservatism

THE JUDGES HAVE AWARDED 1 GOLD CUBE / 2 SILVER CUBES / 10 DISTINCTIVE MERIT WINNERS / 101 MERIT WINNERS IN THIS CATEGORY.

After Neoconservatism / Merit / see page 220

The Ideas Issue / Merit / see page 222 /

Miscellaneous Crap / Merit / see page 244

All Men Are Brothers - Designers' Edition / Merit / see page 236

Typographic / Merit / see page 232

Frost* (Sorry Trees) / Merit / see page 237

87 / Merit / see page 242

Channel 4 Annual Report & Accounts 2006 /
Merit / see page 260

"Potsunen Maru" Produced By
Kentaro Kobayashi / Silver /
see page 205

Quartet: Four Literary Walks Through The V&A / Merit / see page 262

Grid-It! Notepads / Distinctive Merit /
see page 204

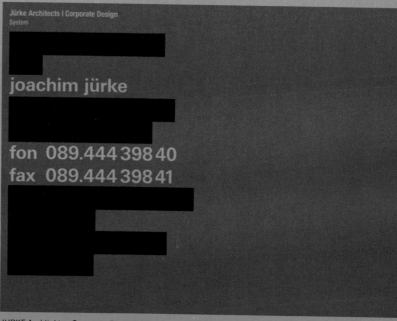

JURKE Architekten Corporate Design / Merit / see page 273

ADC LXXXVI

Graphic Design
Television & Cinema Design
Animation / Single

Gold
Issey Miyake A-Poc Inside

196

**ISSEY MIYAKE
A-POC INSIDE.**

Art Director
Masahiko Sato

Creative Director
Masahiko Sato

Designer
Tomoko Kaizuka, Kohji
Robert Yamamoto

Director
Mio Ueta, Masashi Sato

Production Company
Euphrates

Music
Seiichi Yamamoto

Agency
Euphrates

Client
Issey Miyake Inc.

Country
Japan

In this animation, we were
challenged to create a universal expression, which
can be understood by any
person, belonging to any
race, any religion, or age, by
using the knowledge of cognitive science. The screen
just shows simple information—white dots and lines
on a black flat background,
but the audience easily recognizes the elegant motion
of walking fashion models,
and depth of the screen.
This is a new expression,
which exceeds individuals'
arbitrariness.

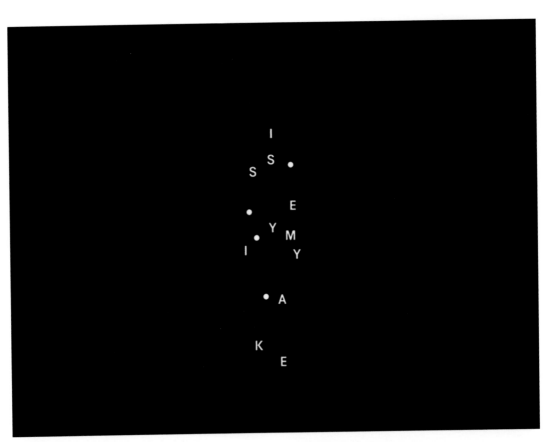

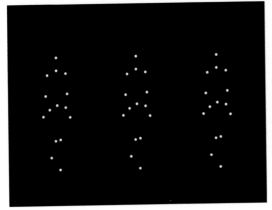

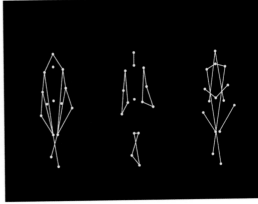

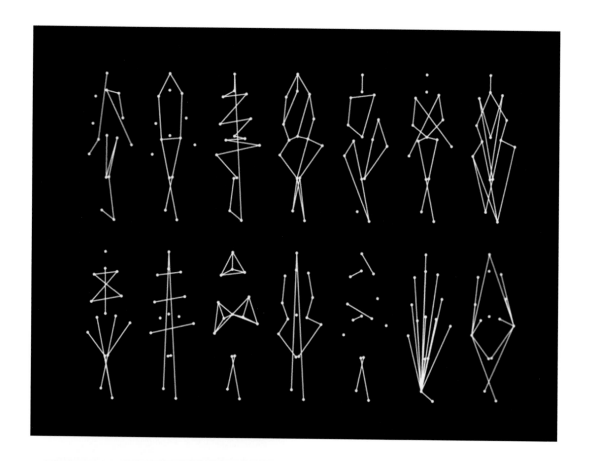

ADC LXXXVI

Graphic Design
Television & Cinema Design
TV Identities, Openings,
Teasers / Single

Silver
MTV 2 Sleep Dance

198

MTV2 SLEEP DANCE

Art Director
David McElwaine

Director
Johnnie Ross

Producer
Janet Shaw (MTV), Helene
Polverelli (Smuggler)

Production Company
Smuggler

Director of Photography
Dave Rodriguez

VP MTV On Air Design
Romy Mann

SVP MTV Design
Jeffrey Keyton

Executive Producer
Kevin Corvetti

Agency
MTV Networks

Client
MTV

Country
United States

Sleep dancing was an idea
that I wanted to do for a
long time; I was just looking
for the right opportunity.
When MTV2 came along
and asked for "power"
themed shorts, I knew what
I had to do. The biggest
challenge was finding
dancers who had the moves.
The concept was simple
enough but it required a rare
talent for limpness and
hang time. We had no idea
how to cast for that. Then
this guy showed up that
claimed to be an Olympic
long jumper. He nearly put
his head through the ceiling
at the casting session and
that was that.

MHD CROW
Creative Director
Marie Hyon, Marco Spier
Production Company
Psyop
Designer
Marie Hyon
Director
Marie Hyon, Marco Spier
Producer
Lucia Grillo
VP MTV On Air Design
Romy Mann
SVP MTV Design
Jeffrey Keyton
Technical Director
Pakorn Bupphavesa
Senior Design Director
Rodger Belknap
Agency
MTV Networks
Client
MTV
Country
United States

*
Graphic Design
Television & Cinema Design
TV Identities, Openings,
Teasers / Single
Silver
MHD Crow
+
Graphic Design
Television & Cinema Design
Animation / Single
Silver
MHD Crow
+
Graphic Design
Television & Cinema Design
TV Identities, Openings,
Teasers / Single
Silver
MHD Crow

ADC LXXXVI   **Graphic Design**   **Distinctive Merit**   202
Corporate & Promotional   Concept Book for Font [Half
Design Booklet / Brochure /   the Moon]
Single

**CONCEPT BOOK
FOR FONT [HALF
THE MOON]**
Art Director
Toshiyasu Nanbu
Copywriter
Toshiyasu Nanbu
Designer
Toshiyasu Nanbu
Agency
Taste Inc.
Client
Taste Inc.
Country
Japan

ADC LXXXVI

Graphic Design
Corporate & Promotional
Design Self-Promotion:
Print / Campaign

Distinctive Merit
Grid-It! Notepads

204

GRID-IT! NOTEPADS
Art Director
Astrid Stavro
Creative Director
Astrid Stavro
Designer
Birgit Pfisterer, Astrid
Stavro
Publisher
Miquelrius
Agency
Astrid Stavro
Client
The Royal College of Art
Country
Spain

Grid-it! notepads are a series of notepads based on the layout grids of famous publications. They are a selection of grids that played a historic role in the development of design systems, covering a wide spectrum of classic and contemporary editorial design. By moving the grids from the background to the foreground, and divorcing them from their content, I pay homage, as well as render the invisible visible. As designers, understanding the advantages, as well as the limitations, of the grid helps us determine what place they should take in our own work. The grid, like any other instrument in the design process, is not an absolute. Like computers, they are simple design tools. It is the process of challenging or questioning these assumptions that is important, because in doing so we reevaluate our perception of the environment and our role within it.

ADC LXXXVI

Graphic Design
Poster Design Promotional /
Single

Distinctive Merit
"Potsunen Maru" Produced
by Kentaro Kobayashi

205

**"POTSUNEN MARU"
PRODUCED BY
KENTARO KOBAYASHI**
Art Director
Manabu Mizuno
Designer
Masaru Uemura
Production Company
Good Design Company
Publisher
Twinkle Corporation Ltd.
Photographer
Lucy Sky
Agency
Good Design Company, Inc.
Client
Twinkle Corporation Ltd.
Country
Japan

ADC LXXXVI

Graphic Design
Poster Design Promotional /
Single

Distinctive Merit
Mesatex Japan Modern Fabric
Collection

206

**MESATEX JAPAN
MODERN FABRIC
COLLECTION**
Art Director
Gaku Ohsugi
Designer
Gaku Ohsugi, Kenji
Iwabuchi
Production Company
702 Design Works Inc.
Director
Mikako Wada
Agency
702 Design Works Inc.
Client
Mesatex Japan Inc.
Country
Japan

This poster was made for
an announcement for a new
work of fabric. Our client,
Mesatex Japan is a fabric
manufacturing and import-
ing company, mainly
focused on curtain materials. The theme of this work
is "modern fabric." We used
visually and sensually simple colored lines, inter-
twined, expressing the attitude of the business to put
out something new, and
moving lively. In the center
are the characters of
Mesatex Japan. From each
character, threads are
released in various direc-
tions, and each bundle is
made up of threads of delicate colors. This design is
made with two thoughts:
for people to feel the hope
and the possibility of one
thin thread getting together
and making Mesatex Japan,
and the mass of colored
threads released from the
characters would be inter-
twined and put out some-
thing fresh and new.

ADC LXXXVI

Graphic Design
Poster Design Public
Service / Non-Profit /
Educational / Single

Distinctive Merit
Who Am I?

207

WHO AM I?
Art Director
Pazu Lee Ka Ling
Copywriter
Pazu Lee Ka Ling
Creative Director
Pazu Lee Ka Ling
Designer
Pazu Lee Ka Ling
Illustrator
Pazu Lee Ka Ling
Photo Editor
Pazu Lee Ka Ling
Photographer
Pazu Lee Ka Ling
Producer
Pazu Lee Ka Ling
Client
Shenzhen Graphic Design
Association
Country
China

TRANSPORT
NETWORK

Art Director
Tim Schierwater

Copywriter
Sebastian Behrendt, Ingmar
Bartels

Creative Director
Lars Ruehmann

Designer
Christoph Bielefeldt,
Stephanie Schneider,
Barbara Schirner, Bertrand
Kirschenhofer

Other
Das Taxi: Christiane Moje
Nolte, Jo Ferschen, Ralf
Elfering, Anne Regine-Rach

Agency
Nordpol Hamburg Agentur
fuer Kommunikation GmbH

Client
Das Taxi

Country
Germany

Das Taxi irritates passengers of Hamburg´s public
transport system. A special
route map hangs right
next to the official route
information of the passenger transport authority on
underground and railway
platforms. The poster
shows all possible destina-
tions and connections you
can reach with Das Taxi,
which means every single
street in Hamburg.

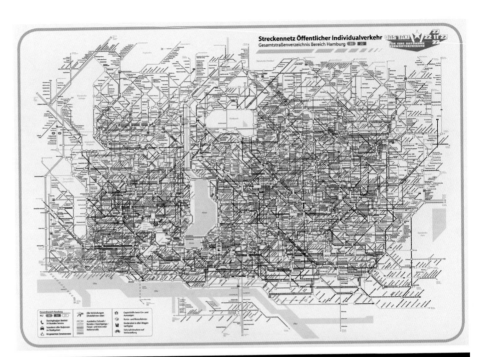

POSTER IN SUBWAY AND RAILWAY STATIONS

THE TAXI ROUTE MAP HANGS NEXT TO THE OFFICIAL PLAN OF HAMBURG'S PASSENGER TRANSPORT AUTHORITY.

EVERY SINGLE STREET IN HAMBURG CAN BE FOUND ON THE MAP. THE LEGEND EXPLAINS THE DIFFERENT TYPES OF STREETS.

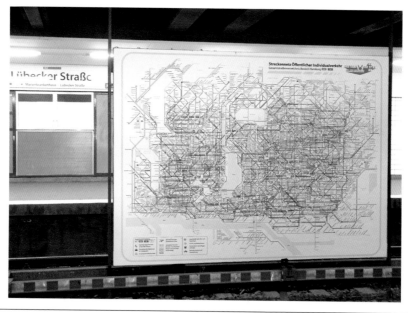

ADC LXXXVI   **Graphic Design**   **Distinctve Merit**   210
Environmental Design   Being Not Truthful
Gallery Museum Exhibit /
Installation / Campaign

BEING NOT TRUTHFUL

<u>Art Director</u>
Stefan Sagmeister, Ralph
Ammer

<u>Copywriter</u>
Stefan Sagmeister

<u>Creative Director</u>
Stefan Sagmeister, Ralph
Ammer

<u>Designer</u>
Stefan Sagmeister,
Matthias Ernstberger

<u>Agency</u>
Stefan Sagmeister

<u>Client</u>
Austrian Cultural Institute

<u>Country</u>
United States

The sentence "Being not
truthful works against me"
is woven into a projected
virtual spider web. As the
viewer passes the web she
rips it apart wherever her
reflection touches it. But it
reconstructs itself time and
again. This interactive
installation was first be
shown at the Austrian
Cultural Forum in New York,
in the spring of 2006."Being
not truthful works against
me" is part of a list in
Stefan's diary titled:
"Things I have learned in
my life so far."

YAHOO! MOVIES
Creative Director
Greg Hahn
Designer
Diana Park, Greg Hahn
Production Company
Gretel
Animator
Joe DiValerio
Agency
Gretel
Client
Yahoo!
Country
United States

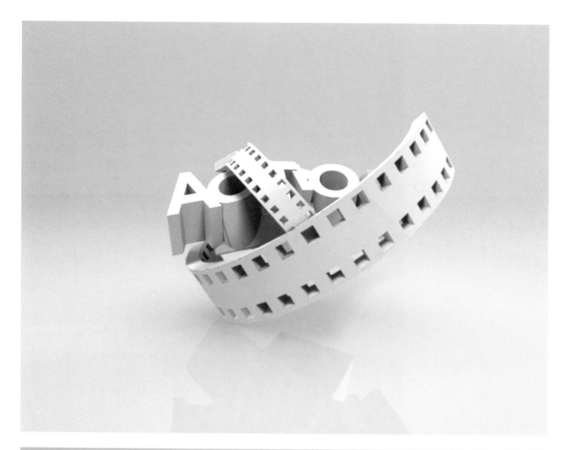

ADC LXXXVI

Graphic Design
Television & Cinema Design
Art Direction / Campaign
Multiple Winner
see page 28

Distinctive Merit
HP Hands

214

HP HANDS
Art Director
Mark Kudsi & Kaan Atilla
(Motion Theory), Stephen
Goldblatt & Pete Conolly
(Goodby Silverstein &
Partners)
Copywriter
Mike McKay, Harry Cocciolo
Creative Director
Mathew Cullen (Motion
Theory); Rich Silverstein,
Steve Simpson, Mike McKay
(Goodby Silverstein &
Partners)
Designer
Mark Kudsi, Kaan Atilla,
Mathew Cullen, Jake
Sargeant, Jesus De
Francisco, Mike Slane, Ron
Delizo, Mark Kulakoff, Matt
Motal, Robin Resella, Paul
K. Lee, Chad Howitt, John
Fan, Christian De Castro,
Gabe Dunne, Josh Nimoy,
Jesse Franklin, Danny
Zobrist, Nick Losq, Chris
Clyne, Andrew Romatz, Ira
Shain, Helen Choi, Grace
Lee, Sarah Bocket
Director
Dayton/Faris (Jay Z),
Mathew Cullen (Pharrell,
Burnett)
Editor
Jason Webb
Producer
Scott Gemmell (Motion
Theory), Hilary Bradley
(Goodby), Ashley Sferro
(Goodby)
Production Company
Motion Theory
Agency
Motion Theory
Client
HP
Country
United States

Visual autobiographies of
Pharrell, Mark Burnett, and
Jay Z come to life through
simple hand gestures and
intricate animation in the
HP "Hands" campaign,
which was directed by
Mathew Cullen of Motion
Theory and Dayton/Faris of
Bob Industries. The spots,
which focus on the hands
rather than the face of each
subject, reveal each well-
known identity through a
series of increasingly specific facts drawn from each
person's computer. The
visual effects department at
the Motion Theory studio
combined 2D and 3D visual
effects, creating a visual
conversation that reflects
each subject's style and
personality.

"Hands Jay Z" JAY Z: I've got my whole life in this thing. Check out this new song I'm mixing. Still rough. All artists say that. Got the new Roc-a-Wear campaign Shot it in Aspen. I think it's kinda cool. Love playin' chess online. Hold on. This game is over. I wonder if he knows. Vacation photos you won't see in tabloids. New Frank Gehry plans for my team in Brooklyn. See that? Cool. Just started organizing my world tour. Tryin to be a rockstar and a role model. Gotta track all my investments because …I'm retired right? *TYPE: Jay Z CEO of Hip Hop.* JAY Z: My passport says Shawn, but you may know me by another name. Holla. *ANNCR: HP Pavilion Entertainment Notebooks with Intel Centrino Duo mobile technology. TYPE: The computer is personal again. LOGO: HP Invent. URL: hp.com/personal. ANNCR: The computer is personal again.*

ADC LXXXVI   **Graphic Design**   **Distinctive Merit**   216
Television & Cinema Design   Open Up
Art Direction / Single

OPEN UP

<u>Art Director</u>
Dominik Anweiler, Bertrand
Kirschenhofer
<u>Copywriter</u>
Ingmar Bartels, Sebastian
Behrendt
<u>Creative Director</u>
Lars Ruehmann
<u>Director</u>
Marc R. Wilkins
<u>Editor</u>
Marty Schenk, Moritz
Steinkohl
<u>Producer</u>
Andrea Roman
<u>Production Company</u>
Big Fish Filmproduktion
GmbH
<u>Music</u>
Marco Meister
<u>Camera</u>
Pascal Walder
<u>Sound Design</u>
Andreas Ersson, Thomas
Nitzsche
<u>Agency</u>
Nordpol Hamburg Agentur
fuer Kommunikation GmbH
<u>Client</u>
Allesklar.com AG
<u>Country</u>
Germany

meinestadt.de (German for
"MyTown.de") is the biggest
town portal in Germany.
Only here, all 12,241 German
towns and cities can be
found. Whether a global
metropolis, big city, small
town or suburb, meines-
tadt.de has all the information you could ever need.
According to this proposi-
tion, the individual access
to all kinds of local and
regional information
becomes the campaign's
core idea: every town open
to every user.

**JAPAN IS STILL
WHALING**

<u>Art Director</u>
Julia Ziegler, Oliver
Froehnel
<u>Copywriter</u>
Daniel Frericks, Jan-Florian
Ege
<u>Creative Director</u>
Goetz Ulmer, Daniel
Frericks, Oliver Voss
<u>Designer</u>
Javier Suarez Argueta
<u>Photographer</u>
Uwe Duettmann
<u>Agency</u>
Jung von Matt AG
<u>Client</u>
NOAH - people for animals
<u>Country</u>
Germany

Graphic Design
Editorial Design Magazine,
Consumer, Full Page / Single
Merit
Japan is Still Whaling
+
Graphic Design
Poster Design Promotional /
Single
Merit
Japan is Still Whaling

ADC LXXXVI

Graphic Design
Editorial Design Magazine,
Consumer, Cover / Single

Merit
The Ideas Issue

219

THE IDEAS ISSUE

Art Director
Arem Duplessis
Creative Director
Janet Froelich
Designer
Gail Bichler
Editor
Gerry Marzorati
Photo
Editor Kathy Ryan
Photographer
Horacio Salinas
Publisher
The New York Times
Agency
New York Times Magazine
Country
United States

The Annual Ideas Issue celebrates some of the most noteworthy ideas of the previous twelve months, covering everything from science and technology to politics and policy. This year, we asked different creatives to come up with visuals that best articulate a specific subject. In the end, the overall issue was based both on visual and written ideas, highlighting the theme in the most appropriate of ways.

ADC LXXXVI

Graphic Design
Editorial Design Magazine,
Consumer, Spread / Multi-
Page / Campaign

Merit
After Neoconservatism

220

**AFTER
NEOCONSERVATISM**
Art Director
Arem Duplessis
Creative Director
Janet Froelich
Designer
Jeff Glendenning
Editor
Gerry Marzorati
Publisher
The New York Times
Agency
New York Times Magazine
Client
The New York Times
Magazine
Country
United States

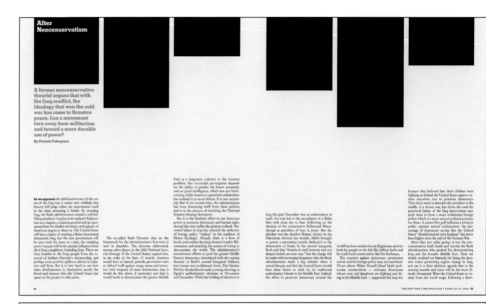

ADC LXXXVI

Graphic Design
Editorial Design Magazine,
Consumer, Spread / Multi-
Page / Campaign

Merit
T Openers

221

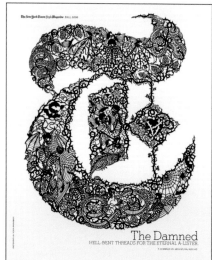

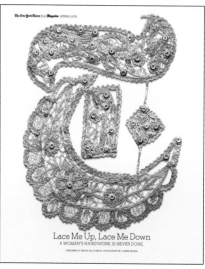

T OPENERS

Art Director
David Sebbah, Christopher
Martinez
Creative Director
Janet Froelich
Editor
Stefano Tonchi
Publisher
The New York Times
Agency
T: The New York Times Style
Magazine
Client
The New York Times
Magazine
Country
United States

Each issue of T opens with
our logo re-imagined by a
noted artist, photographer
or designer. Each of these
logos speaks to the style
news of the particular season—in this case, the modern craftsmanship of
Fernando and Humberto
Campana, the vampire influences on menswear shows
as rendered by the artist
Michael Dal Vecchio, and
the Belle Epoque lace of the
women's fashion season,
created for us by Oscar de
la Renta.

ADC LXXXVI

Graphic Design
Editorial Design Magazine,
Consumer, Spread / Multi-
Page / Campaign

Merit
The Ideas Issue

222

THE IDEAS ISSUE

Art Director
Arem Duplessis
Creative Director
Janet Froelich
Designer
Gail Bichler, Jeff Docherty,
Leo Jung
Editor
Gerry Marzorati
Photo Editor
Kathy Ryan
Publisher
The New York Times
Illustrator
Chester Jenkins, Julia
Hasting, +ISM, Catalog
Tree, Fabrizio Moretti,
Leanne Shapton
Agency
New York Times Magazine
Client
The New York Times
Magazine
Country
United States

The Annual Ideas Issue celebrates some of the most
noteworthy ideas of the previous twelve months, covering everything from science
and technology to politics
and policy. This year, we
asked different creatives to
come up with visuals that
best articulate a specific
subject. In the end, the overall issue was based both on
visual and written ideas,
highlighting the theme in the
most appropriate of ways.

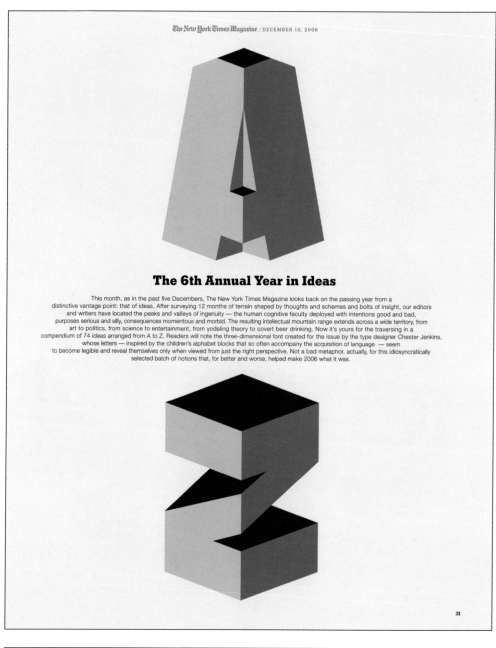

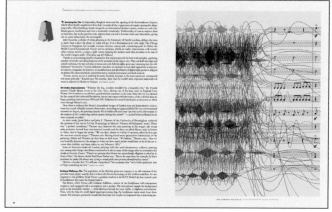

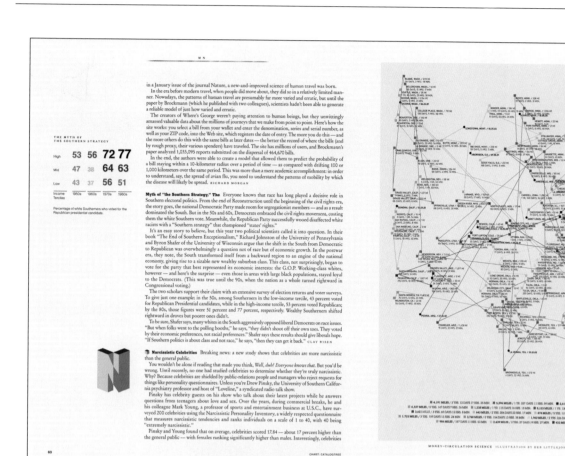

in a January issue of the journal Nature, a new-and-improved science of human travel was born.

In the era before modern travel, when people did move about, they did so in a relatively limited manner. Nowadays, the patterns of human travel are presumably far more varied and erratic, but until the paper by Brockmann (which he published with two colleagues), scientists hadn't been able to generate a reliable model of just how varied and erratic.

The creators of Where's George weren't paying attention to human beings, but they unwittingly amassed valuable data about the millions of journeys we make from point to point. Here's how the site works: you select a bill from your wallet and enter the denomination, series and serial number, as well as your ZIP code, into the Web site, which registers the date of entry. The more you do this — and the more others do this with the same bills at later dates — the better the record of where the bills (and by rough proxy, their various spenders) have traveled. The site has millions of users, and Brockmann's paper analyzed 1,033,095 reports submitted on the dispersal of 464,670 bills.

In the end, the authors were able to create a model that allowed them to predict the probability of a bill staying within a 10-kilometer radius over a period of time — as compared with drifting 100 or 1,000 kilometers over the same period. This was more than a mere academic accomplishment: in order to understand, say, the spread of avian flu, you need to understand the patterns of mobility by which the disease will likely be spread. RICHARD MORGAN

Myth of "the Southern Strategy," The Everyone knows that race has long played a decisive role in Southern electoral politics. From the end of Reconstruction until the beginning of the civil rights era, the story goes, the national Democratic Party made room for segregationist members — and as a result dominated the South. But in the 50s and 60s, Democrats embraced the civil rights movement, costing them the white Southern vote. Meanwhile, the Republican Party championed "states' rights" that championed "states' rights."

It's an easy story to believe, but this year two political scientists called it into question. In their book "The End of Southern Exceptionalism," Richard Johnston of the University of Pennsylvania and Byron Shafer of the University of Wisconsin argue that the shift in the South from Democratic to Republican was overwhelmingly a question not of race but of economic growth. In the postwar era, they note, the South transformed itself from a backward region to an engine of the national economy, giving rise to a sizable new wealthy suburban class. This class, not surprisingly, began to vote for the party that best represented its economic interests: the G.O.P. Working-class whites, however — and here's the surprise — even those in areas with large black populations, stayed loyal to the Democrats. (This was true until the 90s, when the nation as a whole turned rightward in Congressional voting.)

The two scholars support their claim with an extensive survey of election returns and voter surveys. To give just one example: in the 50s, among Southerners in the low-income tercile, 43 percent voted for Republican Presidential candidates, while in the high-income tercile, 53 percent voted Republican; by the 80s, those figures were 51 percent and 77 percent, respectively. Wealthy Southerners shifted rightward in droves but poorer ones didn't.

To be sure, Shafer says, many whites in the South aggressively opposed liberal Democrats on race issues. "But when folks went to the polling booths," he says, "they didn't shoot at their own toes. They voted by their economic preferences." Shafer says these results should give liberals hope. "If Southern politics is about class and not race," he says, "then they can get it back." CLAY RISEN

Narcissistic Celebrities Breaking news: a new study shows that celebrities are more narcissistic than the general public.

You wouldn't be alone if reading that made you think, *Well, duh! Everyone knows that.* But you'd be wrong. Until recently, no one had studied celebrities to determine whether they're truly narcissistic. Why? Because celebrities are shielded by public-relations people and managers who reject requests for things like personality questionnaires. Unless you're Drew Pinsky, the University of Southern California psychiatry professor and host of "Loveline," a syndicated radio talk show.

Pinsky has celebrity guests on his show who talk about their latest projects while he answers questions from teenagers about love and sex. Over the years, during commercial breaks, he and his colleague Mark Young, a professor of sports and entertainment business at U.S.C., have surveyed 200 celebrities using the Narcissistic Personality Inventory, a widely respected questionnaire that measures narcissistic tendencies and ranks individuals on a scale of 1 to 40, with 40 being "extremely narcissistic."

Pinsky and Young found that on average, celebrities scored 17.84 — about 17 percent higher than the general public — with females ranking significantly higher than males. Interestingly, celebrities

THE MYTH OF
THE SOUTHERN STRATEGY

	1950s	1960s	1970s	1980s
High	53	56	72	77
Mid	47	38	64	63
Low	43	37	56	51

Income Terciles

Percentage of white Southerners who voted for the Republican presidential candidate.

60

CHART: CATALOGTREE

MONEY-CIRCULATION SCIENCE ILLUSTRATION BY DER LITTLEJOHN/SANTIAGO PIEDRAFITA

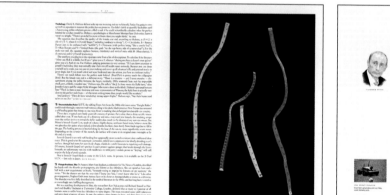

ISSUE 4 -
THE GLOSSY ZINE

Art Director
Katia Kuethe, Philipp
Muessigmann

Designer
Anne-Catherine Wehrli,
Sidsel Solmer Eriksen

Editor
Katia Kuethe, Philipp
Muessigmann

Illustrator
Bernd Schifferdecker,
Tiffany Malakooti

Photo Editor
Carole Reid

Photographer
Alan Castro, Alex Freund,
Ben Pogue, Keith Kleiner,
Vincent Skeltis

Copywriter
Adrian Almquist, KT
Auleta, Alan Castro,
William Hall, Havana
Laffitte, Jason Crombie,
Sven O. Ahrens, Katia
Kuethe, Philipp
Muessigmann

Creative Director
Katia Kuethe, Philipp
Muessigmann

Publisher
Studio Von Birken

Agency
Studio Von Birken

Client
E&A Editor & Art Director

Country
United States

E&A is Fashion, Pop & Art.
It is a zero budget, oversize
newspaper zine published
in Brooklyn, New York. This
fourth issue was all about
"Hecho en U.S. of A." And
America being a big coun-
try, this had to be an
extremely big issue, to be
precise, a broadsheet. We
ran a lengthy article about
the dark side of American
agriculture throughout the
magazine - we wanted peo-
ple to read it and we
thought we make this more
likely by distributing it all
over the issue instead of
putting it somewhere in one
long piece. Heavy reading
meets pleasant pictures.
We worked with the
theme of pop art & cus-
tomized a vintage font, the
"SVB Lapidaire Monstre
Americaine". Dedicated to
Paz, our firstborn son, who
was a month old when we
put this issue together.

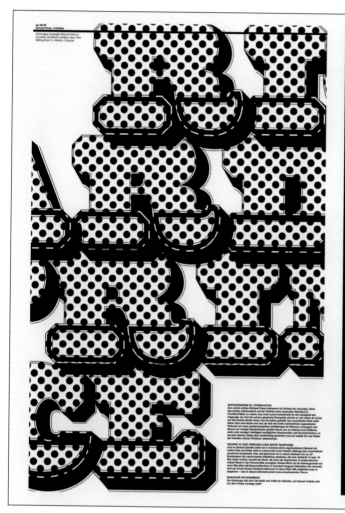

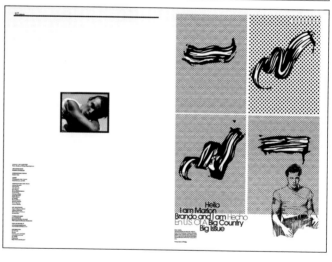

ADC LXXXVI

Graphic Design
Editorial Design Magazine,
Consumer, Full Issue / Single

Merit
Kid's Wear Vol. 23 Autumn /
Winter

226

**KID'S WEAR VOL. 23
AUTUMN/ WINTER**
2006/ 2007
Art Director
Mike Meirè
Designer
Tim Giesen
Photo Editor
Ann-Katrin Weiner
Publisher
Achim Lippoth
Agency
Kid's Wear Verlag
Client
Kid's Wear Magazine
Country
Germany

kid's wear

Vol.23

FASHION, LIFE AND CULTURE

Nan Goldin

(Autumn/Winter 2006/07)

MILES FROM NOWHERE **Anton Corbijn**, MOONSHADOW **Achim Lippoth**,
ON THE ROAD TO FIND OUT **Takashi Homma**, MAYBE YOU'RE RIGHT **Lise Sarfati**,
HOME IN THE SKY **Julie Morstad**, (REMEMBER THE DAYS OF THE)... **Mike Meiré**,
I WISH, I WISH **Ari Marcopoulos**

PHOTO ESSAY
Mark Borthwick

ESSAYS
Joseph Beuys, Jiddu Krishnamurti, Lacaton & Vassal

NEW YORK
TIMES

Nan Goldin

(elio & lorenzo)
Vint Takä To Wien

Smile
Art

Merry Project
by
Koji Mizutani

text Koji Yoshida

What can art do for the Earth? In his pursuit of the answer to that question, Koji Mizutani, a Japanese artist, has come to believe that a "smile is the sole universal means of communication". Based on this belief, he initiated an art project called "Merry" in 1999 and has since photographed the smiling faces of people around the world together with their handwritten messages of what happiness means to them. In his efforts to search for smiling faces, he dared to visit the areas where smiles seem to be disappearing, such as New York after the terrorist attacks, Moscow, and African nations.

At the request of the 2005 World Exposition in Aichi, Japan, he travelled to 23 countries around the world, including America, England, Germany, Italy, Cuba, Kenya, Vietnam, and the Kingdom of Tonga and collected the smiles and messages of over 20,000 people. His particular focus was on children's smiles because he viewed them as the light shining over the future of the Earth. Children's smiles were projected on a large screen installed in the main plaza of the expo with their handwritten messages, which attracted much attention.

When we face a large number of smiling faces, we are awed at the mysterious power of a face = a human's ultimate tool of expression. As we continue staring at it in its entirety, we feel as if electricity were generated in our brains. What Mizutani learned in the process and was deeply moved by was the fact that the severer the environment where children live, the brighter the smiles as they truly relish the happiness of living "now".

Recently, he has been working hard to raise funds to build schools in South Africa and has contributed to the cause all the profits made from publishing Merry Expo, a photo collection of children's smiles, in return for the beaming smiles he received from these children.

Further information on the "Merry" project: www.21merry.net

03

03

ADC LXXXVI

Graphic Design
Editorial Design Magazine,
Consumer, Full Issue /
Campaign

Merit
34

228

34

Art Director
Republica

Creative Director
Republica

Editor
Adam Eeuwens

Producer
Ottto Publications

Publisher
Ottto Publications

Agency
Republica

Client
Ottto Publications

Country
Turkey

34 is Turkey's first global
lifestyle magazine. It rede-
fines the parameters of
global lifestyle, proving that
style and substance can
exist side by side. It is not
just a magazine about style
but also a magazine about
the philosophy of style. It is
intelligent and unapologeti-
cally vain. It is educated and
beautiful a 21st century
marriage of form and con-
tent. 34's niche is that it can
cover East and West with
equal vigor and authority.
We have one foot in Europe
and the other in Asia, literally. 34's headquarters is
situated in the heart of
Istanbul, the city where
Eastern and Western philosophy, design and style function simultaneously. 34
caters to the eclecticism of
the new century and
acknowledges that contem-
porary consumers enjoy
both Eastern and Western
influences in their interiors,
their fashion and their lives.

TO EXPLORE

34 times middle east chic

Curated with the help of Anna Sussman, Anneloes van Gaalen, Betsy Kohen, Jenn Harger, Lucy White, Rebeca Méndez and Sevil Delin.

With the World Wide Web as the gift that keeps on giving, our global 34 team set out to scour the Middle East for all it deemed Chic, as that is the theme for this issue. At first it was difficult to look beyond a lifetime of news of endless wars on the Middle Eastern front. How can such an abandoned place be considered abundant? Smart Google keywords, and click upon serendipitous click lead to a collection of artists, designers, media, objects, foods and places from the region, offering both recognition and fresh insights.

Respectable sources from the BBC to the Encyclopaedia Britannica and Wikipedia to the World Bank seem to disagree on the parameters of the Middle East. Some say it just the Arabian Peninsula plus Israel. Some add Iran and Turkey and Egypt. Others go as far west as Morocco and far east as Afghanistan and Pakistan. On top of that, Middle Eastern culture is everywhere in the world: hookah bars are opening up all over Los Angeles where it is the 'in' thing to do. It gets even trickier when 'chic' is added to the mix: is chic a dinner menu without a price list, or is it effortless elegance and refined taste? From ignorant to cognizant in 34 little stories of oriental opulence—you do the rest. Adam Eeuwens

RESTAURANT CHIC

Imagine a restaurant in the very heart of a large Northern European city full of Moroccan lamps, Arabian cocktails and belly dancers. Sounds like a tourist trap, right? Or, even worse, one of those awful theme restaurants with food catered to Western palettes and décor that is equally bland. While Amsterdam-based Nomads does indeed feature Moroccan lamps and belly dancers, it is neither a tourist trap nor a theme restaurant but rather an Arabian oasis offering lavish décor and authentic Eastern cuisine. Inspired by the Bedouin culture of North Africa and Arabia, Nomads is a popular destination for those looking for good Arabian-inspired food and luxurious design. Nomads guests are invited to make themselves comfortable on an original Egyptian kelim while enjoying a vast array of authentic Arabian mezzes as prepared by Lebanese chef Ali Balout and his team. The restaurant itself is designed by architectural firm Concrete, the same team responsible for the Supperclub concept. Anneloes van Gaalen

Contributors
1. What is your favourite smell?
2. What is your chicest possession?
3. What is your favourite oriental object/person/place/experience?

Bonus question: Would you like to say something to the Middle East?

Lucy White
Partying this December like it's the Christmas holidays every day, Lucy is Gallery Director of The Third Line (TTL) gallery in Dubai, representing select artists originating from or working in the Middle East. With a regular schedule of art exhibitions both in the gallery warehouse and outside locations, TTL attempts to create a platform for the furthering of contemporary art in Dubai and the surrounding cities. Its goal is to engage in dialogue and decrease between the artists and the people of the region, and to serve a growing collector base.

1) Citronella. Reminds me of French camping holidays as a child.

2) An original 1920s kimono-style silk robe. It makes me feel like I'm in a Josef von Sternberg film.

3) Surin Island, Thailand. Cycling around the vast acres of fallen trees took my breath away (literally, I'm not very fit).

Bonus: It's a bit sandy.

Aaron Betsky
Aaron is the Director of the Netherlands Architecture Institute in Rotterdam, The Netherlands. Before that, he was the Curator of Architecture and Design at the San Francisco Museum of Modern Art for the period 1995-2001. Aaron has published several books on architecture and design, including Building Sex: Men, Women, Architecture and the Construction of Sexuality (1995), Queer Space: Architecture and Same Sex Desire (1997), Architecture Must Burn (2000) and False Flat: Why Dutch Design is So Good (2004).

1) My husband

2) My mind

3) Zaha Hadid

Bonus: Beyond political devastation, the real story is environmental warfare: what was once the birthplace of civilisation might be its tomb.

Anneloes van Gaalen
The brainchild of Anneloes is Paperdoll Writing Services, a text agency that writes, translates and edits for among others the U.S. Embassy in The Netherlands and the European Parliament. Her freelance writing has been published in a wide variety of international publications, including Wired, Black Book, Dazed & Confused, I.D., Clear Magazine and Amsterdam Weekly. And 34.

1) I tend to like the corny stuff: the smell of rain after a hot summer day, fresh cut grass, my boyfriend and this lovely Pacifica Mediterranean Fig candle.

2) I'm afraid that 'freelance writer' and 'chic possessions' are two mutually exclusive concepts.

3) I don't like pinning myself down to one specific kind of object/person/place/experience although I am kind partial to Middle Eastern ceramics and Moroccan mint tea.

AMPERSAND
Art Director
Vince Frost
Creative Director
Vince Frost
Designer
Vince Frost, Anthony
Donovan, Ben Backhouse
Publisher
D&AD
Copywriter
Lakshmi Bhaskaran
Agency
Frost Design
Client
D&AD
Country
Australia

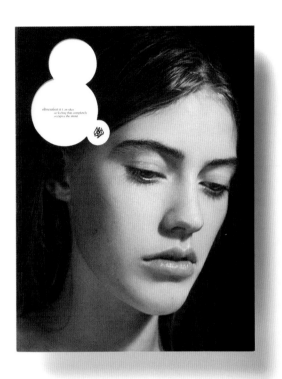

TYPOGRAPHIC
<u>Art Director</u>
Paul Belford, David Jury
<u>Creative Director</u>
Paul Belford, David Jury
<u>Designer</u>
Paul Belford, David Jury
<u>Editor</u>
David Jury
<u>Photo Editor</u>
David Jury
<u>Photographer</u>
Paul Cohen, David Jury
<u>Production Company</u>
Simmons Print
<u>Publisher</u>
ISTD
<u>Agency</u>
This is Real Art
<u>Client</u>
ISTD
<u>Country</u>
United Kingdom

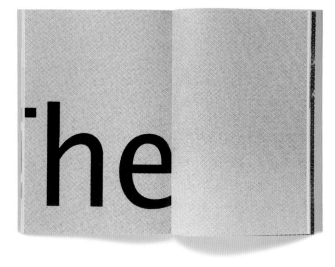

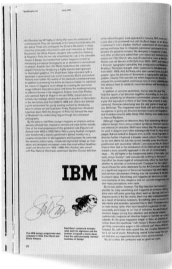

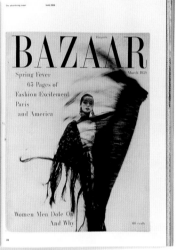

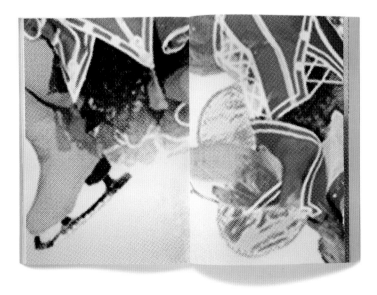

ADC LXXXVI

Graphic Design
Design Special Trade Book
(Image-Driven) / Single

Merit
Duf

234

DUF

Art Director
Suzanne Hertogs
Copywriter
Suzanne Hertogs
Creative Director
Suzanne Hertogs
Designer
Suzanne Hertogs
Director
Suzanne Hertogs
Editor
Suzanne Hertogs, Petra
Boers, Nicole Ros
Photo Editor
Suzanne Hertogs
Producer
Suzanne Hertogs
Production Company
Print: Zwaan Printmedia,
NL
Publisher
Suzanne Hertogs,
Ontwerphaven
Client
Independent Publication
Country
Netherlands

DUF - Serendipity; the
occurrence and develop-
ment of events by chance in
a happy or beneficial way.
You are DUF (dull) if: you
know how to record onto a
cassette tape; your first
music album was an LP; you
remember not having a cell
phone; you've never seen a
Playstation... then DUF isn't
for you! DUF, the brainchild
of Suzanne Hertogs
(designer, art director), is
an independently published
"bookazine" created to
entice Dutch teenagers to
read more. DUF has a high
"ZAP-factor," with a wide
variety of information presented in a playful and
exciting manner for young-
sters. DUF is an adventure,
just like reading should be.
Topics covered range from a
7 page article on a Jeroen
Bosch painting to a "fuck
without worries" item. The
various writing styles
include the short story,
prose, poetry and
reportages. DUF is fun!

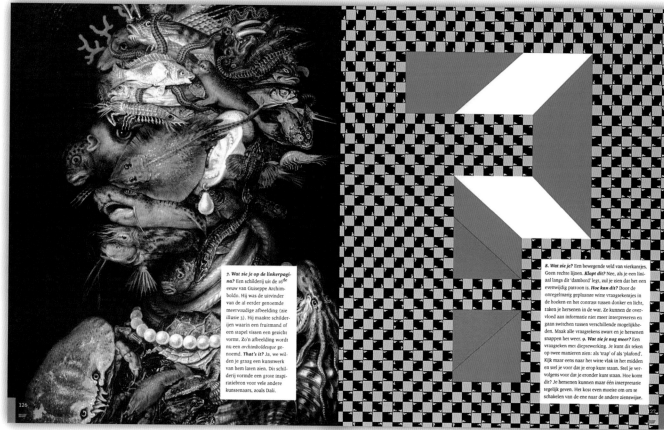

**ALL MEN ARE
BROTHERS -
DESIGNERS' EDITION**
Art Director
Jianping He
Creative Director
Jianping He
Designer
Jianping He
Editor
Jianping He
Publisher
Hesign Publishing
Agency
Hesign
Client
Hesign Publishing
Country
Germany

"All Men Are Brothers -
Designers' Edition" is an
achievement for us, in which
the contemporary heroes of
the graphic design scene
could gather together.

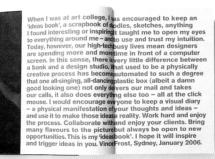

FROST* (SORRY TREES)

Art Director
Vince Frost

Copywriter
Lakshmi Bhaskaran

Creative Director
Vince Frost

Designer
Anthony Donovan

Publisher
Frost Design

Agency
Frost Design

Client
Frost Design

Country
Australia

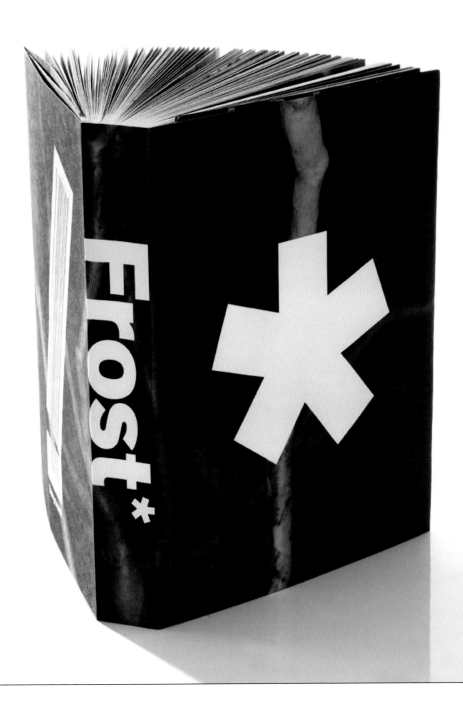

ADC LXXXVI

Graphic Design
Book Design Limited Edition,
Private Press or Special
Format Book / Single

Merit
Vie.w

238

VIE.W
Art Director
Jun Tamukai
Copywriter
Kensaku Kamada
Creative Director
Tatsuo Ebina
Production Company
E. Co.,Ltd.
Agency
E.Co.,Ltd.
Client
E. Co., Ltd
Country
Japan

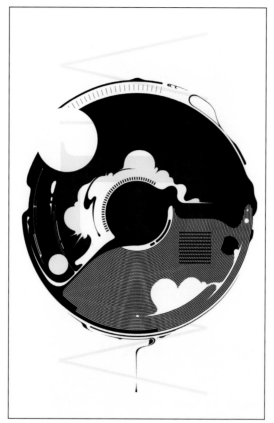

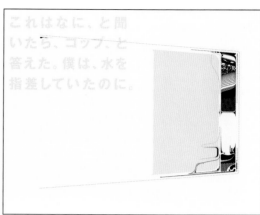

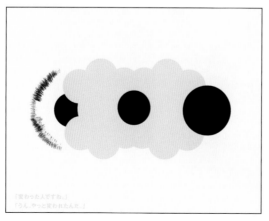

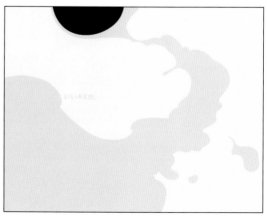

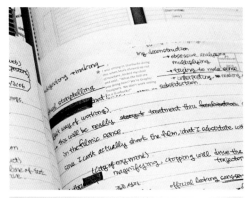

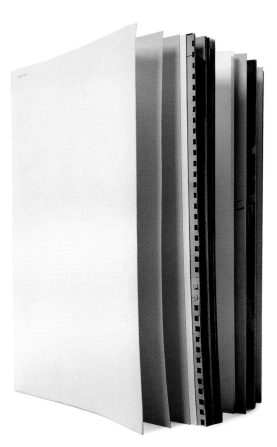

MAGNIFYING
Art Director
Elizabeth Yerin Shim
Copywriter
Elizabeth Yerin Shim
Creative Director
Elizabeth Yerin Shim
Designer
Elizabeth Yerin Shim
Editor
Elizabeth Yerin Shim
Photographer
Elizabeth Yerin Shim
Illustrator
Elizabeth Yerin Shim
Photo Editor
Elizabeth Yerin Shim
Producer
Elizabeth Yerin Shim
Country
Republic of Korea

Magnifying is a portfolio book with warmth and humor. It reveals a closer, personal look on design projects by unfolding their behind stories. Three interweaving voices tell these stories: three different formal languages, three different colored paper stock, and three varying sheet widths. The project-related silly little quotes from people around me are on pink, the processes are rough and free on gray, and the finished presentations are clean and simple on white. Within the process pages are tiny asides hidden in the layout, some of which are numbered to guide the reader through the transformation of that particular seed of an idea. The set up plays with hierarchy. Pages showcasing finished projects are short-sheeted and hidden after the gray process pages, planting them as precious surprises. The goal of the design and the structure was to create layers and layers of stories and information, whispers and nudges—to provide the reader with a captivating treasure hunt.

ADC LXXXVI

Graphic Design
Book Design Limited Edition,
Private Press or Special
Format Book / Single

Merit
PT Ram Book Projekttriangle
Design Works 1999-2006

240

**PT RAM BOOK -
PROJEKTTRIANGLE
DESIGN WORKS
1999-2006**
Designer
Danijela Djokic, Martin
Grothmaak, Juergen Spaeth
Agency
Projekttriangle
Informationdesign
Client
Projekttriangle
Country
Germany

The Pt Ram Book is an exhibition catalogue of the exhibition "Ram Random
Access Memory" of
Projekttriangle Design
Studio. Seven years of work
in the 3 areas interaction
design/red color, information design/green color and
contemporary graphic
design/blue color.
We wanted to create a
unique form and format of
this piece. It contains a CD
with spoken information of
the various projects
described in the 3 different
booklets. As an add-on
there are 3 piano music
pieces and an electronic
music track on the CD,
especially composed for
this project.

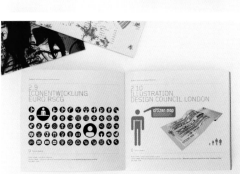

ADC LXXXVI

Graphic Design
Book Design Limited Edition,
Private Press or Special
Format Book / Single

Merit
Monsters Ink

241

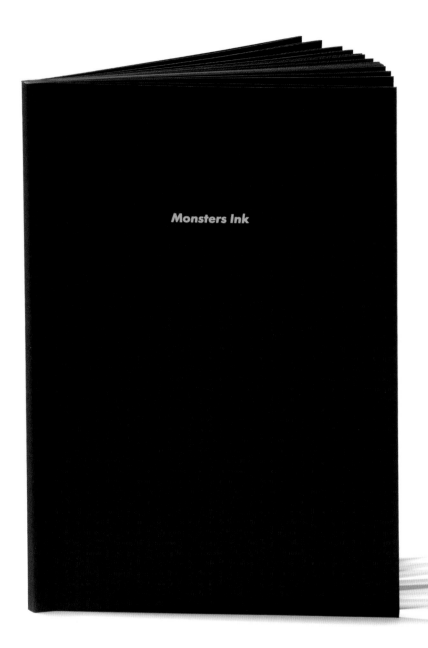

MONSTERS INK
Art Director
Nick Finney, Ben Stott,
Alan Dye
Designer
Nick Finney, Jodie
Wightman
Illustrator
James Graham
Copywriter
Vivienne Hamilton
Agency
NB:Studio
Client
NB:Studio
Country
United Kingdom

Monsters Ink is a self-initi-
ated project created as a
giveaway for an NB:Studio
Halloween party. The book
also acts as a promotional
piece for copywriter
Vivienne Hamilton and illustrator James Graham.
Monsters stir our hearts
with an uncommon intensi-
ty. They lend a vital edge to
our daily lives—a vague
malevolence in the office, a
creeping uneasiness on our
walk home and a disquieting
sense of danger at bedtime.
In the interest of "feeling
the fear and doing it anyway," we brought together
an indispensable guide to
all that's ghastly, mis-
shapen, ghoulish and gener-
ally hideous. After
researching mythical mon-
sters throughout different
cultures, we commissioned
James Graham to illustrate
a selected few in his eccen-
tric and eclectic hand drawn
style. Text and image was
lovingly screen printed in
white onto black paper to
give a really contrasting and
dark feel to the book.

87

Art Director
Jonathan Ellery

Copywriter
Jonathan Ellery

Creative Director
Jonathan Ellery

Designer
Jonathan Ellery, Rachel
Veniard

Editor
Jonathan Ellery

Producer
Kendra Futcher

Production Company
Printer: Westerham Press

Publisher
Ellery / Browns

Agency
Browns

Client
Browns

Country
United Kingdom

With this book, Jonathan
Ellery looks at numbers,
form, pace, rhythm and the
tactile qualities of the book
itself. This conceptual piece
forms part of "Unrest," a one
man show at the Wapping
Project / London in 2007.

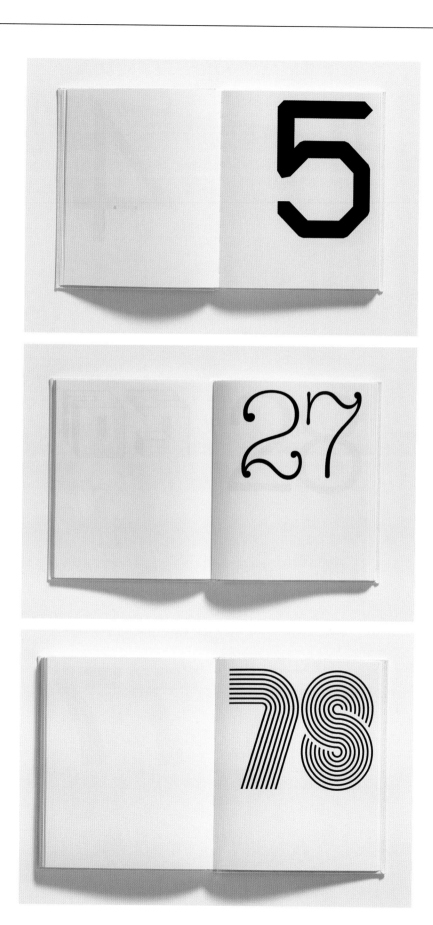

MISCELLANEOUS CRAP

Designer
Sue Joo Kim
Faculty Advisors
Michael Vanderbyl,
Leslie Becker
Agency
Sue Joo Kim
Client
Sue Joo Kim
Country
United States

This book celebrates miscellaneous things, random items that we accumulate and put away because we do not know what to do with them, nor how to organize them. Things like glow-in-the-dark lizards and an unlabeled burnt CD. Originally produced as my undergraduate thesis at the California College of the Arts, this book features over 75 absurd ways to organize 170 items that were found in a box labeled "misc" after my last move. To reinforce the idea of organization, the book itself is highly organized. Each spread contains the category title (i.e. things that weigh more than a gerbil), an item count (35) and a related fact (an adult male gerbil weighs about 3 ounces). A corresponding grid displays items that belong in the category, each item occupying the same grid position throughout the book. A tiny red number in each grid cell serves as a running item count. The book concludes with an index that doubles as an item count histogram.

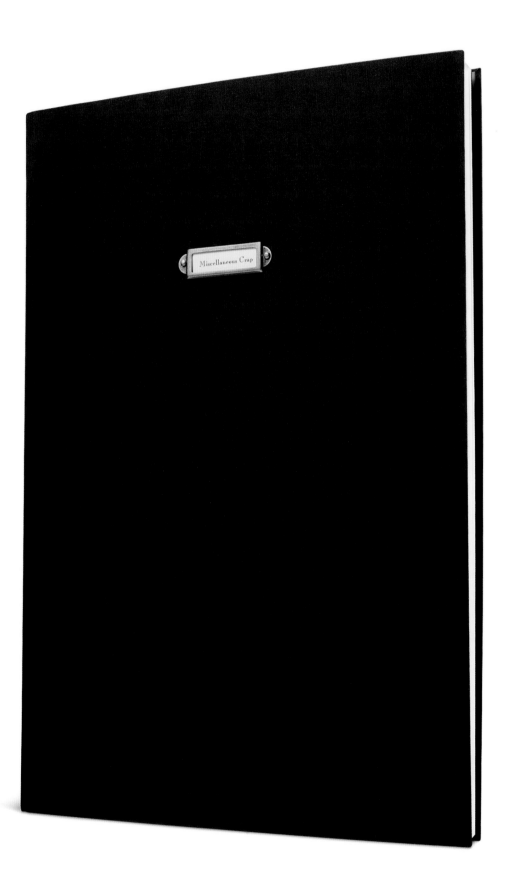

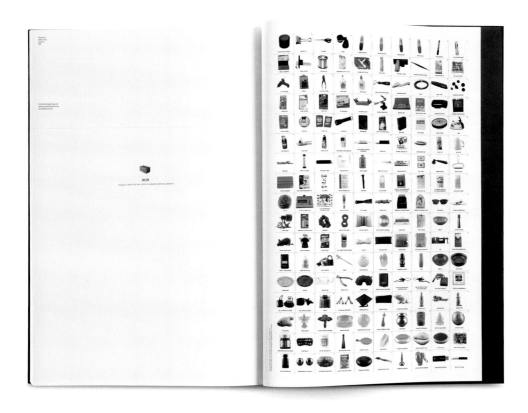

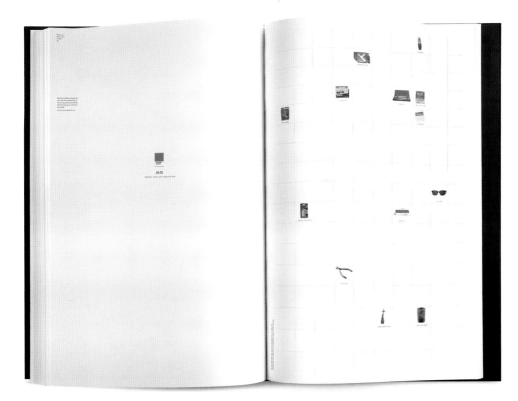

ADC LXXXVI

Graphic Design
Book Design Public Service /
Non-Profit Book / Single

Merit
Asian Field / Makers & Made

246

ASIAN FIELD / MAKERS & MADE

Art Director
Xu Wang

Designer
Xu Wang

Editor
Zhang Wei, Hu Fang

Photographer
Zhang Haier

Production Company
WX-design

Publisher
Hand Books

Other
Artist: Antony Gormley

Agency
WX-design

Client
Antony Gormley

Country
China

ADC LXXXVI

Graphic Design
Book Design Public Service /
Non-Profit Book / Single

Merit
Liu Xiaodong: Painting
from Life

247

**LIU XIAODONG:
PAINTING FROM LIFE**
Art Director
Xu Wang
Designer
Ying Hou
Editor
Guangdong Museum of Art
Producer
Reliance Printing
(Shenzhen) Co., Ltd.
Production Company
WX-design
Publisher
Lingnan Art Publishing
House
Agency
WX-design
Client
China Mingsheng Banking
Corp., Ltd.
Country
China

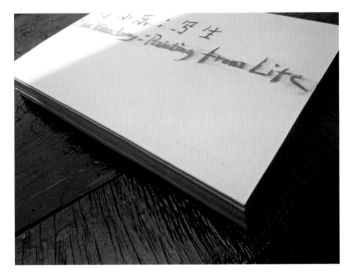

**PRINTED IN
HOLLAND......
DESIGNED IN CHINA**
Art Director
Ineke Teeninga
Creative Director
Ineke Teeninga
Director
Fokko Tamminga
Producer
Ando bv
Production Company
Ando bv
Agency
Drift grafisch ontwerpen
Client
Ando bv
Country
Netherlands

This agenda is "printed in
Holland, designed in China."
These days, you see a lot of
print work done in China.
We'd like to say, "Please go
for quality, for your design
as well as for your print-
work!" The agenda has a
Chinese look, 50 grs paper,
gold print, a silky cover, a
weekly Chinese superstition
and 60 pages each part
(related to the well-known
Chinese cycles).

ADC LXXXVI

Graphic Design
Book Design Museum, Gallery
or Library Book / Single

Merit
Whitney Biennial 2006:
Day for Night

249

WHITNEY BIENNIAL 2006: DAY FOR NIGHT

Creative Director
Mary Delmonico

Designer
Purtill Family Business

Director
Rachel Wixom

Editor
Michelle Piranio

Production Company
Mary Delmonico and Purtill
Family Business

Publisher
Whitney Museum of
American Art, New York

Agency
Whitney Museum of
American Art

Client
WMAA

Country
United States

The 2006 Whitney Biennial
catalogue's innovation is the
co-existence of two funda-
mental book spaces simultaneously presented, each
having an entirely different
scale, dynamic, and content.
One space represents the
traditional group exhibition
catalogue including the work
of 100 artists alongside
essays. It was important that
the book embody its own
ephemerality as a document
of the show that occurs
every two years and so the
curators Chrissie Iles and
Philippe Vergne, invited each
artist to reduce the last two
years into one image, word,
text, or object to be included
in the book as a running
visual essay. The resulting 99
posters were bound by glue-
pad glue on one fold—allowing one to remove one or all
posters. The folded and
bound posters create a 398-
page book form where the
traditional catalogue content
(essays and plates) is found.
The resulting form adds
complexity to a straightfor-
ward, group exhibition catalogue presentation.

ADC LXXXVI   **Graphic Design**   **Merit**   250
Book Design Museum, Gallery   No Art
or Library Book / Single

NO ART

Art Director
Barbara Baettig, Markus
Buesges, Fons Hickmann
Copywriter
Niklaus Troxler, Klaus
Hesse, Gabriele Werner,
Fons Hickmann
Creative Director
Fons Hickmann
Designer
Barbara Baettig, Fons
Hickmann
Production Company
Universitaetsdruckerei
Mainz
Publisher
Verlag Hermann Schmidt
Mainz
Producer
Fons Hickmann m23
Editor
100 Bester Plakate e.V.
Agency
Fons Hickmann m23
Client
100 Best Posters Org.
Country
Germany

No Art - The 100 best
posters from Austria,
Germany and Switzerland
The jury held its meeting,
and the 100 best posters of
the last year are chosen:
innovative, provocative,
advertising and cultural.
Everything is connected—
communicative quality at
the highest stage. Attempts
that make you want to have
a closer look, that attract,
that make one's point.
Messages which stay in
mind of the observer. This is
accomplished for sure, but
is it also art? The never-end-
ing debate about art and
design, freedom and to
serve a purpose, usefulness
and beauty, individuality
and ideals versus commerce
and the financial balance
finds entry in this year's
competition documentation
in citation form. A theoreti-
cal text of the picture scientist Gabriele Werner will let
you discover the posters in
a new context and the chary
design of Fons Hickmann
make this book to - bookart!

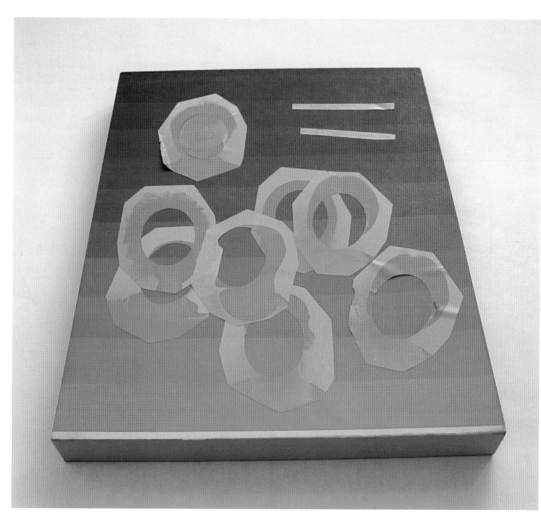

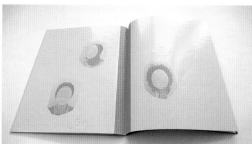
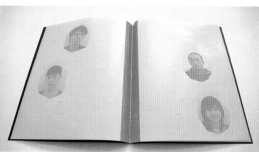

N12 NO.4
Art Director
Jun He
Copywriter
N12
Creative Director
Jun He
Designer
Jun He
Director
N12
Photographer
Ben Zheng
Producer
N12
Production Company
C5 Gallery
Agency
MEWE D A
Client
N12
Country
China

N12 is a painter's association founded by 12 members. They started to hold annual exhibitions 4 years ago. At the 4th annual exhibition, one of the artists was absent. As all works from one artist have been displayed in a separate space, a booklet is made for each artist, and bound by strings. The colors of the booklet's cover compose a gradient; the blank pages are left for the absent artist. All information regarding the artists and works are printed on a separate booklet on stickers. The artists and readers can complete this art book according to their own taste and understanding. In this process, readers may get better knowledge about the artists and their works. It also implies the process of those artists from being nobody to somebody. As a tradition, every year's art book is named "N12" and by a specially made typography. This year, "N" and "12" are composed by the photograph of the book itself.

XING HAILONG— IN BETWEEN: INK PAINTINGS

Art Director
Yu Guang

Copywriter
onemoon

Creative Director
Yu Guang

Designer
Yu Guang

Director
Jan Leaming

Editor
Xing Hailong,
Jan Leaming, Ren li

Producer
Jan Leaming

Production Company
Onemoon

Publisher
Onemoon

Agency
MEWE Design Alliance

Client
Onemoon

Country
China

MEWE Design Alliance is actually not a "well-defined" organization. Its name suggests a few "ME"s constructing a "WE." ME dictates the independence of individuals, whereas WE indicates forces. Therefore, MEWE means open and multi-dimensional. The members of MEWE design association come from different fields of visual art. In this "ensemble" state, they are in hope of changing the landscape of contemporary design. The three graphic designers of MEWE mentioned here have similar backgrounds, but have different orientations in design work. Their works cover almost every aspect of graphic design. "This is a logical reasoning process that makes the result well known. What people are expecting is how you wisely put everything in the right place." One of them has said so.

N12 VOL.3

Art Director
Zhizhi Liu

Copywriter
N12

Creative Director
Zhizhi Liu

Designer
Zhizhi Liu

Director
N12,Jainjun Xiu

Editor
Zhizhi Liu, N12

Photo Editor
Zhizhi Liu, N12

Photographer
N12

Producer
N12

Production Company
N12

Publisher
N12

Agency
MEWE

Client
N12

Country
China

The main challenge is a very limited budget, thus the idea of printing on the waste paper. The outcome is satisfactory, both the appearance and the attitude expressed.

ADC LXXXVI

Graphic Design
Book Design Museum, Gallery
or Library Book / Campaign

Merit
2006 New Wight Biennial

254

**2006 NEW WIGHT
BIENNIAL**

Designer
Henri Lucas,
David Whitcraft
Editor
Jesse Green
Agency
Willem Augustus
Client
UCLA Department of Art
Country
United States

Facing a minimal budget,
we tried to stretch our
resources as much as
possible. The client asked
for a brochure, but we also
wanted to give them a
poster. We arranged the
press sheet so that when it
was unfolded and uncut it
could function as a poster.
The hybrid feel of this
design was enhanced by
using the first page of the
brochure as an image for
the design of postcard.

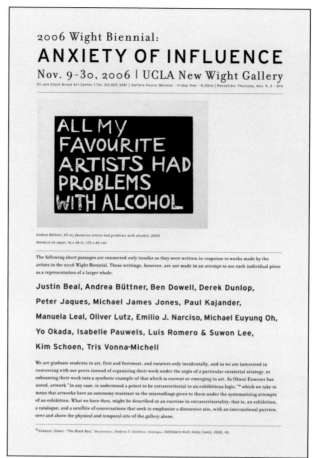

Graphic Design
Book Design Museum, Gallery
or Library Book / Campaign

Merit
Kristian Kozul

255

KRISTIAN KOZUL
Art Director
Ivana Vucic, Orsat Frankovic
Creative Director
Ivana Vucic, Orsat Frankovic
Designer
Ivana Vucic, Orsat
Frankovic, Sasa Stubicar
Editor
Jasna Jaksic
Illustrator
Kristian Kozul
Photo Editor
Ivana Vucic
Photographer
Tomislav J. Kacunic, Ivana
Vucic, etc.
Producer
Museum of Contemporary
Art Zagreb
Production Company
Laboratorium
Publisher
Museum of Contemporary
Art Zagreb
Agency
Laboratorium
Client
Museum of Contemporary
Art Zagreb
Country
Croatia

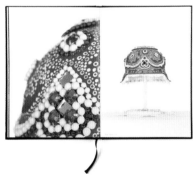

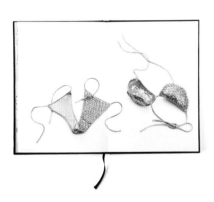

INVISIBLE MIGHT
<u>Creative Director</u>
Helicopter, LLC
<u>Designer</u>
Mike Perry for
Helicopter, LLC
<u>Editor</u>
Tim Nye
<u>Photographer</u>
Adam Reich
<u>Production Company</u>
Helicopter, LLC
<u>Publisher</u>
Tim Nye
<u>Copy Editor</u>
Christina Cho
<u>Agency</u>
Helicopter
<u>Client</u>
Nyehaus/ Foundation 20 21
<u>Country</u>
United States

The concentration on the
materiality of light, its
strength and subtlety, great-
ly influenced the creation of
the show's catalog. Instead
of simply printing each
artist's name at the intro-
duction of their work, the
letters were knife-cut into
the paper itself, while the
essay text was printed in
metallic ink and the cap-
tions printed only in two
coats of varnish; all techniques which allow for light
to affect the transference of
information. Also, all of the
photographs of the work
are each contained behind
a one-sided gatefold, making the book, at first glance,
to appear to be void of
imagery. Yet, once those
gatefolds are lifted, and
the artwork revealed, the
images become almost
hyper-real due to a spot
gloss varnish applied to
the matte paper of the book.
Although the techniques
employed are individually
inconspicuous, their com-
bined effect becomes both
smart and compelling.

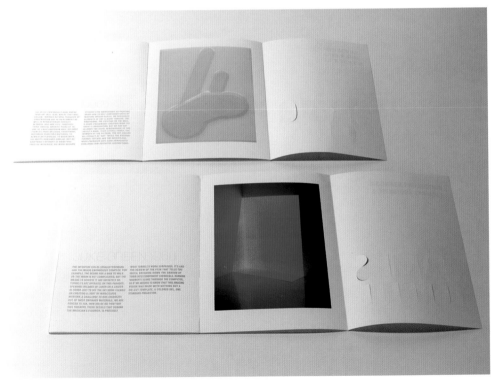

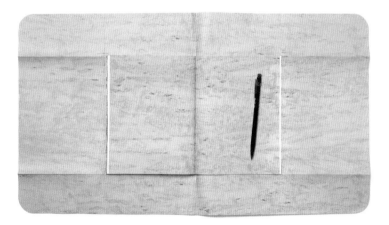

BRUNO MATHSSON

Art Director
Lisa Careborg

Creative Director
Anders Kornestedt

Photographer
Jesper Sundelin / Henry
Thelander / Åke E:son
Lindman

Printer
Goteborgstryckeriet

Writer
Hedvig Hedqvist, Karin
Åberg Waern, Thomas
Sandell

Agency
Happy Forsman
& Bodenfors

Client
The Swedish Museum of
Architecture

Country
Sweden

Bruno Mathsson is one of
Sweden's most famous
architects and furniture
designers. His interiors are
designed to make living
convenient and easy—with
ergonomic seats and a lot of
small tables. The catalogue
cover is a photo of one of
his most popular tables (in
actual size).

ADC LXXXVI

Graphic Design
Corporate & Promotional
Design Annual Report /
Single

Merit
Baumax Imagebrochure 2006
"Fast Growing Success"

258

**BAUMAX
IMAGEBROCHURE
2006 "FAST GROWING
SUCCESS"**
Art Director
Andreas Miedaner
Copywriter
Franziskus Kersenbrock
Creative Director
Andreas Miedaner,
Dominik Cofalka
Designer
Sonja Handl, Sascha
Schaberl, Werner Singer,
Beatrix Hepting
Editor
Dr. Monika Voglgruber
Photographer
Manfred Klimek, Klaus
Vyhnalek
Producer
Mensalia GmbH—
Daniela Böhm
Production Company
AV-Druck (Print)
Consulting
Mensalia
Unternehmensberatung
GmbH
Agency
Büro X Design GmbH
Client
bauMax AG—
www.baumax.at
Country
Austria

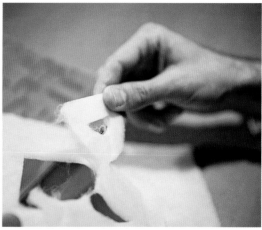

ADC LXXXVI

Graphic Design
Corporate & Promotional
Design Annual Report /
Single

Merit
Excerpt of the Eternal Debate
About the Heart

259

**EXCERPT OF THE
ETERNAL DEBATE
ABOUT THE HEART**

Art Director
Davor Bruketa &
Nikola Zinic

Copywriter
Davor Bruketa, Nikola Zinic,
Imelda Ramovic, Mirel
Hadzijusufovic

Creative Director
Davor Bruketa, Nikola Zinic

Designer
Davor Bruketa, Nikola Zinic,
Imelda Ramovic, Mirel
Hadzijusufovic

Editor
Drenislav Zekic

Photographer
Domagoj Kunic, Marin Topic

Producer
Boris Matesic

Production Company
Lbl

Publisher
Podravka

Agency
Bruketa & Zinic

Client
Podravka

Country
Croatia

Podravka is one of the
biggest food companies in
the region. The main idea of
Podravka is company with
heart. The belief that everything needs to be done by
heart can be seen every-
where—from the logo of the
company to the production
process that often includes
handmade techniques.
Except the usual data
about the company, the
annual is full of proves why
it is important to cook with
heart. The central illustration of this idea is the auto-
biographical handwriting of
the Croatian writer Ante
Tomic which describes his
childhood full of Podravka's
products that became more
than food but a group of
scent and taste sensations
that remind millions of people of home and growing up.

ADC LXXXVI

Graphic Design
Corporate & Promotional
Design Annual Report /
Single

Merit
Channel 4 Annual Report &
Accounts 2006

260

**CHANNEL 4 ANNUAL
REPORT & ACCOUNTS
2006**
Art Director
Jonathan Ellery
Copywriter
Channel 4 Television
Creative Director
Jonathan Ellery
Designer
Jonathan Ellery,
Rachel Veniard
Illustrator
Josie Jammet
Producer
Philip Ward
Production Company
Printer: Westerham Press
Publisher
Channel 4 Television
Agency
Browns
Client
Channel 4 Television
Country
United Kingdom

This is the fourth report
that we have designed for
UK television station
Channel 4. The report has
been designed using four
different covers, which
highlight key programs of
the previous season.
Artwork is by fine artist
Josie Jammet and was pro-
duced in acrylics. The aesthetic of the reports is in
dramatic contrast to a traditional annual report and
challenges the usual formu-
la. The reports epitomize the
brand through being unconventional and dynamic in
their approach.

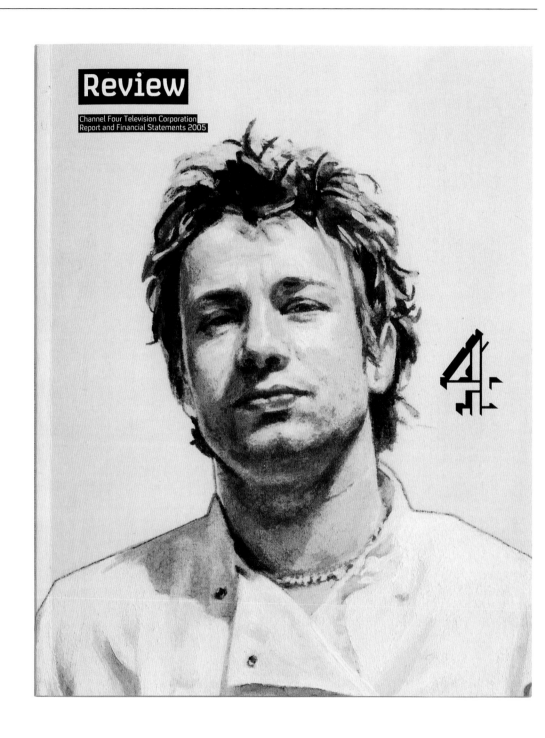

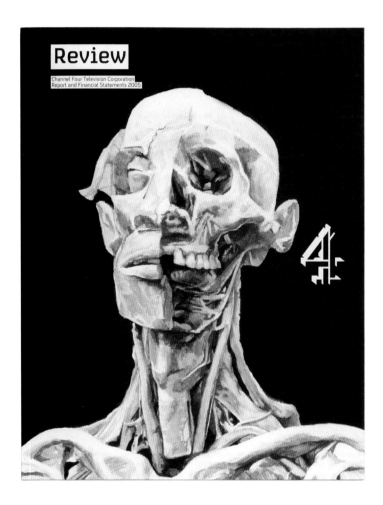

ADC LXXXVI

Graphic Design
Corporate & Promotional
Design Booklet / Brochure /
Single

Merit
Quartet: Four Literary Walks
Through The V&A

262

**QUARTET: FOUR
LITERARY WALKS
THROUGH THE V&A**
Creative Director
Matt Willey, Zoë Bather
Designer
Matt Willey, Zoë Bather
Editor
Dan Crowe
Agency
Studio8 Design
Client
Victoria & Albert Museum /
Sony PSP
Country
United Kingdom

'Quartet: Four Literary
Walks Through The V&A'
contains short stories by
Nicholas Royle, Lucy
Caldwell, Peter Hobbs and
Shiromi Pinto, who were
commissioned to write stories for a one-off event at
the museum. Inspired by the
museum and its collections,
the four stories in 'Quartet'
were annotated with direc-
tions, mapping the routes
described in the writers'
narratives and thus
enabling readers to follow
the stories as they moved
through the museum. The
routes were also made
available as downloads for
Sony PlayStation Portable
consoles.

QUARTET:
FOUR
LITERARY
WALKS
THROUGH
THE V&A
27.01.06

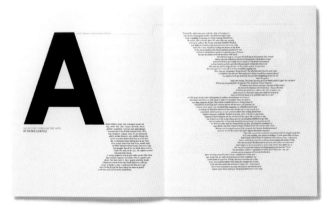

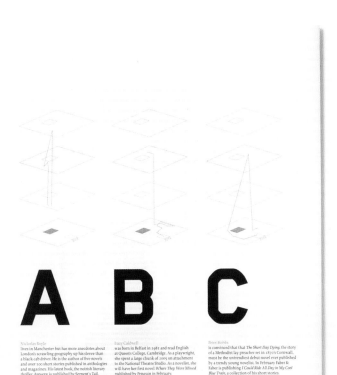

A B C D

Created exclusively for Born Free
Friday Late January 27 2006 at the
V&A in partnership with PSP

Edited by
Dan Crowe & Philip Oltermann
Email: contact@lanternlit.co.uk

Design
Studio8 Design
www.studio8design.co.uk

Print
Principal Colour
(01842) 835005

V&A

PSP™
PlayStation•Portable

With kind support from

PRINCIPALCOLOUR

Nicholas Royle
lives in Manchester but has more anecdotes about London's scrawling geography up his sleeve than a black-cab driver. He is the author of five novels and over 100 short stories published in anthologies and magazines. His latest book, the noirish literary thriller *Antwerp*, is published by Serpent's Tail.

Lucy Caldwell
was born in Belfast in 1981 and read English at Queen's College, Cambridge. As a playwright, she spent a large chunk of 2005 on attachment to the National Theatre Studio. As a novelist, she will have her first novel *Where They Were Missed* published by Penguin in February.

Peter Hobbs
is convinced that that *The Short Day Dying*, the story of a Methodist lay preacher set in 1870's Cornwall, must be the untrendiest debut novel ever published by a trendy young novelist. In February Faber & Faber is publishing *I Could Ride All Day in My Cool Blue Train*, a collection of his short stories.

Shiromi Pinto
is part Sri Lankan, part Londoner and part reluctant Canadian. Originally, she was going to write her story in the style of George Macdonald Fraser's *Flashman Papers*, but decided that she wasn't racist or sexist enough. Her racy and sexy first novel *Trussed* will be published in March by Serpent's Tail.

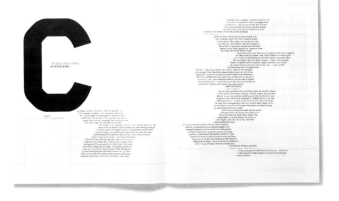

ADC <u>LXXXVI</u>   **Graphic Design**   **Merit**   264
Corporate & Promotional   Programs
Design Booklet / Brochure /
Campaign

PROGRAMS
<u>Art Director</u>
Kirsten Dietz
<u>Creative Director</u>
Kirsten Dietz, Jochen
Raedeker
<u>Designer</u>
Anders Bergesen, Kirsten
Dietz, Anika Marquardsen
<u>Illustrator</u>
Anders Bergesen & others
<u>Agency</u>
Strichpunkt
<u>Client</u>
Wuerttembergisches
Staatstheater / Schauspiel
Stuttgart
<u>Country</u>
Germany

ADC LXXXVI

Graphic Design
Graphic Design Corporate &
Promotional Design Booklet /
Brochure / Single

Merit
Nintendo 2007 Recruitment
Booklet

265

**NINTENDO 2007
RECRUITMENT
BOOKLET**
Art Director
Takashi Maeda
Creative Director
Shin Kojo
Designer
Takashi Maeda, Yurie Sato
Publisher
Nintendo co., Ltd.
Agency
Nintendo
Client
Nintendo
Country
Japan

This was distributed to
students preparing to graduate who submitted job
applications to Nintendo.
It includes photos of the
video game studio, idea
notes, rough drawings, pro-
totypes of game controllers
etc. Our purpose was to
convey Nintendo's strong
commitment to video game
development.

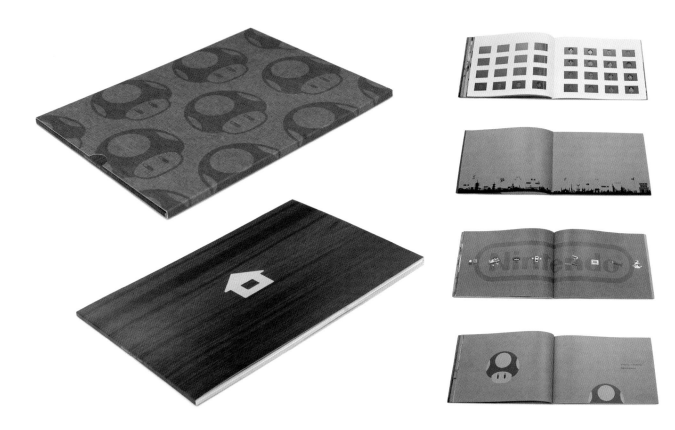

**THE NETWORKED
CITY**

<u>Art Director</u>
Claire Dawson, Fidel Pena
<u>Copywriter</u>
Stuart Ross
<u>Creative Director</u>
Claire Dawson, Fidel Pena
<u>Designer</u>
Claire Dawson, Fidel Pena
<u>Printer</u>
Andora Graphics Inc.
<u>Agency</u>
Underline Studio
<u>Client</u>
InterAccess Electronic
Media Arts Centre
<u>Country</u>
Canada

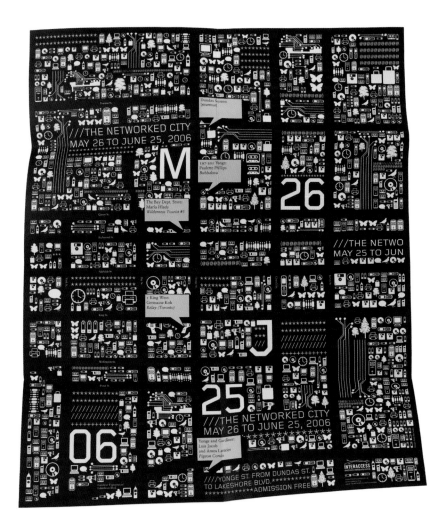

ADC LXXXVI

Graphic Design
Corporate & Promotional
Design Booklet / Brochure /
Single

Merit
See: The Potential of Place,
Fifth Issue

267

SEE: THE POTENTIAL OF PLACE, FIFTH ISSUE

Art Director
Bill Cahan, Steve Frykholm,
Todd Richards

Copywriter
Pamela Erbe, Nancy
Ramsey, Debra Wierenga,
Linton Weeks, Brian Carter

Creative Director
Bill Cahan

Designer
Todd Richards

Illustrator
Artemio Rodriguez, Joseph
Hart, Brian Carter

Photographer
Heimo Schmidt, Vivienne
Flesher, Robert Schlatter,
Catherine Ledner, Andy
Sacks, Colin Faulkner, Brian
Carter

Agency
Cahan & Associates

Client
Herman Miller

Country
United States

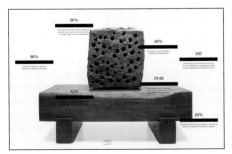

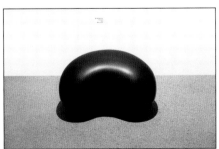

ADC LXXXVI

Graphic Design
Corporate & Promotional
Design Newsletter, Journal,
or House Publication / Single

Merit
Below the Fold: Issue No. 3

268

BELOW THE FOLD: ISSUE NO. 3

Art Director
William Drenttel, Jessica Helfand, Lorraine Wild
Copywriter
William Drenttel, Jessica Helfand, Lorraine Wild
Creative Director
William Drenttel, Jessica Helfand, Lorraine Wild
Designer
Geoff Halber
Illustrator
Imre Reiner
Publisher
Winterhouse Institute
Agency
Winterhouse
Client
Winterhouse Institute
Country
United States

Below the Fold: is an occasional journal of graphic design and visual culture published by the Winterhouse Institute.

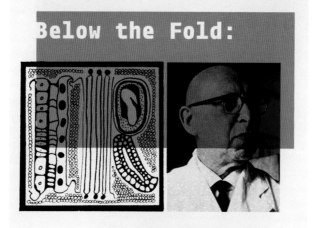

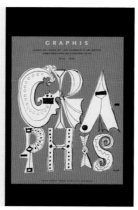
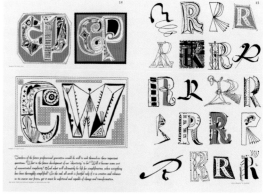

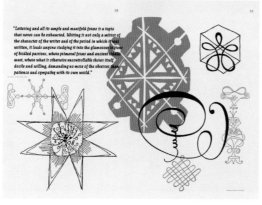
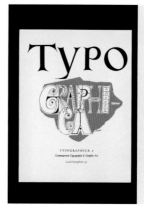

SKITTLES BRAND BOOK

Art Director
Craig Allen
Copywriter
Ashley Davis
Creative Director
Gerry Graf, Ian Reichenthal,
Scott Vitrone
Designer
Hans Seeger
Illustrator
Jay Ryan, Cody Hudson
Photographer
Magnus Magnusson, Kipling
Swhela, Ola Bergengren
Art Buyer
Hillary Frileck
Agency
TBWA / Chiat / Day
Client
Masterfoods
Country
United States

We were asked to create a
brand book that would
define Skittles brand guidelines for the agency, all
worldwide agency offices
and partners, and the
clients themselves. Most
brand books very bluntly
define the brand, and set
strict guidelines. However,
Skittles is unlike most other
brands, and therefore could
not look or read like most
other brand books. Rather
than telling readers flatfoot-
edly what the brand is and
what it stands for, we chose
to show them, allowing
them to experience the
brand and form their own
conclusions.

ADC LXXXVI

Graphic Design
Corporate & Promotional
Design Corporate Identity
Program / Campaign

Merit
Walter Moore Identity
Program

270

WALTER P MOORE IDENTITY PROGRAM

Art Director
Thomas Hull

Copywriter
Joann Stone

Creative Director
Lana Rigsby

Designer
Thomas Hull, Daniel Pagan

Photographer
Terry Vine

Production Company
EMCO Printing

Agency
Rigsby Design

Client
Walter P Moore

Country
United States

ADC LXXXVI   **Graphic Design**   **Merit**   271
Corporate & Promotional   (RED) Identity
Design Corporate Identity
Program / Campaign

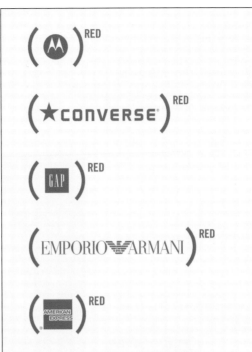

(RED) IDENTITY

Art Director
Todd Simmons

Copywriter
Todd Simmons, Sam Wilson

Creative Director
Karl Heiselman, Eric Scott

Designer
John Paul Chirdon,
Christian Butte

Illustrator
Christian Butte, Henri
Kusbiantoro

Photographer
Annie Leibovitz (Gap
Advertising Campaign)

Producer
Creative Director for
Gap Advertising
Campaign: Trey Laird
(Laird+Partners, New York)

Agency
Wolff Olins

Client
(RED)

Country
United States

A revolutionary organiza-
tion conceptualized by
Bono, (RED) is a union of
businesses, people and
ideas. The assignment
required creating a brand to
identify (RED), (RED) products marketed in conjunc-
tion with partners, and to
represent the (RED) ambi-
tion. The challenge involved
uniting two brands visually
and communicating the
power of this union.
Replacing traditional co-
branding models where
marks live side by side,
Wolff Olins' solution took
the form of brackets that
embraced partner marks.
The outcome is a modified
version of the partner mark
that emphasizes one entity.
Bono launched (RED) at the
World Economic Forum in
2006. (RED) charmed com-
panies and consumers alike.
In just six weeks, (RED)
sales raised enough money
to doctor 40,000 Africans in
dire need.

ADC LXXXVI

Graphic Design
Corporate & Promotional
Design Corporate Identity
Program / Campaign

Merit
FAIF Corporate Identity
Program

272

**FIAF CORPORATE
IDENTITY PROGRAM**
Designer
Philippe Apeloig,
Ellen Zhao, Ronny Quevedo,
Elamine Maecha
Art Director
Philippe Apeloig
Creative Director
Philippe Apeloig
Editor
Lisa Dupont
Photographer
Argenis Apolinario, Maria
Mikulasova (Calendar
Cover)
Production Company
Studio Apeloig
Agency
French Institute Alliance
Francaise
Client
French Institute Alliance
Francaise (FIAF)
Country
United States

Corporate & Promotional   J¸RKE Architekten |
Design Corporate Identity   Corporate Design
Program / Campaign

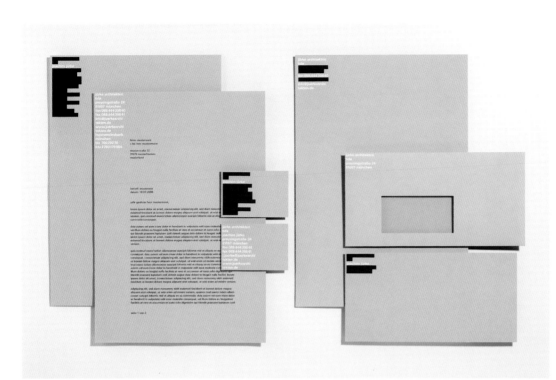

J¸RKE ARCHITEKTEN | CORPORATE DESIGN

Art Director
Julia Just

Copywriter
Dr. Axel Sanjosé

Creative Director
Michael Keller

Other
Production Management:
Christina Baur

Agency
KMS Team GmbH

Client
Jürke Architekten

Country
Germany

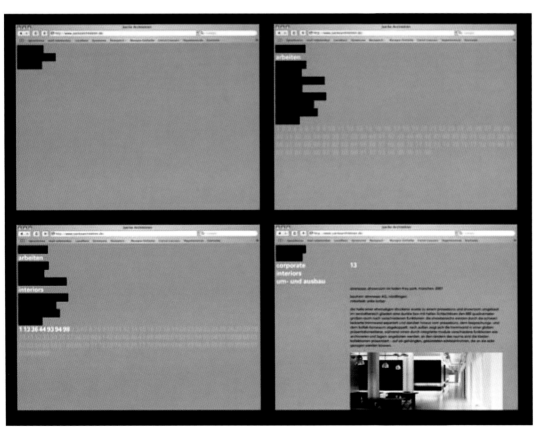

**PEACE OVER VIOLENCE
INTEGRATED BRAND
PROGRAM**
Art Director
Rebeca Méndez
Copywriter
Adam Eeuwens, Kibi
Anderson
Creative Director
Rebeca Méndez
Designer
Rebeca Méndez
Director
Rebeca Méndez
Editor
Rebeca Méndez
Photo Editor
Michael D. Powers
Photographer
Michael D. Powers
Producer
Rebeca Méndez, Adam
Eeuwens
Production Company
Rebeca Méndez
Communication Design
Publisher Peace Over
Violence
Assistant Designers
Ryan Weafer, Roxane
Zargham
Agency
Rebeca Méndez
Communication Design
Client Peace Over Violence
Country
United States

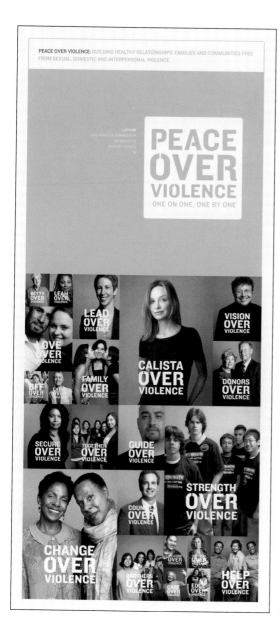

In 2004, my studio made a heartfelt decision to donate our creative services to the Los Angeles Commission on Assaults Against Women, a non-profit, multi-cultural, volunteer organization whose mission is building healthy relationships, families and communities, free from sexual, domestic and interpersonal violence. We became the agency's brand stewards and continue to lead them through their re-branding process. We helped them in repositioning their mission, gave them a new name and visual vocabulary so it more accurately represents the agency's expanded mandate of not only intervening in sexual assault and domestic abuse cases against women, but also actively preventing violence through education programs for youth, including girls and boys, and informing public policy and opinion on a local, state and federal level. The re-brand launched on October 27, 2006 at their Annual Humanitarian Awards event in Los Angeles. That night the organization received 50% more donations than they have ever received since their existence. Peace Over Violence executive director Patti Giggans attributes great part of their success to our rebranding efforts. The integrated brand program we created for Peace Over Violence includes a new positioning and mission statement, new name and tagline, new graphic identity and application guidelines, advertising campaign including two public service announcements, a brand video, website, capabilities brochures and all printed communication templates. We also established an internship program with students from UCLA Design | Media Arts department. The work that follows is what we have accomplished with extremely limited funds, yet with tireless dedication of great men and women who believe that violence is preventable and peace achievable.

ADC LXXXVI

Graphic Design
Corporate & Promotional
Design Corporate Identity
Program / Campaign

Merit
CA Vision Book & Posters

276

CA VISION BOOK & POSTERS

Art Director
Dana Gonsalves
Copywriter
David Konigsberg, Melanie
Engerski, Chris Korbey
Creative Director
Chris Korbey
Designer
Dana Gonsalves
Agency
Sequel Studio
Client
CA
Country
United States

One year after launching a
revitalized brand, the
"Celebrating CA" campaign
was rolled out to internal
audiences globally. The goal
was to introduce employees
to a new set of messages
and visuals that comprised
the new identity. Opting to
shed the typical show-and-
tell brand book format, the
campaign featured a story-
book account of employees
embodying the essence of
the brand positioning. In
addition, a series of posters
was used to educate and
generate excitement. The
campaign launched with a
global web cast hosted by
the CEO.

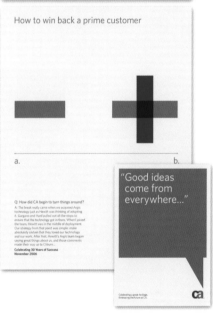
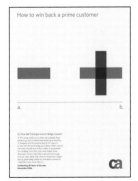

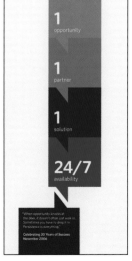

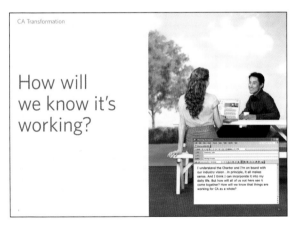

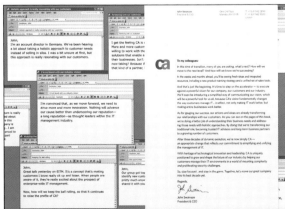

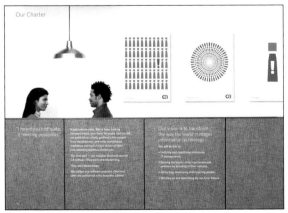

ADC LXXXVI

Graphic Design
Corporate & Promotional
Design Corporate Identity
Program / Campaign

Merit
DELC

278

DELC
Art Director
Andréas Netthoevel, Martin
Gaberthüel
Copywriter
Irene Krause
Creative Director
Andréas Netthoevel, Martin
Gaberthüel
Designer
Andréas Netthoevel, Martin
Gaberthüel
Printer
Ediprim
Agency
Secondfloorsouth
Client
Dr. Med. Adrian Krähenbühl
Country
Switzerland

The DELC Derma Estetic
Laser Center is one of the
leading dermatology cen-
ters for skin care and beauty in Switzerland. In
February 2006, DELC
opened its wonderful refur-
bished center in a new
location and on that occa-
sion all of its communication tools were redesigned.
In the middle of the new
appearance there is a mirror, which is reproduced
with an orange and light
blue frame in large formats
on the walls of the practice
rooms and on all the com-
munication tools described
and illustrated below.
Letterhead, envelope, business and appointment card.
brochure "the skin – 2m2 of
feeling" containing DELC's
offers regarding the various
topics of aesthetic dermatology. From the envelope
to the last page: different
paper strengths support the
haptic theme. Gift certifi-
cate: beauty is the essence
of the world. Enjoying
beauty means understand-
ing the world.

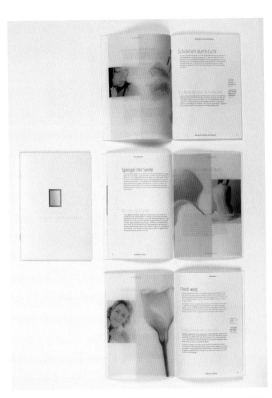

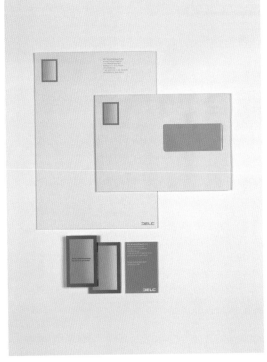

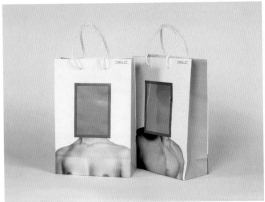

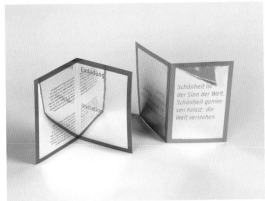

ADC LXXXVI

Graphic Design
Corporate & Promotional
Design Logo / Trademark /
Single

Merit
Christel Palace

279

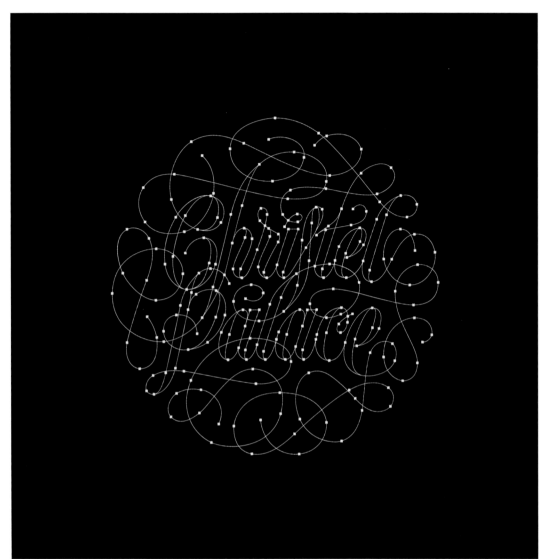

CHRISTEL PALACE
Art Director
Niels Shoe Meulman, Peter
Heykamp
Creative Director
Enrico Bartens
Designer
Niels Shoe Meulman
Agency
Unruly
Client
Christel Palace
Country
Netherlands

ADC LXXXVI

Graphic Design
Corporate & Promotional
Design Self-Promotion:
Print / Single

Merit
Art + Commerce Promotion

280

**ART + COMMERCE
PROMOTION**
Creative Director
Lisa Naftolin
Designer
Shigeto Akiyama
Photo Editor
Michael Van Horne
Other
Printer: Taylor Tocci & Co.
Agency
Art + Commerce
Client
Art + Commerce
Country
United States

Art + Commerce was
founded in the early 1980s
to represent outstanding
image makers in a range of
creative disciplines. In early
2006, the identity and website were redesigned to
reflect an expanded pro-
gram of activities. As part
of the relaunch, these post-
cards were produced for
marketing and promotion.
The postcard format is effi-
cient, allowing various
methods of distribution —
in portfolios; as small promos highlighting specific
groups of artists; or as a
"brick" covering the whole
agency. The guiding design
principle is "high end/low
key" and this economical,
relatively modest approach
differentiates Art +
Commerce in a field in
which slick promos are
commonplace.

ADC LXXXVI

Graphic Design
Corporate & Promotional
Design Self-Promotion:
Print / Single

Merit
Hormon Paper

281

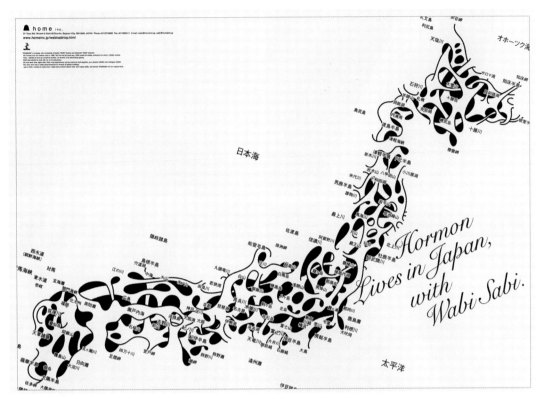

HORMON PAPER

<u>Art Director</u>
Ryohey wabi Kudow,
Kazushi sabi Nakanishi
<u>Designer</u>
Ryohey wabi Kudow,
Kazushi sabi Nakanishi
<u>Production Company</u>
Home Inc.
<u>Publisher</u>
Home Inc.
<u>Agency</u>
Home Inc.
<u>Client</u>
Home Inc.
<u>Country</u>
Japan

Maybe this kind of font has-
never existed before. Each
letter of the alphabet is like
a cell. You can create any
action or feeling by putting
together these 26 cells. All
alphabets are already living
before they are put together, as if they ask us to make
messages by putting them
together, pulling them
apart, sticking them out,
denting, etc.

ADC LXXXVI

Graphic Design
Corporate & Promotional
Design Self-Promotion:
Print / Single

Merit
Paprika Wrapping Paper

282

**PAPRIKA
WRAPPING PAPER**
Creative Director
Louis Gagnon
Designer
Richard Bélanger, René
Clément, David Guarnieri
Art Director
Richard Bélanger, René
Clément, David Guarnieri
Agency
Paprika
Client
Paprika
Country
Canada

Last year, we teamed up
with printer Transcontinen-
tal Litho Acme for the
creation of our annual
Christmas gift. We wanted
to create a piece that
showed and promoted both
our talents, as graphic
designers and printers. Our
artistic directors ended up
interfering directly in the
printing process, by changing colors and patterns on
the press. The results are
series of double-sided
sheets designed from
remaindered paper and ink.
We then placed a roll of
about 20 sheets in a ran-
dom order, in a specially
designed box. Each box had
wrapping papers with dif-
ferent designs, making
each gift unique.

ADC LXXXVI

Graphic Design
Corporate & Promotional
Design Self-Promotion:
Print / Single

Merit
Work 3

283

WORK 3
Art Director
DesignDavey
Copywriter
Trevor Harvey
Designer
Jeffrey Davey
Photographer
Simon Hewson
Agency
DesignDavey
Client
DesignDavey
Country
Australia

Work 3 is a graphic representation of the creative journey traveled by a small Sydney based design agency. Its purpose is to create interaction with the reader, in order to inform and provoke reaction.

ADC LXXXVI

Graphic Design
Corporate & Promotional
Design Announcements /
Single

Merit
Verite Symposium Invitation

284

**VERITE SYMPOSIUM
INVITATION**
Art Director
Mimi Jung
Copywriter
Colin Ilsley
Creative Director
Brian Hurewitz
Executive Creative Director
Jimmie Stone
Designer
Mimi Jung
Producer
Alan Stuart
Agency
Green Team
Client
Verite
Country
United States

Verite is a non-profit organization whose mission is to ensure that people worldwide work under safe and legal conditions. They paired with Calvert Group and UNIFEM for a symposium on how the advancing of women in the workplace improves corporate performance. We stitched our invitation message on an oversized clothing tag because a major offender of fair treatment is the textile industry. 8"x21" piece of satin fabric folded in half and stitched closed.

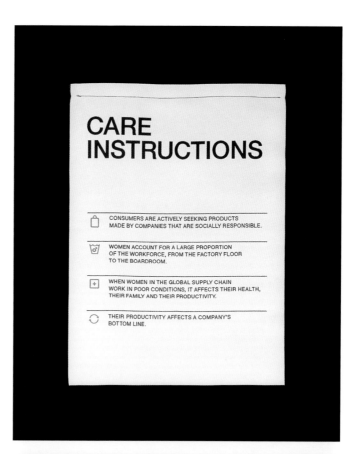

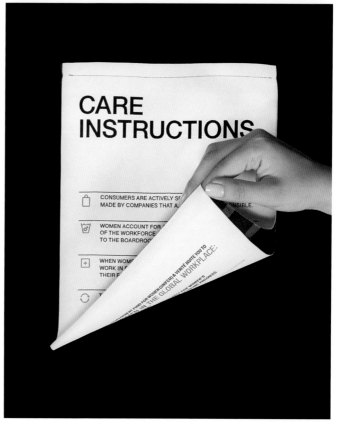

BLACK INVITATION

Creative Director
Louis Gagnon

Art Director
David Guarnieri

Designer
David Guarnieri

Agency
Paprika

Client
Commissaires

Country
Canada

Commissaires, a very
unique gallery-boutique
located in Montreal, wanted
an invitation to launch its
second exhibit, "La couleur
de l'ombre" ("The colour of
shadow"), in which every
presented piece was black.
The invitation has been
silkscreened on an oversize
sheet of black tissue paper,
which then could be held up
to the light to reveal the
black on black text.

ADC LXXXVI

Graphic Design
Corporate & Promotional
Design Postcard, Greeting
Card, or Invitation Card /
Single

Merit
Flying Card

286

FLYING CARD
Art Director
Tetsuya Tsukamoto
Copywriter
Hidetoshi Kuranari
Creative Director
Hidetoshi Kuranari, Tetsuya
Tsukamoto
Designer
Tetsuya Tsukamoto
Producer
Kazuo Iitaka
Production Company
Seio Printing Co., Ltd.
Agency
Dentsu
Client
Rewind
Country
Japan

This card was released first
in the Design Festival,
called Design Tide and now
sold in design shops and
museum shops only in
Japan. We are now search-
ing for shops in foreign
countries which will deal in
our cards.

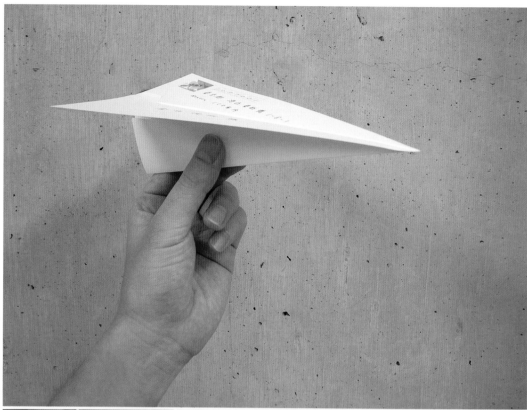

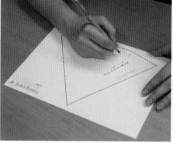

ADC LXXXVI

Graphic Design
Corporate & Promotional
Design Postcard, Greeting
Card, or Invitation Card /
Single

Merit
180 Christmas Card

287

180 CHRISTMAS CARD
Art Director
Garech Stone
Copywriter
Richard Bullock,
Garech Stone
Creative Director
Garech Stone
Designer
Garech Stone
Illustrator
Garech Stone
Producer
Marlon Lee
Project Manager
Dennis van Weerdenberg
Agency
180 Amsterdam
Client
180 Amsterdam
Country
Netherlands

ADC LXXXVI

Graphic Design
Corporate & Promotional
Design Calendar or
Appointment Book / Single

Merit
365 on Death Row

288

365 ON DEATH ROW

Art Director
Veronika Broich

Copywriter
Helmut Huber

Creative Director
Christoph Everke

Designer
Anja Krumrein, Ivo Hlavac,
Massimo Petrolli

Publisher
Pinsker Druck

Other
Account Executive:
Carla Nothhelfer

Agency
Serviceplan Gruppe fuer
innovative Kommunikation
GmbH & Co. KG

Client
Alive e.V. gegen Todesstrafe

Country
Germany

Our objective was to bring
people's attention to the
plight of prisoners on death
row and generate support
for Alive e.V. To bring it emo-
tionally as close as possible
to the recipients we wanted
to create something which
involves the addressee physically. We came up with this
tear-off calendar which
demonstrates that people
are being executed under the
death penalty every day and
how easy it is to literally
throw away someone's life.
Beside the investigation-
workload, which went on for
over a year, one special point
turned out to be the real
challenge for every team-
member: the unexpected
authenticity and emotional
closeness of this project.

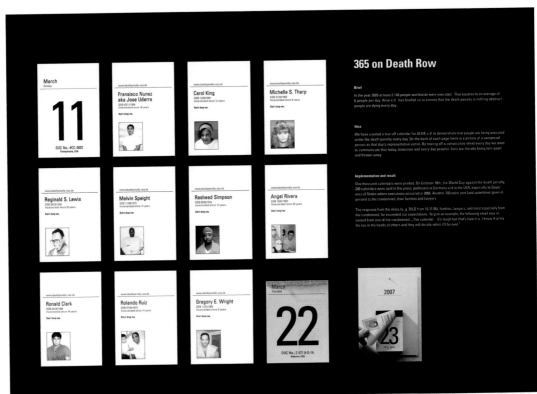

THE VERY FIRST
MAGAZINE 2006
Art Director
Javin Mo
Designer
Javin Mo
Editor
Milkxhake
Publisher
Antalis (HK) Ltd.
Copywriter
Milkxhake
Agency
Milkxhake
Client
Antalis (HK) Ltd.
Country
China

ADC **LXXXVI**

Graphic Design
Corporate & Promotional
Design Calendar or
Appointment Book / Single

Merit
Cryptology Calendar

290

**CRYPTOLOGY
CALENDAR**

Art Director
Xiaoying Zhang

Creative Director
Xaioying Zhang

Designer
Xiaoying Zhang

Agency
Zhifan design Ltd.

Country
China

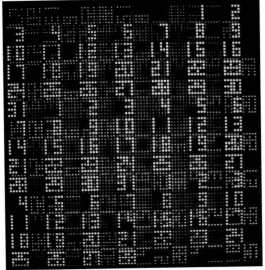

ADC LXXXVI

Graphic Design
Corporate & Promotional
Design Miscellaneous
(Stamps, Menus, Etc.) / Single

Merit
Super-Bastard Box Art
Characters

291

SUPER-BASTARD BOX ART CHARACTERS

Art Director
Undoboy
Copywriter
Undoboy
Creative Director
Undoboy
Designer
Undoboy
Illustrator
Undoboy
Production Company
Asia Pacific Offset
Agency
Undoboy
Client
Undoboy
Country
United States

We created Super-Bastard
Box Art Characters for self-
promotion. They consist of
16 unique toys, with 4
unique characters on each
of the face of the box, which
are pop icons. The toys are
designed so that you can
detach the head or the
pants. Once removed, it
reveals either a skull or
underwear. What makes it
exciting isn't how funny
their underwear is, but that
collectors can interchange
their heads and pants. Can
a George W. Bush head go
with a Saddam Hussein
commander suit? The objective is to bring happiness to
collectors, having fun with
this conceptual toy and create a brand identity of our
design studio.

ADC LXXXVI

Graphic Design
Corporate & Promotional
Design Miscellaneous
(Stamps, Menus, Etc.) / Single

Merit
Mit Handen Sehen

292

MIT HÄNDEN SEHEN
Art Director
Christof Gassner
Designer
Christof Gassner
Director
Ulrike Bohm
Production Company
Bagel Security-Print
Publisher
Bundesministerium der
Finanzen
Agency
Christof Gassner
Client
Bundesministerium der
Finanzen
Country
Germany

A special edition stamp
titled "Seeing with your
hands" promotes two
anniversaries: "200 years of
Blind School Berlin" and
"150 years of Nikolaus Care
Charity". The scholastic
education of blind children
started with the foundation
of the first German School
of the Blind in Berlin-
Steglitz through Johann
August Zeune in 1806. The
Nikolaus Care is a clerical
charity that supports the
scholastic and professional
education as well as the
social integration of blind
and visually impaired
human beings. The graphic
design takes on the theme
"Seeing with your hands" in
a variety of perception levels addressing the sense of
touch and vision. The text is
set for normal readers in 6
point. For the blind it comes
with the key message
"Seeing with your hands" in
the Braille type face, value
digit "55". The large, hazy
"55" in the background visu-
alizes a vision impairment.

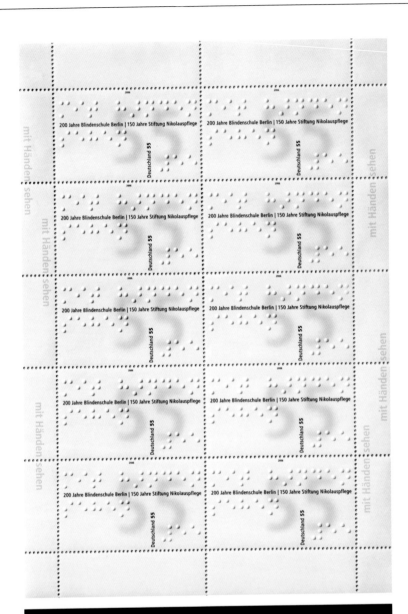

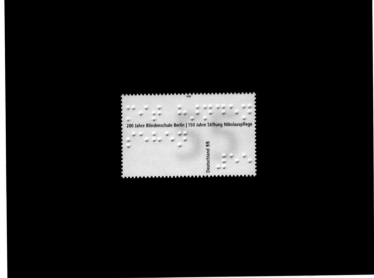

Graphic Design
Corporate & Promotional
Design Miscellaneous
(Stamps, Menus, Etc.) /
Campaign

Merit
Ecole Buissonniere Year
School Book 2006-2007

293

ECOLE BUISSONNIERE YEAR SCHOOL BOOK 2006-2007

Art Director
René Clement
Creative Director
Louis Gagnon
Designer
René Clement
Photographer
Monic Richard
Agency
Paprika
Client
Ecole Buissonniere
Country
Canada

It is now a tradition at École Buissonnière, a private elementary school: at the beginning of every school year, each kid receives a "year school book" to facilitate contacts between kids outside school. Every year, we create a totally different concept. For the 2006-2007 edition, we took pictures of the kids making funny faces and placed them in an oversize document. The kids had fun posing and it shows; the result is a grimace book that they will not only use as a reference document, but as a funny picture book they'll like to consult also.

ADC LXXXVI

Graphic Design
Poster Design Promotional /
Campaign

Merit
Couqo

294

COUQO

<u>Art Director</u>
Hiroki Yamamoto
<u>Creative Director</u>
Joan McCulloch
<u>Designer</u>
Hiroki Yamamoto, Kaori
Murakami
<u>Agency</u>
Marvin
<u>Client</u>
Couqo
<u>Country</u>
Japan

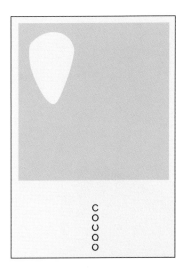

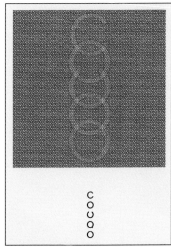

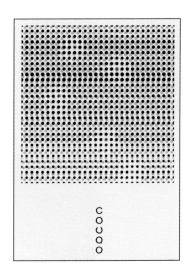

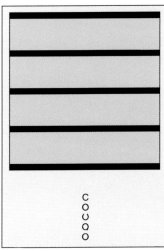

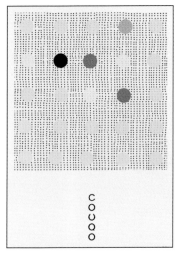

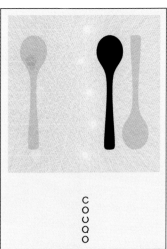

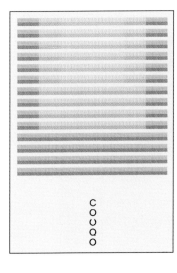

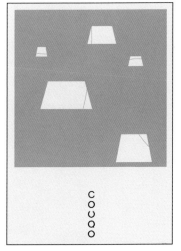

ADC LXXXVI

Graphic Design
Poster Design Promotional /
Single

Merit
Arahata Fresh Meat Co. Ltd.

295

**ARAHATA FRESH
MEAT CO.,LTD**
Art Director
Koichi Nakano
Copywriter
Koichi Nakano
Creative Director
Koichi Nakano
Designer
Koichi Nakano
Illustrator
Koichi Nakano
Production Company
Creative Mind Co., Ltd.
Agency
Creative Mind Co., Ltd.
Client
Arahata Fresh Meat Co.,
Ltd.
Country
Japan

ADC LXXXVI

Graphic Design
Poster Design Promotional /
Campaign

Merit
Nullin Osaka Nagoya

296

**NULL IN OSAKA &
NAGOYA**

Art Director
Shun Kawakami

Creative Director
Shun Kawakami

Designer
Shun Kawakami

Production Company
Artless Inc

Agency
Artless Inc

Client
Artless Inc

Country
Japan

This poster is made for
exhibitions of graphic art
and interactive art in Osaka
and Nagoya, organized by a
design group called
"Artless Inc." The Japanese
expression "ON-KO-CHI-
SHIN" is the design con-
cept. It means "learn from
the past, and create new
things." The artwork is printed on a traditional
Japanese paper called
"Washi" and original wood
paper using a slice of two
different kinds of traditional
Japanese wood, which is
processed for printing. As
for main graphic, I re-
designed an old Japanese
map and it is pointing at
Osaka and Nagoya.

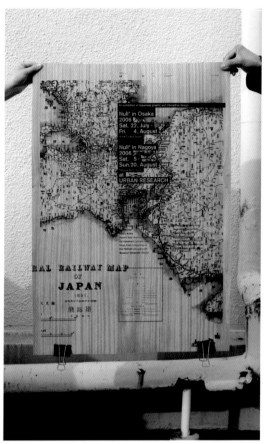

ADC LXXXVI

Graphic Design
Poster Design Promotional /
Campaign

Merit
Build Your Body With Good
Water

297

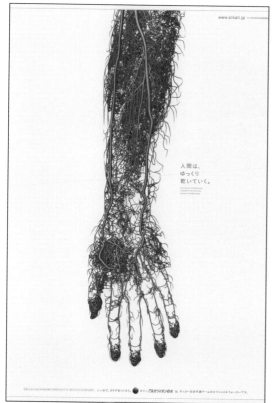

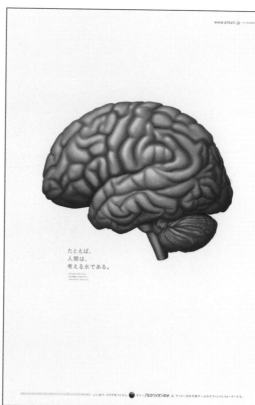

**BUILD YOUR BODY
WITH GOOD WATER!**

Art Director
Yukimi Sano

Copywriter
Tetsuya Sakota

Creative Director
Yukimi Sano, Tetsuya
Sakota

Designer
Yukimi Sano, Ritsuko
Watanab

Illustrator
Hitoshi Asano

Production Company
ADK Inc.

Agency
ADK Inc.

Client
Kirin McDanone Waters
Co.,Ltd.

Country
Japan

ADC LXXXVI

Graphic Design
Package Design
Entertainment / Single

Merit
Akikoyano Hajimete Noyano
Akiko

298

**AKIKO YANO -
HAJIMETE NO YANO
AKIKO**

Art Director
Atsuki Kikuchi

Designer
Atsuki Kikuchi

Production Company
Yamaha Music
Communications Co. Ltd.

Publisher
Yamaha Music
Communications Co. Ltd.

Agency
Bluemark Inc.

Client
Yamaha Music
Communications Co. Ltd.

Country
Japan

Akiko Yano is a major
recording artist in Japan.
The album "Hajimete no
Yano Akiko" is an anniver-
sary album which features
friends of Akiko Yano as
guest artists. The concept of
different musicians coming
together on one album was
picked up in the sleeve
design where different
shapes on different layers
form new shapes, shadows
and spaces.

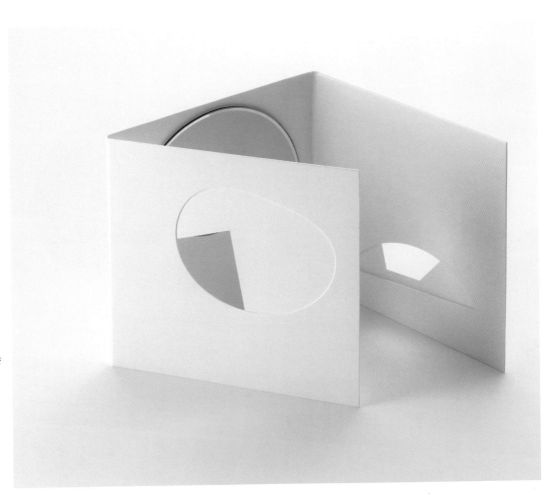

WARM
Art Director
Daigo Daikoku
Creative Director
Daigo Daikoku
Designer
Daigo Daikoku
Agency
Nippon Design Center
Client
Warm Project
Country
Japan

ADC LXXXVI   **Graphic Design**   **Merit**   300
                                Poster Design Promotional /   Cut It Out!
                                Campaign

CUT IT OUT!

Art Director
Hideto Yagi
Copywriter
Jeremy Perrott
Creative Director
Jeremy Perrott
Photographer
Munenori Nakamura
Designer
Kentaro Kasahara
Producer
Tetsuichi Segawa,
Toshiaki Tanaka
Translator
Ayumi Tsuzuki
Agency
McCann Erickson
Japan Inc.
Client
OLFA
Country
Japan

The challenge was to demonstrate the product use without any of the expected cliche images. It came very simply. What if you could cut out all the things that upset you or annoyed you or just plain didn't like? So we did. And the result was many executions but a budget only for three posters. Originally designed to be in magazines with the actual areas cut out, the final result were these in-store and outdoor posters. Art direction and attention to detail bring out the simple but very demonstrative images of the OLFA blade knife. A simple line "cut it out," doubled as the call to action in an equally understated manner.

WMW

Art Director
Michal Kacperczyk
Designer
Michal Kacperczyk
Production Company
The Silkscreen Center of
Academy of Fine Arts in
Lodz
Publisher
Inselgalerie, Berlin
Agency
Michal Kacperczyk
Client
Inselgalerie, Berlin
Country
Poland

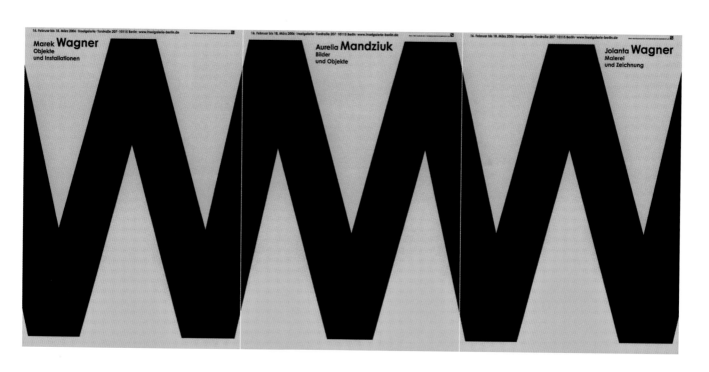

ADC LXXXVI

Graphic Design
Poster Design Promotional /
Campaign

Merit
Die Couch: Vom Denken Im
Liegen

302

**DIE COUCH: VOM
DENKEN IM LIEGEN**
Art Director
Abbott Miller
Creative Director
Abbott Miller
Designer
Abbott Miller, Kristen
Spilman
Agency
Pentagram Design
Client
The Sigmund Freud
Museum
Country
United States

ADC LXXXVI

Graphic Design
Package Design Food /
Beverage / Campaign

Merit
Mini Garage Super

303

MINI GARAGE SUPER

<u>Art Director</u>
Reginald Wagner, Benjamin
Pabst
<u>Copywriter</u>
Sabine Manecke
<u>Creative Director</u>
Katrin Oeding
<u>Designer</u>
Sonja Kliem
<u>Producer</u>
Marc Schecker, Martin
Luehe
<u>Agency</u>
Kolle Rebbe Werbeagentur
GmbH
<u>Client</u>
Anthony's Mini Garage
Winery
<u>Country</u>
Germany

The task was a product
redevelopment for a range
of fruit brandies. Name
development, design and
container form should be
completely unusual and
should be strongly convinc-
ing to both bar / restaurant
goers and owners alike. We
conceived and realized the
ANTHONY'S SUPER
range, contained in a
uniquely developed and
handy schnapps canister,
which can stand prominent-
ly alongside the other alco-
holic drinks at the bar. The
packaging concept encom-
passes the name develop-
ment and the design for
ANTHONY'S SUPER Z
("Zwetschgenbrand" or
plum brandy), SUPER K
("Kirschbrand", or cherry
brandy) and SUPER W
("Williams" pear spirit).

Graphic Design
Poster Design Promotional /
Single

Merit
"Takeoff" Produced By
Kentaro Kobayashi

304

**"TAKEOFF" PRODUCED
BY KENTARO
KOBAYASHI**

Art Director
Manabu Mizuno

Designer
Masaru Uemura, Shinya
Nakayama

Production Company
Good Design Company

Publisher
Twinkle Corporation Ltd.

Agency
Good Design Company, Inc.

Client
Twinkle Corporation Ltd.

Country
Japan

I AM LIVING
Art Director
Pazu Lee Ka Ling
Copywriter
Pazu Lee Ka Ling
Creative Director
Pazu Lee Ka Ling
Designer
Pazu Lee Ka Ling
Director
Pazu Lee Ka Ling
Illustrator
Pazu Lee Ka Ling
Photo Editor
Pazu Lee Ka Ling
Photographer
Pazu Lee Ka Ling
Agency
Pazu Lee Ka Ling
Client
Shenzhen Graphic Design
Association
Country
China

ADC <u>LXXXVI</u>

Graphic Design
Poster Design Public
Service / Non-Profit /
Educational / Single

Merit
Conference for Stopping Dog
Droppings Left

306

**CONFERENCE FOR
STOPPING DOG
DROPPINGS LEFT**
<u>Art Director</u>
Junya Kamada
<u>Designer</u>
Junya Kamada
<u>Production Company</u>
Levan, Inc.
<u>Agency</u>
Levan, Inc.
<u>Country</u>
Japan

ADC LXXXVI

Graphic Design
Poster Design Public
Service / Non-Profit /
Educational / Campaign

Merit
Staircase, Hump, Slope

307

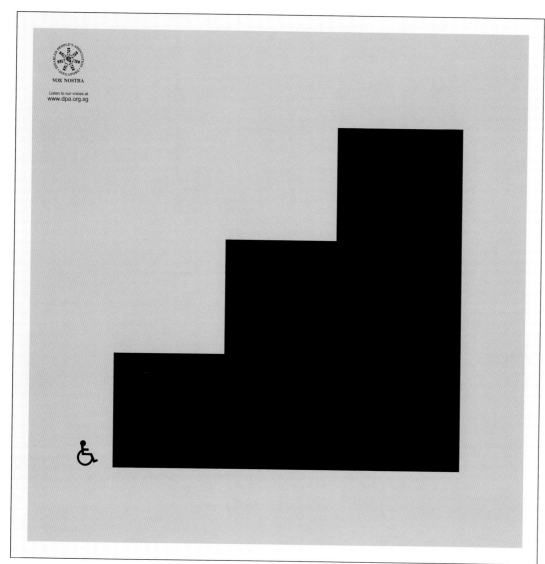

STAIRCASE, HUMP, SLOPE

Art Director
Leo Teck Chong

Copywriter
Alfred Teo, Louise Bolo

Creative Director
Leo Teck Chong

Illustrator
Leo Teck Chong

Producer
Simon Chan

Other
James Tan

Agency
Ad Planet Group

Client
Disabled People's
Association Singapore

Country
Singapore

This campaign originated
from the observation that
most "abled" people are
ignorant of the plight of
"disabled" people. What
most of us take for granted
can actually be a huge
obstacle for the physically
handicapped. We chose to
use common traffic icons
juxtaposed with the wheel-
chair icon to communicate
this fact. The use of traffic
icons is also a way to sym-
bolize the arduous journey
of life that the "disabled"
community has to endure
while trying to fit into the
"abled" society. It is a journey that most of us turn a
blind eye to. The DPAS's
motto "VOX NOSTRA"
perfectly captured this need
of theirs to be finally heard
and seen.

ADC LXXXVI

Graphic Design
Poster Design Billboard /
Campaign

Merit
The World Translated by
Lagenscheidt

308

**THE WORLD.
TRANSLATED BY
LANGENSCHEIDT.**

Art Director
Vera Schuchardt

Copywriter
Dietmar Neumann

Creative Director
Matthias Eickmeyer

Illustrator
Vera Schuchardt

Photographer
Markus Meuthen

Agency
BBDO Duesseldorf GmbH

Client
Langenscheidt KG

Country
Germany

How do you communicate
the benefits of
Langenscheidt dictionaries
to people who don't speak a
second language? Our solution needed to be solely
visual: We used the infa-
mous yellow and blue color
code of Langenscheidt on
various national flags. A
simple way of illustrating
how easy it is to translate
any language in the world –
with Langenscheidt.

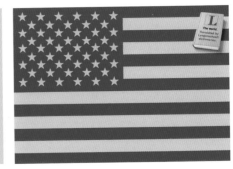

ADC LXXXVI

Graphic Design
Package Design
Entertainment / Single

Merit
Schonberg Ensemble Edition

309

**SCHÖNBERG
ENSEMBLE EDITION**
Art Director
Will de l'Ecluse
Designer
Will de l'Ecluse, Tim
Baumgarten, Julius van der
Woude , Tiny Risselada
Production Company
Cyber Music
Publisher
Drukkerij Mart. Spruijt
Other
Production Radio
Recordings Radio
Nederland Wereldomroep
Agency
UNA (Amsterdam)
Designers
Client
Schönberg Ensemble
Country
Netherlands

The Schönberg Ensemble
CD-box consists of 22 CDs,
3 DVDs and a book. The
book comprises work of
founders of the 20th century
music such as Stravinsky,
Schönberg and Webern.
By using a colored pattern
of horizontal lines we have
tried to visualize the contemporary music. The color
moves along per CD resulting in a harmonious entity.
The typography is also
adjusted to suit each CD.
The amount of text deter-
mines the typeface size to
be used for each composer.
In the 600 pages of the book
we have used the same
design to indicate the different chapters. On the
fore-edge of the book the
lines reappear in a playful
manner. The material for the
cover of both the book and
box are the same.

ADC LXXXVI   **Graphic Design**   **Merit**   310
Package Design   Two Pianos
Entertainment / Single

TWO PIANOS

Art Director
Vladan Srdic

Creative Director
Vladan Srdic

Designer
Vladan Srdic

Producer
Nada Jeraj Velan

Production Company
TheSign / Studio 360 d.o.o.

Publisher
RTV Slovenija

Agency
Studio 360 d.o.o.

Client
Gorisek / Lazar

Country
Slovenia

Gorisek / Lazar "Two Pianos" is one of the rare piano duos in Europe, playing an extraordinary mixture between contemporary classical and jazz music. The challenge in designing this CD sleeve was to get maximal visual and emotional output using minimal graphics. We wanted to highlight the vibrating energy of piano duo using a single thin line "traveling" through the sleeve, expressing an amplitude of common and, in the same time, individual musical voyage.

ADC LXXXVI

Graphic Design
Package Design
Entertainment / Single

Merit
Sonic Brat HI.A.TUS CD

311

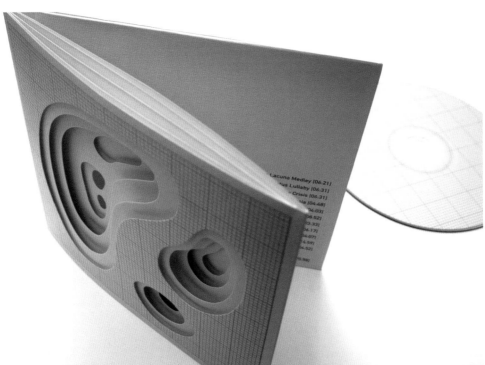

SONIC BRAT
HI.A.TUS CD
Art Director
Cara Ang
Creative Director
Chris Lee
Production Company
Asylum Sounds
Agency
Asylum Creative Pte Ltd
Client
Sonic Brat
Country
Singapore

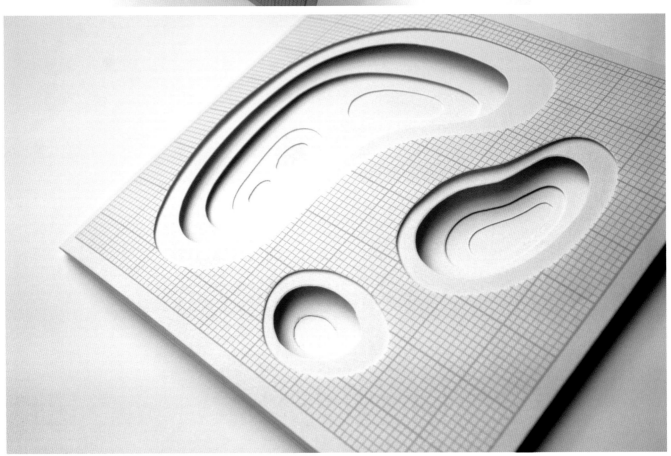

ADC LXXXVI

Graphic Design
Package Design Food /
Beverage / Single

Merit
Uonumasan Koshi-Hikari
(Package)

312

**UONUMASAN
KOSHIHIKARI
(PACKAGE)**
Art Director
Masahiko Gonda
Creative Director
Masahiko Gonda
Designer
Masahiko Gonda
Agency
P913 Inc.
Client
Ja-Kitauonuma
Country
Japan

ADC LXXXVI   **Graphic Design**   **Merit**   313
Package Design Food /   Fukunishiki Japanese Sake
Beverage / Single

**FUKUNISHIKI
JAPANESE SAKE**

Art Director
Issay Kitagawa
Designer
Issay Kitagawa, Manabu
Inoue
Producer
GRAPH Co.,Ltd.
Agency
GRAPH Co.,Ltd.
Client
Fukunishiki Co., Ltd.
Country
Japan

Designs for sake bottles
often use Chinese calligraphy. The package design for
Fukunishiki allows the company mark and the types of
sake to stand out, rather
than the written name,
Fukunishiki. The mark represents a head of rice seeds
(sake is brewed from rice)
and the three circles sym-
bolize rice, water and people, the three basic ele-
ments in making sake. The
mark is also a configuration
of the Japanese hiragana
alphabet, FU of FUkunishiki.
Hence, if you are in a liquor
store, the design of the bottle stands out, as there is no
calligraphy used in the
packaging. The smallest
bottle also has a distinct
form, unusual for a sake
bottle. The design is simple
and fresh, to show the elegance of sake.

DELISHOP PACKAGING

Art Director
Enric Aguilera

Creative Director
Enric Aguilera

Designer
Jordi Carles, Merçè
Fernández

Agency
Enric Aguilera Asociados

Client
Delishop

Country
Spain

The objective of this project
was very simple, to make
labels for all packaging
products with a minimum
cost. As a solution, we pro-
posed to convert the bar-
code in the graphic system

delishop

**Cacao
puro en polvo**
Pure cocoa powder

delishop

**Bombones
tequila, ron
y café**
Tequila, rum and coffee
chocolates

delishop

**Cobertura de
chocolate negro**
Dark chocolate chips

delishop

**Chocolate
de tiramisu**
White chocolate
tiramisu

ADC LXXXVI

Graphic Design
Package Design Food /
Beverage / Campaign

Merit
The Cost Vineyard Wine
Bottles

316

**THE COST VINEYARD
WINE BOTTLES**

<u>Art Director</u>
Steve Sandstrom

<u>Copywriter</u>
Lane Foard

<u>Creative Director</u>
Steve Sandstrom

<u>Designer</u>
Starlee Matz, Steve
Sandstrom

<u>Producer</u>
Prue Searles

<u>Agency</u>
Sandstrom Design

<u>Client</u>
The Cost Vineyards

<u>Country</u>
United States

The Cost Vineyards pro-
duces only 350 cases of
Willamette Valley Pinot
Noir, a renowned wine
region in Oregon. A willing
client and low yield allowed
us a unique creative opportunity. We created a different label for each bottle in a
case (12 total) using digital
printing. Each label is a clipping from a section of what
appears to be a local newspaper. One is from the front
page, another from the
advice column, and another
from the classified ads and
so on. Somewhere in the
clipping a mention of the
wine appears and is encir-
cled or underlined with pen.
The made up articles are
humorous and encourage
the consumer to seek out
other labels. A consumer
isn't likely to get the same
label twice from a restaurant or a select grocer
because each merchant can
only receive a limited number of cases. One restau-
rant has framed the entire
collection of labels for their
guests to enjoy. The next
vintage and 12 new clip-
pings await.

ES, OCTOBER 2, 2005

Things To Do This Weekend

The Purple Nurples Rockin' Tour Live
at Rose Coliseum

Purple Nurple characters combine some well-known silly songs and plenty of wacky G-rated humor in this moral-laden show that emphasizes the Nurple message that sometimes it's okay to be an underachiever. 1:30 and 5:30 p.m. Sun $15 - $35

"Donuts While You Sleep" Gallery Opening
at The Auguste Gallery

The work of surging Austrian artist Kathrin Zefferer comes to the Pacific Northwest. Her surreal paintings of pastries under bed sheets are otherworldly. Hors'doeuvres will include Dancing Monk cheeses and The Cost Vineyard's highly touted 2004 Willamette Valley Pinot Noir. 1:00 p.m. - 5:00 p.m. Saturday and Sunday. Free admission.

You Can! Gosh-Darnit, We All Can!!!
at Sleep Right Inn's Grand Ballroom

Motivational speaker Prue

MES, OCTOBER 2, 2005

THEATER REVIEW

No Wisdom Here
BY NATHAN RAMSEY

If you ever have a chance to see the play, "The Wisdom of the Rhinoceros," well, be sure to pass on that. To say that this production leaves much to be desired would be to engage in gross understatement. First of all, it's not even about rhinoceroses (it's about horses). The dialogue is putrid and the acting is early eighth grade drama department. I now have no reason to visit any of the inner rings of hell, as this play replicated it perfectly.

In fact, the only redeeming moment of the entire evening was intermission. I had the pleasure of sampling The Cost Vineyard's 2004 Willamette Valley Pinot Noir. Outstanding. Soul-touching. Superb. It's what they're serving right now up in heaven. It

(continued D9)

IN CONCERT
The
Purple
Nurple

ADC LXXXVI

Graphic Design
Package Design Fashion /
Apparel / Wearable / Single

Merit
Net Backing

318

NET BACKING
Art Director
Eiji Yamada
Designer
Chiharu Kondo, Yuriko Seki
Agency
UltRA Graphics
Client
Takeo
Country
Japan

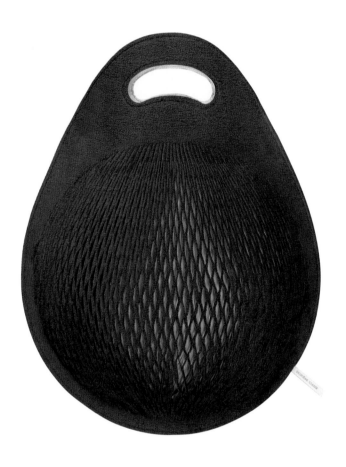
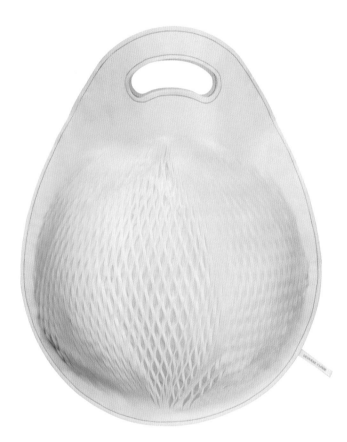

ADC LXXXVI   **Graphic Design**   **Merit**   319
Environmental Design   Scratchers Room
Gallery Museum Exhibit /
Installation / Campaign

SCRATCHERS ROOM

Art Director
Ante Rasic, Oleg Hrzic

Designer
Ante Rasic

Creative Director
Ante Rasic

Producer
Studio Rasic

Multimedia
Ivan Marusic Klif

Agency
Studio Rasic

Client
HOZ, MUO, Zagreb

Country
Croatia

"Scratchers room" was in
the third part (Methods of
communication) of the exhibition "Art of Persuading."
A complete wall in this
room was covered with
thousands of pictures with
sponsors' logos and cov-
ered with a silver film.
Visitors were able to
scratch individual fields
that contained one logo and
win many various prizes.
The wall also contained
sensors on the winning
fields, so when a winning
field was scratched, a
recording of applause was
triggered in the room. We
needed to create a piece of
artwork that would symbol-
ize the phenomenon of
advertising (symbolically
how huge and influential it
is in today's world), as well
as it had to be something
that all visitors could interact with. We wanted to show
that the visitors themselves
are an inevitable part of the
exhibition (advertising)
because they are the cre-
ators of the final piece
(product). A huge "scratch-
er" directly involved visitors
with the exhibition as well
as it directly involved them
in advertising by trying to
win the prizes.

ADC LXXXVI

Graphic Design
Package Design Cosmetics /
Perfume / Campaign

Merit
Prosays

320

PROSAYS'
Creative Director
Tommy Li
Designer
Tami Leung
Photographer
Danny Chiu
Copywriter
Mabel Leung
Agency
Tommy Li Design
Workshop Ltd
Client
Jun & Peace Limited
Country
Hong Kong

Unlike most cosmetic products that use logos repeat-
edly, different objects were
used as main visuals in the
"Black Humor" concept.
They were applied throughout the packaging series to
avoid confusion and to create an outstanding, high
quality and unique image.

ADC LXXXVI

Graphic Design
Package Design Gift /
Specialty Product / Campaign

Merit
Paper Bubble Wrap

321

PAPER BUBBLE WRAP

Art Director
Kotaro Hirano
Production Company
Hakuhodo Inc., Nippon
Paper Industries, Co.,Ltd.
Creative Director
Kotaro Hirano
Agency
Hakuhodo Inc.
Client
Fuji Television Network, Inc.
Country
Japan

The aim was to add to the emotional, positive anticipation of sending or receiving a gift. Air cellular cushioning material, or bubble wrap, as it is more commonly recognized, is a functional item to merely wrap an item safely and securely. By changing the material from plastic to paper, we deliver a Japanese, premium quality. Also, by intentionally making it nontransparent, it builds the excitement of opening the gift. The design comes in a theme of four distinct seasons, which makes it appropriate for the Japanese gift giving culture throughout the year. The world's most elastic paper (as of June, 2006) is used. A totally new packaging material was invented, which is molded with cast, just as regular bubble wraps are made.

ADC LXXXVI   **Graphic Design**
Package Design Gift /
Specialty Product / Single
    Merit
Wrapping Print Furoshiki
    322

WRAPPING PRINT FUROSHIKI

Art Director
Yuki Sugiyama

Creative Director
Masaru Kitakaze

Designer
Yuki Sugiyama, Shinji Ueno

Illustrator
Shoko Yokota

Agency
Hakuhodo Inc.

Client
Ministry of the Environment

Country
Japan

The objective was to create an environmentally friendly bag to help reduce usage of plastic bags. Our solution was to reintroduce a forgotten Japanese tradition, Furoshiki. It is just a square piece of cloth, but by tying the cloth in different ways, it can wrap anything. We created "Wrapping Print Furoshiki" which has 12 different ways of tying the furoshiki printed onto the cloth so everyone can use "Wrapping Print Furoshiki" with ease. The Ministry of Environment handed out "Wrapping Print Furoshiki" at the Torino Winter Olympics and spread this traditional Japanese wisdom to the world. I hope that this Japanese tradition will be used around the world to help the world to be environmentally friendly.

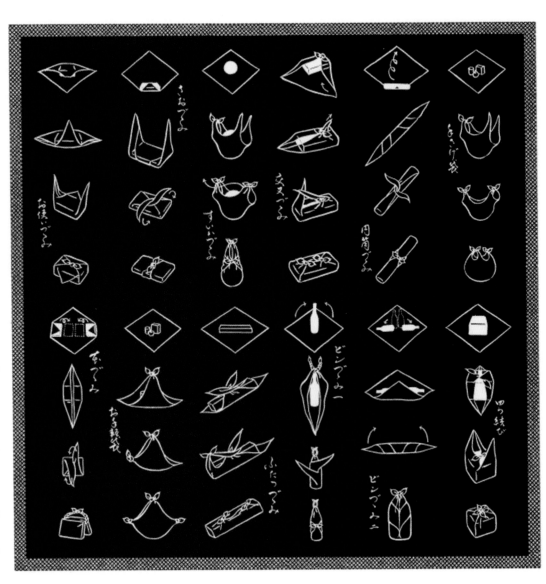

ADC <u>LXXXVI</u>

Graphic Design
Package Design Gift /
Specialty Product / Single

Merit
Card Type Package

323

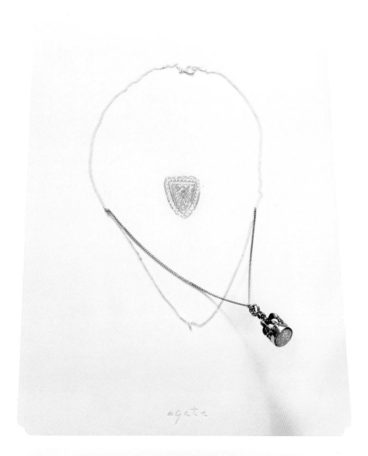

CARD TYPE PACKAGE
<u>Art Director</u>
Eiji Yamada
<u>Designer</u>
Chiharu Kondo
<u>Agency</u>
UltRA Graphics
<u>Client</u>
Agato
<u>Country</u>
Japan

ADC <u>LXXXVI</u>

Graphic Design
Package Design Gift /
Specialty Product / Single

Merit
Glasses Case

324

GLASSES CASE
<u>Art Director</u>
Satoru Kubo
<u>Designer</u>
Satoru Kubo
<u>Production Company</u>
This Way Inc.
<u>Agency</u>
This Way Inc.
<u>Client</u>
Takeo Co. Ltd.
<u>Country</u>
Japan

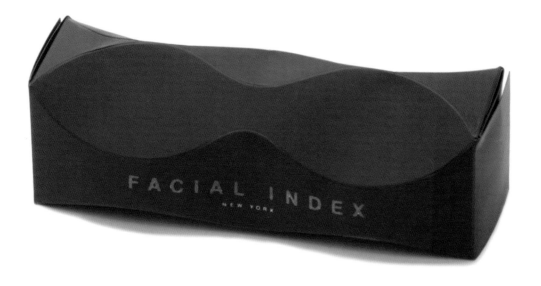

Graphic Design
Package Design
Miscellaneous / Campaign

Merit
Issimbow "Katachi-Koh"

ISSIMBOW "KATACHI-KOH"

<u>Art Director</u>
Shin Matsunaga
<u>Creative Director</u>
Shin Matsunaga
<u>Designer</u>
Shin Matsunaga
<u>Agency</u>
Shin Matsunaga Design Inc.
<u>Client</u>
Issimbow, Inc.
<u>Country</u>
Japan

The biggest characteristic of this project was that a single graphic designer was involved from beginning to end in bringing it to fruition, including the processes of planning, production, direction and design. And finally, this project led to the creation of Issimbow, Inc. The concepts of product creation were "healthier," "more beautiful," and "more energetic" in other words, "Wellness that will eliminate stress, the eternal goal of modern man." The first product of these is Katachi-koh, a completely new type of incense. In future, through collaboration with various corporations that share this concept, we aim to expand into a variety of brands. Not only is this a suitable theme to tackle at the beginning of the 21st century, but I also feel that this may be one of the happiest events in my entire life as a designer.

ADC LXXXVI

Graphic Design
Package Design
Miscellaneous / Single

Merit
Brick-Like Designed
Tissue Box

326

BRICK-LIKE DESIGNED TISSUE BOX

Art Director
Masamichi Katayama
(Wonderwall)

Copywriter
Susumu Namikawa

Creative Director
Susumu Namikawa,
Hidetaka Ando

Designer
Groovisions

Production Company
Pict Inc.

Agency Producer
Takuo Ozawa

Account Executive
Kaoru Kowaguchi

Agency
Dentsu Inc. Tokyo

Client
Oji Nepia Co.,Ltd.

Country
Japan

This is a project by Oji Nepia Co., Ltd., a paper products company, to make tissue paper and toilet paper rolls that are good for the environment and which feel good. The theme is LOHAS, or Lifestyles Of Health And Sustainability. Each month, the company asks various people to submit product ideas, makes products out of these ideas, and actually sells them one by one. A wide variety of people send in their ideas, including musicians, students, comedians, artists, children, and others. This is a new form of communication to unleash craftsmanship to the world and make the company Oji Nepia Co., Ltd. better known in society through craftsmanship.

ADC LXXXVI

Graphic Design
Package Design
Miscellaneous / Single

Merit
Amnesty International
"Torture Meets Modern Art"

327

Torture meets modern art   (1)

Torture meets modern art   (2)

H1/105

This is just a duplicate.
The original hangs in a prison cell somewhere
in China, Indonesia or the Middle East. Without
witnesses. Without hope. Help us to stop this
happening: www.amnesty-international.com

Torture meets modern art   (3)

Brief
The Amnesty section of Mannheim (Germany) wanted to create new and
strong public interest in their town. Because people often avoid the
classical Amnesty information desks in pedestrian zones and shopping malls.

Idea
We disguised torture as a modern art sculpture and exposed it in the most
unusual context, the big local Art Museum (Kunsthalle Mannheim).
Because in museums you'll find people of higher education and income than
in ordinary contexts – the profile of potential Amnesty supporters. The artist
Christian Schönwälder created the sculpture for us.

Results
1. Over 7000 Visitors during the first four weeks.
2. Large PR coverage in local and national newspapers.
3. Extra PR in magazines where Amnesty normally would never get in:
   Art Magazines and Marketing Periodicals.
4. The clickrates on amnesty-international.de during the promotion were
   16% higher than in the previous months.
5. The local Amnesty Group in Mannheim doubled the number of members
   in 2006.

**AMNESTY
INTERNATIONAL
"TORTURE MEETS
MODERN ART"**

Art Director
Christian Mommertz
Copywriter
Dr. Stephan Vogel
Creative Director
Christian Mommertz, Dr.
Stephan Vogel
Designer
Friedrich Detering
Artist
Christian Schoenwaelder,
Gallery Diskus
Agency
Ogilvy Frankfurt
Client
Amnesty International,
Mannheim / Germany
Country
Germany

In some countries prisoners
are still being brutally tor-
tured. Today. In the 21st century, of course people are
shocked when they learn
about this fact. Fortunately,
Amnesty International is
raising awareness, trying to
put an end to torture.
Unfortunately, most people
don't know this, because
they tend to avoid the information desks AI puts up in
the pedestrian areas of big
cities, for example. So when
AI Mannheim wanted to run
an Anti-Torture-Campaign
in 2006, Ogilvy Frankfurt
came up with the idea to
confront people with the
message in an unexpected
way. We chose an art exhibition in a popular museum.
There we put up an exhibit
of our own: A wooden
sculpture of a man hanging
upside down in a dirty bag.
And a small plaque next
to it telling visitors that
this was only a copy; the
original being held in some
unknown torture chamber
in China, Iran etc.

ADC LXXXVI

Graphic Design
Environmental Design
Gallery Museum Exhibit /
Installation / Campaign

Merit
A Sign of Democracy

328

**A SIGN OF
DEMOCRACY**

Creative Director
Jonathan Alger

Designer
Bettina Berg

Manufacturer
Solari di Udine, S.p.A.

Agency
C&G Partners

Client
National Center for the
Preservation of Democracy

Country
United States

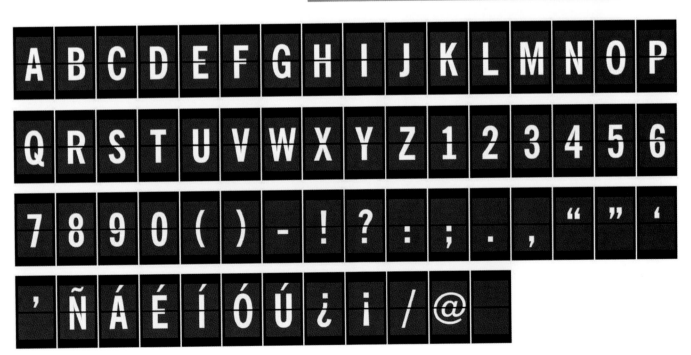

ADC LXXXVI

Graphic Design
Environmental Design
Wayfinding Systems /
Signage / Directory / Single

Merit
Signage System Cardealer
Pappas, Salzburg

329

signage system
car dealer pappas
salzburg
2006

**SIGNAGE SYSTEM
CARDEALER PAPPAS,
SALZBURG**
Designer
Beate Gerner (Project
Manager), Prof. Andreas
Uebele
Agency
Buero Uebele Visuelle
Kommunikation
Client
Pappas Group, Salzburg
Country
Germany

ADC LXXXVI

Graphic Design
Television & Cinema Design
Animation / Single

Merit
Factory of Idea

330

FACTORY OF IDEA

Art Director
Masahiko Sato, Euphrates
Creative Director
Masahiko Sato
Designer
Masaya Ishikawa, Kohji
Robert Yamamoto, Tomoko
Kaizuka
Director
Masashi Sato, Mio Ueta
Producer
Toshiyuki Sasaki
Production Company
Euphrates
Music
Takayuki Hattori
Agency
Euphrates
Client
Dai Nippon Printing Co.,
Ltd.
Country
Japan

What would it look like—a
factory that produces concepts that really exist? In
this film we were chal-
lenged to express a virtual
factory as the most ideal
form. The fine, and some-
times bold, transformation
process of the "words" is a
new type of expression.

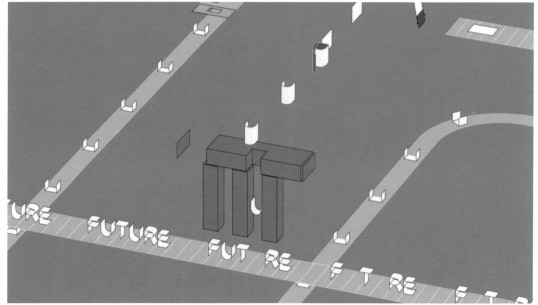

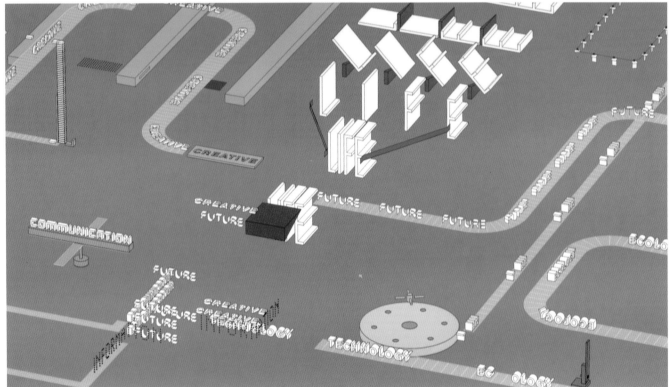

HAIR

Art Director
Jaclyn Rink

Copywriter
Chip Rich, Anselmo Ramos

Chief Creative Officer
Mark Wnek

Executive Creative Director
Fernanda Romano

Creative Director
Eddie Van Bloem, DJ Pierce

Designer
Ken Rabe, Katie Potochney,
Sean Moroney

Editor
Michael McKenna
(Version 2)

Producer
Jill Meschino

Production Company
One Division New York

Agency
Lowe New York

Client
XM Satellite Radio

Country
United States

XM Satellite Radio has 170
channels, far more than traditional radio. In this spot,
we needed to establish XM
as the superior service and
show why it's worth the sub-
scription fee. So we let the
XM logo showcase a wide
breadth of channels that
gives everyone the chance
to get inspired.

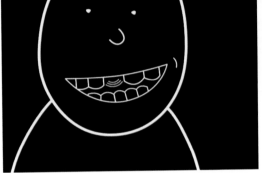

ADC LXXXVI   **Graphic Design**   **Merit**   333
Television & Cinema Design   Nike Golf
Art Direction / Campaign

NIKE GOLF

Art Director
Mark Kudsi (Motion Theory),
Ken Mayer
(Wieden+Kennedy)

Copywriter
Tatum Shaw

Creative Director
Mathew Cullen (Motion
Theory), Hal Curtis
(Wieden+Kennedy)

Designer
Mark Kudsi, Robin Resella,
Shawn Le, Vi Nguyen, Chris
Leone, Josh Nimoy, Michael
Chang, Gabe Dunne, Matt
Motal

Director
Frank Todaro

Editor
Mark Hoffman

Producer
James Taylor (Motion
Theory), Jeff Selis
(Wieden+Kennedy)

Production Company
Motion Theory

Compositing
1.1 VFX

Agency
Motion Theory

Client
Nike, Inc.

Country
United States

The athletic genius of Tiger
Woods combines with the
scientific prowess of Nike
engineers Tom Stites and
Rock Ishii, with the goal of
creating better golf equipment. Motion Theory
designers and programmers
created design that inter-
acts fluidly with the footage,
representing the thought
process, the science, and
the imagination that goes
into Nike's efforts to
improve golf equipment. The
real-life engineering data,
which might be indecipher-
ably complex on the page,
becomes delicate forms
dancing around the heads of
the engineers during a
brainstorm, or the feedback
of Tiger as he talks about
his experience with the new
equipment. The design
fuses art and science, con-
stantly striving to convey
the essence of invention.

INTERACTIVE /
ADC LXXXVI

THE JUDGES HAVE
AWARDED 1 GOLD CUBE /
3 SILVER CUBES /

Jonathan Yuen / Distinctive Merit / see page 348

4 DISTINCTIVE MERIT
WINNERS /
35 MERIT WINNERS IN
THIS CATEGORY.

Water Purifier / Merit /
see page 347

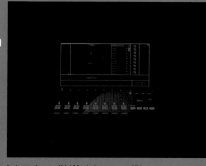

Lebron James IV / Merit / see page 374

Scholz & Volkmer Geschenkedenken / Merit / see page 376

Adidas Y-3 Reflections / Merit / see page 371

The Creative Mind / Merit / see page 359

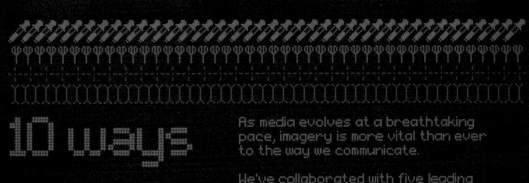

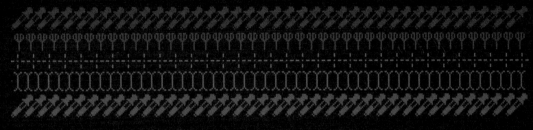

10 ways

As media evolves at a breathtaking pace, imagery is more vital than ever to the way we communicate.

We've collaborated with five leading designers to create 10 ways: interactive experiences that explore what makes visual language so powerful, and where it can take us.

Interact, play, experience...

10 Ways / Merit / see page 375

Primal Screen 2006 Show Reel / Merit / see page 352

The Hunt / Merit / see page 357

Interactive Model of Lower Manhattan / Merit / see page 354

NIKE+
Copywriter
Josh Bletterman,
Alison Hess
Creative Director
Kris Kiger, Nick Law,
Richard Ting, Gui Borchert,
Natalie Lam, Jill Nussbaum,
Michael Spiegel
Designer
Jeff Baxter, Wade Convay,
Gary Van Dzura, Ed Kim,
Michael Reger, Elena
Sakevich, Claudia Bernett,
Joe Tobens
Producer
Matt Howell, Brock Busby,
Daniel Jurow, James Kuo,
David Ross
Technology Lead
Nick Coronges
Technical Director
Sean Lyons
Programmer
Aaron Ambrose, Noel Billig,
Matthias Hader, Asako
Kohno, William Lee, Michael
Mosley, Michael Piccuirro,
Geoffrey Roth, Ben
Sosinski, John Tubert, Stan
Wiechers
Quality Assurance
Nauman Hafiz, Michele
Roman, August Yang
Animator
Mark Voelpel, Kiril Yeretsky
Agency
R/GA
Client
Nike
Country
United States

Nike+ is reinventing running
as a fun, social, digitally-
enhanced sport. A sensor in
Nike+ running shoes tracks
distance and speed and
transmits the data to a run-
ner's Apple iPod nano,
which is automatically
uploaded to nikeplus.com.
At nikeplus.com, runners
can compare runs, track
their progress, set and man-
age goals, and connect and
compete with Nike+ runners
around the world.

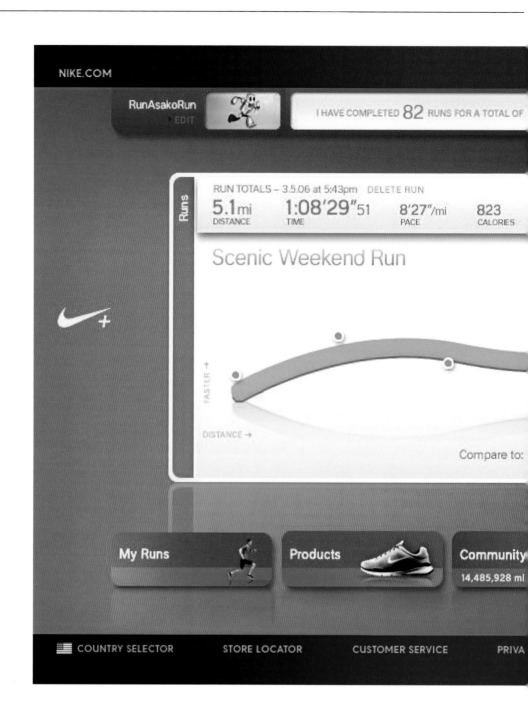

*
Interactive
New Media Innovation
and Development / Single
Gold
Nike+
+
Interactive
Web Application / Single
Distinctive Merit
Nike+

ADC LXXXVI

Interactive
Website Design—Non-Profit /
Reference / Education / Single

Silver
Semillero

338

SEMILLERO
Art Director
Miguel Calderon
Copywriter
Ruben Ruiz
Creative Director
Miguel Calderon
Designer
Cesar Moreno
Programmer
Raul Uranga
Multimedia Production
Ulises Valencia, Cesar
Moreno, Sebastian Mariscal
Agency
GrupoW
Client
Semillero, Creatives School
Country
Mexico

Semillero is the website for
a School of Creatives in
Mexico named "El
Semillero" (seed plot),
where trainee students can
attend courses and have the
preparation they need to be
part of a publicity agency.
The site is about a growing
seed that happens to be a
marvelous plant with brain-
bugs, hand-flowers and
hearts with human-caterpil-
lars that give life to this
implausible world. The
objective was to create a
site where people could
know about Semillero; its
people, courses, costs of
inscription, location, etc.
The site is innovative
regarding the concept of
navigation, where parting
from a seed the user will
accede to different topics
going up in a plant that
grows. Inside of every topic
the interactive experience
will allow him to find
abstract elements such as
brain-insects or the teach-
ers from the school inter-
acting with them.

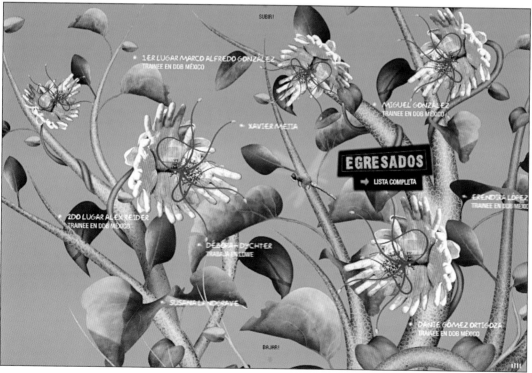

ADC <u>LXXXVI</u>

Interactive
Online Branded Content:
Product / Promotion / Campaign
Multiple Winner
see page 24

Silver
Milk Interactive "Aliens"
Campaign

340

MILK- INTERACTIVE "ALIENS" CAMPAIGN

<u>Art Director</u>
Robert Lindstrom, Feh Tarty
<u>Copywriter</u>
Ronny Northrop, Pat McKay,
Paul Charney, Nat Lawlor
<u>Creative Director</u>
Jeff Goodby,
Will McGinness
<u>Editor</u>
Rob Perkins
<u>Producer</u>
Mike Geiger, David
Eriksson, Roger Stighall
<u>Production Company</u>
North Kingdom
<u>Other</u>
Account Manager:
Martha Jurzynski, Debbie
Lee; Director of Interactive
Prodution: Mike Geiger
<u>Agency</u>
Goodby, Silverstein
& Partners
<u>Client</u>
California Fluid Milk
Processors Advisory Board
<u>Country</u>
United States

It's tough out there for Milk.
It now competes with things
it didn't used to compete
with. Water. Energy drinks.
Orange juice. Orange juice
with added calcium.
Calcium with added calci-
um. Yeah. Tough. And yet,
Milk has more to offer than
any of them. More than just
the strong bones thing,
which is what everyone
assumes. And that, right
there, is why we used aliens.
Aliens can't assume any-
thing about Milk. Because
they've never seen Milk.
And when they finally do,
they call it just how it
appears: miracle elixir. The
reason my partner Feh,
myself, Will, and Ronny
pushed so hard to take the
aliens beyond traditional
media was because, one, we
had the opportunity. And,
two, we liked the idea of
doing more targeted work.
Finding people in more
focused ways. And after ten
straight months of better
Milk sales, we're feeling not
too shabby about it.

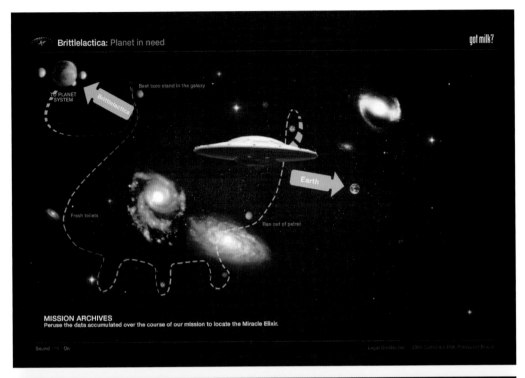

ADC LXXXVI

Interactive
Website Design—Product /
Service Promotion / Single

Silver
Come into the Closet

342

COME INTO THE CLOSET

Art Director
Forsman & Bodenfors
Copywriter
Forsman & Bodenfors
Designer
Forsman & Bodenfors
Production Company
Camp David
Agency
Forsman & Bodenfors
Client
Ikea Sweden
Country
Sweden

Walk-in closets are the next
big thing in home decora-
tion. At Ikea, you can find
everything you need to create your own personal solution. And at www.komini-
garderoben.se
(www.comeintothecloset.se)
you'll get to peek in on five
different people who have
already created closets to
fit their unique needs

ADC LXXXVI

Interactive
Interactive Kiosk /
Installation / Single

Distinctive Merit
Saturn Green Line Nextfest

344

**SATURN GREEN LINE
NEXTFEST**
Art Director
Chris Valencius
Copywriter
Toria Emery
Creative Director
Jeff Goodby, Keith
Anderson, Will McGinness
Associate Creative
Director
Toria Emery
Producer
Hilary Bradley, Brit
Charlebois
Production Company
Obscura Digital, The
Barbarian Group
Account Manager
Julie Evans
Account Director
John Weber
Director of Interactive
Production
Mike Geiger
Agency
Goodby, Silverstein &
Partners
Client
Saturn
Country
United States

Goodby, Silverstein & Partners' installation at WIRED NextFest 2006 focused on Saturn's Green Line hybrid vehicles. Because the Green Line is designed to be affordable, Saturn has democratized hybrid technology for the good of the planet and customers' wallets. GSP, Obscura Digital and The Barbarian Group teamed up to create a display that was equally inclusive and inviting. A 45-foot-wide, high-resolution reactive and interactive wall of animated, stylized grass anchored the 4,000-square-foot space. Via a kiosk, visitors were asked, "What if everyone drove a hybrid?" For each answer, a blade of grass grew on the screen and connected with the user's thought—creating a user-generated, product-relevant art display. To highlight specific features and hybrid components, super high-definition CAD-based animations were mapped and projected onto the cars. The effect was like pulling back the sheet metal or seeing the car with x-ray vision. Finally, a motion-sensitive hologram of a life-sized man was on hand to explain the hybrid technology in greater detail using Minority Report-style floating graphics. Combined with information from the car projections and holograms, visitors discovered something they hadn't known before: Saturn is more forward-thinking than they had realized.

**BODYGROOM
ELECTRIC SHAVER**

Art Director
Daniel Modell, January
Vernon
Copywriter
Brook Lundy,
Scott Ginsberg
Executive Creative Director
Steve Nesle
Creative Director
Brook Lundy
Producer
Chaz Mee
Production Company
Struck Design, Salt Lake
City
Director
Adam Jones
Agency
Tribal DDB New York
Client
Philips Norelco
Country
United States

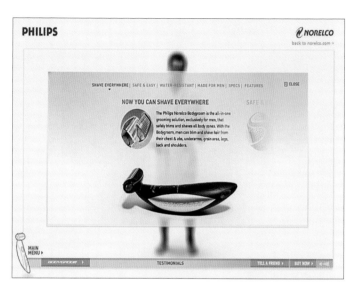

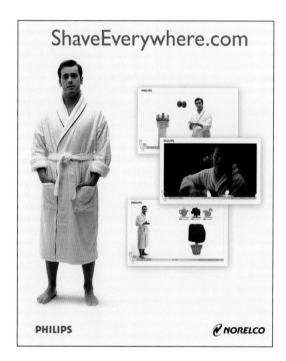

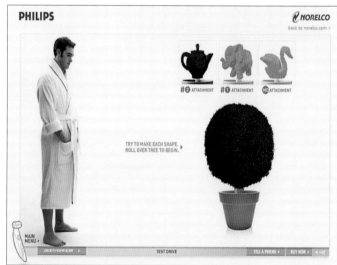

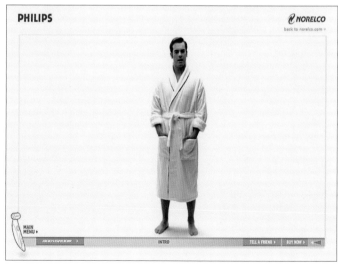

*
Interactive
Viral and Email—Product /
Service Promotion / Single
Merit
Bodygroom Electric Shaver
+
Interactive
Minisite—Product / Service
Promotion / Single
Distinctive Merit
Bodygroom Electric Shaver

ADC LXXXVI

Interactive
Banners—Product / Service
Promotion / Single

Merit
Water Purifier

347

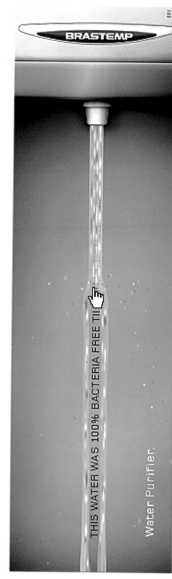

WATER PURIFIER

Art Director
Fabiano de Queiroz

Copywriter
Jones Krahl Jr.

Creative Director
Ricardo Figueira

Producer
Talita Chachamovitz, Bruna
Comin, Karina Frabetti

Programmer
Andre Cardozo, Andre
Brunetta

Account Executive
Ana Maria Nubie, Marcelo
Prais, Caroline Bassi

Technology Director
Abel Reis, Alexandre
Santos

Agency
AgenciaClick

Client
Brastemp

Country
Brazil

A simple interactive piece
gets efficiency when the
experience reproduces the
product benefit in the core
idea. It isn't only about copy,
art direction, interaction or
a message, it is about everything merged.

ADC LXXXVI

Interactive
Website Design—
Self-Promotion / Single

Distinctive Merit
Jonathan Yuen

348

JONATHAN YUEN (2006)
Art Director
Jonathan Yuen
Creative Director
Jonathan Yuen
Designer
Jonathan Yuen
Programmer
Jonathan Yuen
Copywriter
Jonathan Yuen
Agency
Jonathan Yuen
Client
Jonathan Yuen
Country
Singapore

Jonathan Yuen is a multi-disciplinary graphic designer based in Singapore and jonathanyuen.com is a self-promotional portfolio website. The website is designed as an interactive visual narrative journey, with each segment using illustrated visual metaphors to conceptually signify the attributes and information about the designer, e.g. his creativity, curiosity, ambition, works and observation. The metaphorical segmentation engages the viewer to relate to the philosophical concepts behind the visuals with the contents. The viewer will experience a harmonious blend of traditional aesthetics of Chinese inking illustration and contemporary digital animation in a minimalist and simple graphical approach. It also lends a unique visual narrative experience to the presentation.

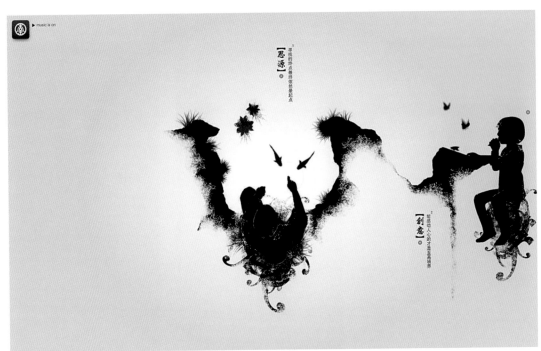

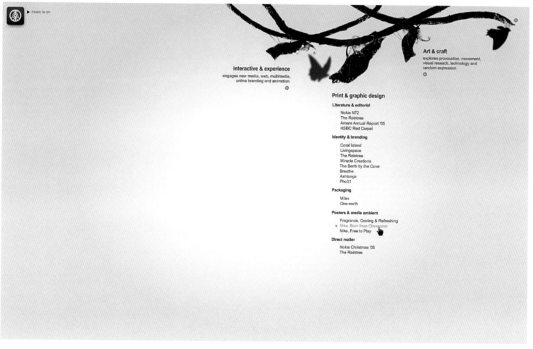

ADC LXXXVI

Interactive
Banners—Product / Service
Promotion / Single

Merit
Crash

350

CRASH

Art Director
Sandro Rosa

Copywriter
Rafael Taiar

Creative Director
Sergio Valente, Mauricio
Mazzariol

Producer
Roberta Padilla,
Leslie Foresta

Programmer
Mauricio Massaia, Wagner
Nunes

Other
Sound Design:
VBF Comunicacao

Agency
DDB Brasil

Client
Itau Insurance

Country
Brazil

The piece shows a damaged car and invites users to dial Itau Insurance telephone number. Each time a number key on the keyboard is pressed, one of the dents and scratches disappears. When the user finishes dialing Itau Insurance phone number, the car is completely fixed. The purpose here is to prove the efficiency of Itau Insurance's Rapid Claims Center.

SEE YOUR OWN WISH

Art Director
Paul Collins
Copywriter
Goran Akestam
Production Company
B-reel
Account Supervisor
Magnus Hamberg
Web Director
Paul Collins
Production Leader
Agneta Oppenheim
Other
Advertiser's Supervisor:
Jonas Jureen
Agency
Åkestam Holst
Client
Posten (The Swedish Post
Office)
Country
Sweden

Our objective was to drive
traffic to the "real-wish
site." Imagine that you
could expose your wish in a
banner; well that's exactly
what we did. This small
application we developed
for the Swedish Post office
enables people to write a
wish, which then can be
seen directly in banners all
over Sweden.

ADC LXXXVI

Interactive
CD / DVD—Self-Promotion /
Single

Merit
Primal Screen 2006 Show
Reel

352

**PRIMAL SCREEN 2006
SHOW REEL**

Art Director
Rick Newcomb

Creative Director
Douglass Grimmett

Producer
Susan Shipsky

Character Design
Ward Jenkins

Animators
Jeremy Seymour, Joe
Kubesheski, Ward Jenkins

Composer
Stephen Mank

Compositing & Authoring
Nate Foster

Agency
Primal Screen

Country
United States

In its 12 years as a broadcast design studio, Primal
Screen has risen to become
a leader in branding, animation, sound and broadcast
design. But designing for
everyone else doesn't make
it any easier to design for
yourself. Most of the studio's client base is split
between children's broad-
casters and those wanting a
little more edge. The animation caters to diverse audiences by representing the
categories with characters
who are cute but who suffer
for their work. Clicking on
each character triggers
unique animation and
reveals new kooky worlds.
To go to a new realm altogether, click on Primal
Screen's mascot in the
upper left. The DVD itself
was intended to demon-
strate capabilities as much
as the work contained within does. All work on the
DVD was done in-house by
Primal Screen staff. This
includes design, hand-
drawn animation, compos-
ite, music composition and
performance, foley/sound
design, and DVD
coding/authoring.

ADC LXXXVI

Interactive
Interactive Kiosk /
Installation / Campaign

Merit
Body in Motion

353

BODY IN MOTION

Art Director
Henry Brook

Creative Director
Mike Bennett

Designer
Tom Hartshorn

Producer
Sarie Gilbert, Simon
Beddoe

Production Company
Digit

Programmer
Lars Jessen, Jamie Ingram,
Tom Bandy, Liam Walsh, Ian
Smith

Agency
Digit

Client
Sony Ericsson

Country
United Kingdom

The brief was to bring to life the qualities of the new Sony Ericsson Cyber-shot K800i phone and in particular the functionality of BestPic™. Digit created a solution that brought the product to life on a grand scale. Body in Motion's power lay in its integration—the experience on the ground, the action shot to take away and the unique ID to take you to your shot on the website—which hosts an archive of the images taken in all ten cities. Once the experience was scaled up the technology itself became invisible and the experience itself more intuitive and playful. Passers-by could enjoy themselves without needing to know about any underlying technology or functionality. Altogether, it was a powerful 360 consumer experience and bang-on message.

ADC LXXXVI

Interactive
Interactive Kiosk /
Installation / Single

Merit
Interactive Model of Lower
Manhattan

354

**INTERACTIVE
MODEL OF LOWER
MANHATTAN**

Art Director
Lisa Strausfeld

Creative Director
Lisa Strausfeld

Designer
Lisa Strausfeld, Nina
Boesch

Programmer
Nina Boesch

Project Coordinator
Kate Wolf, Leslie Kang

Direction, Content and
Script
James Sanders

Narrator
John Hockenberry

Sound Production
John Kilgore

Music and Sound Design
Scott Lehrer

Model
Awad Architectural Models

A/V Consultant
Electrosonic Systems

Agency
Pentagram Design

Client
Wall Street Rising

Country
United States

Wall Street Rising is a not-
for-profit organization that
was founded in the wake of
9-11 with the mission of promoting Lower Manhattan.
For the group's Downtown
Information Center, we created an interactive architectural model of the area that
provides information as varied as the historical background of Lower Manhattan,
its monuments, streets and
buildings; practical information on museums, cultural
institutions, restaurants,
shops and other points of
interest; and updates on
neighborhood events and
new residential and com-
mercial development in the
area. These graphics are all
seamlessly projected onto
the model from two digital
projectors hung from the
ceiling. Using a gyro-
mouse, users can highlight
streets, buildings and other
points of interest, or view
historic and contemporary
scenes. The city's history is
inscribed on the area of
Lower Manhattan, and the
interactive model was
developed as a table: a
communal space that visi-
tors could gather around
and experience together.

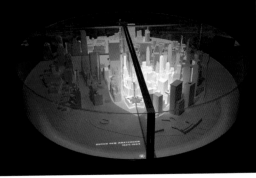

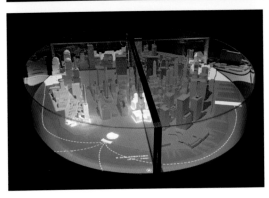

ADC LXXXVI

Interactive
Interactive Kiosk /
Installation / Single

Merit
Insynch Wall

355

INSYNCH WALL
Art Director
James Zucco
Copywriter
Brian Tierney
Group Creative Director
Todd Riddle
Designer
Freeset
Editor
Blue 60
Agency Producer
Amanda Revere
Interactive Producer
David Annis
Production Company
Freeset, Blue 60
Programmer
Freeset
Agency
Fallon
Client
Travelers
Country
United States

Travelers created the In-
synch Wall as a unique,
interactive way to introduce
employees to a new tagline:
"Insurance. In-Synch." The
idea that your insurance
stays in step, in-synch, with
your changing life. The first-
of-its-kind installation was
an innovative way to let
employees feel like they
were literally a part of their
new campaign.

ADC LXXXVI

Interactive
Interactive Kiosk /
Installation / Single

Merit
HSBC Live Window Theatre

356

**HSBC LIVE WINDOW
THEATRE**
Art Director
Damian Totman
Copywriter
Peter Seterdahl
Executive Creative Director
Walt Connelly, Toby Barlow
Designer
Jesse Nemeth
Editor
Cut and Run
Director of Production
Xander Strohm, Marrissa
Shrum, Marcy Pianin
Production Company
JWT / Cunning
Communications
Chief Creative Officer
Ty Montague
Agency
JWT New York
Client
HSBC
Country
United States

Banks can be some of the
most dull and underwhelm-
ing, and unexploited, shop-
front real estate in all of
NYC. We decided, therefore,
to take this problem and
stand it on its head by turning HSBC windows into live
theater spaces that drama-
tize the HSBC brand propo-
sition: Everyone looks at the
world from a different point
of view. We featured a beauty pageant, sports fans, and
an abstract artist.
Passersby texted their p.o.v
on each of these specta-
cles. "Crazy," "Beautiful,"
"Pathetic"— whatever their
opinion, it was instanta-
neously displayed within the
theater space. Live feeds
worldwide enabled people
globally to tap into this theater via the Web.

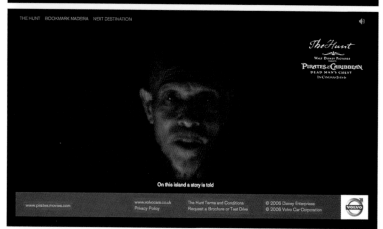

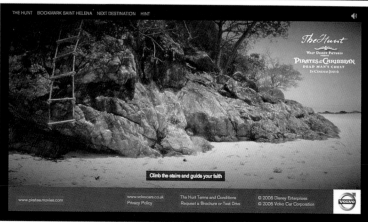

THE HUNT

Art Director
Martijn Sengers
Copywriter
Bram de Rooij
Creative Director
Sicco Beerda, Jason
Holzman
Designer
Antonio Costa, Feike
Kloostra, Edwin Nikkels,
Jurgen Nedebock
Production Company
FramFab Gothenburg
Account Director
Sabine Steinhaus
Account Manager
Janette Decaire
Agency
Euro RSCG 4D
Client
Volvo Cars Corporation
Country
Netherlands

Sponsoring Disney's
Pirates of the Caribbean:
Dead Man's Chest, Volvo
organizes a global treasure
hunt. A television commercial shows a unique Volvo
XC90 being buried: find it
and it's yours. Having
picked up a treasure map at
your dealership, The Hunt
continues online. Hopping
from website to website a
30-day journey across the
Seven Seas unfolds.
Unravel an old man's tale
on Madeira, match broken
china off Africa's coast,
decipher Maya murals on
Cozumel and be the first to
return in Port Royal harbor.
The increasing difficulty of
the puzzles urges partici-
pants to seek assistance
from each other resulting in
a multitude of user-generated forums and blogs. Seven
finalists are flown to an
island in the Bahamas for
the final event: the recovery
of the buried car.

*
Interactive
Online Branded Content—
Games / Movies / Webisodes /
Entertainment / Single
Merit
The Hunt
+
Interactive
Minisite—Product / Service
Promotion / Single
Merit
The Hunt

ADC LXXXVI

Interactive
Minisite—Product / Service
Promotion / Single

Merit
On Toyota's Mind

358

ON TOYOTA'S MIND

Art Director
Staffan Lamm

Copywriter
Anders Lidzell

Creative Director
Bjarne Melin, Ulf Enander

Designer
Andreas Hellström, Daniel
Wallström, Mathias
Lindgren

Producer
Rebekah Kvart, Bitte
Söderlind

Production Company
North Kingdom, SWE

Programmer
Klas Kroon, Isak Wiström

Other
Simon Stefansson, Mikael
Forsgren, Anders, Mille
Bruket

Agency
North Kingdom

Client
Toyota Sweden

Country
Sweden

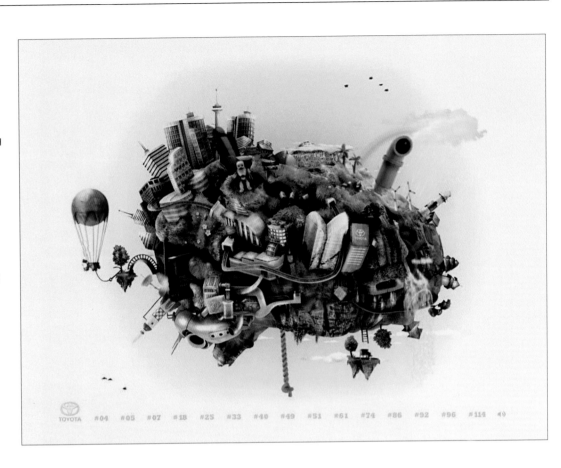

ADC LXXXVI

Interactive
Minisite—Product / Service
Promotion / Single

Merit
The Creative Mind

359

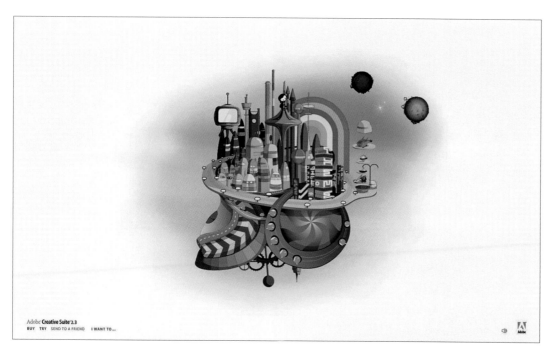

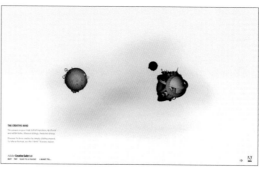

THE CREATIVE MIND

Art Director
Mark Sikes

Copywriter
Spencer Riviera

Creative Director
Keith Anderson

Producer
Kenna Takahashi

Production Company
Unit-9

Account Manager
Mike Barbeau

Director of Interactive
Production
Mike Geiger

Agency
Goodby, Silverstein &
Partners

Client
Adobe Systems

Country
United States

For the release of Adobe
Creative Suite 2.3, we had
one simple rule: speak to
designers in their own language. So instead of just
talking about the technical
capabilities of the Adobe
software package, we
decided to demonstrate
them in as visually com-
pelling a context as possible. This led us to the
Creative Mind site—an
abstract representation of
the mental universe inside a
designer's head. Filled with
ideas, inspiration, a touch of
absurdity, and examples-a-
plenty of how Adobe soft-
ware can bring it all to life.

ADC LXXXVI

Interactive
Minisite—Product / Service
Promotion / Single

Merit
Culture Fool

360

CULTURE FOOL

Art Director
Devin Sharkey, Stefan
Copiz

Copywriter
Dan Rollman

Creative Director
Will McGinness, Jamie
Barrett, Mark Wenneker

Producer
Brit Charlebois

Production Company
The Barbarian Group,
Number-9

Director of Interactive
Production
Mike Geiger

Agency
Goodby, Silverstein &
Partners

Client
Comcast

Country
United States

To promote Comcast On
Demand, we created the
Culture Fool Challenge. This
Mr. T-hosted experience let
users take a pop culture
quiz to find out their Culture
IQ. Questions were based
on content from within the
On Demand library. Did Mr.
T pity the fool who
answered questions incor-
rectly? Absolutely, sucka.
He told those turkeys to quit
their jibba-jabba, prescribed
a healthy dose of On
Demand viewing, and
reminded them, "Don't be a
culture fool!"

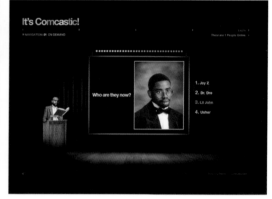

ADC LXXXVI

Interactive
Minisite -Games / Movies /
Webisodes / Entertainment /
Single

Merit
Cluedo Cop Star

361

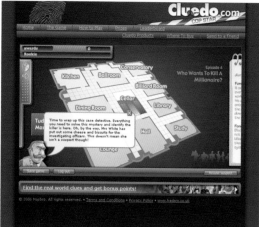

CLUEDO COP STAR

Art Director
Ben Clapp, Simon Richings
Copywriter
Simon Richings, James
Leach
Creative Director
Ben Clapp
Designer
Paul Robinson
Producer
Cynthia O'Murchu, Stephen
Diffey
Programmer
Sam Briggs, Jamie
Copeland
Other
Craig Morgan, James
Garcia-Luengo, Greg Sue
Agency
Tribal DDB London
Client
Hasbro
Country
United Kingdom

ADC LXXXVI

Interactive
Minisite—Games / Movies /
Webisodes / Entertainment /
Single

Merit
The Concretes in Color

362

THE CONCRETES, IN COLOUR

Art Director
Tom Jennings
Creative Director
John Denton
Designer
John Denton
Programmer
Xavier Monvoisin, Iain Lobb,
Steve Hayes
Other
Eric Winbolt, Rick Palmer
Agency
Bloc Media
Client
EMI Records
Country
United Kingdom

BLOC were challenged to
create an interactive audio
player that surpassed the
audiences expectation of an
online album sampler,
engaging users and encouraging creativity and a sense
of community amongst
users. By offering a positive
and engaging interactive
experience, which captivat-
ed the audience with intrigu-
ing interaction full of lots of
hidden secrets, BLOC were
able to entertain users
whilst they listened to the
album samples. BLOC also
wanted to encourage cre-
ativity amongst the audience
and a sense that they could
have a positive personal
contribution to the album. To
that end BLOC also devised
a tool set that offers users
the chance to get creative
and make their own
Concretes artwork to con-
tribute to the site and pass
amongst friends and family.
Artwork created by users
could then be saved to a
public gallery on the site,
downloaded as PC, PSP
and mobile phone wallpa-
pers, or emailed to friends
and family. This provided
the perfect environment
from which to create a personal greeting or message
for a loved one, whilst in turn
promoting the album and
artist to a wider audience
and ultimately driving sales.

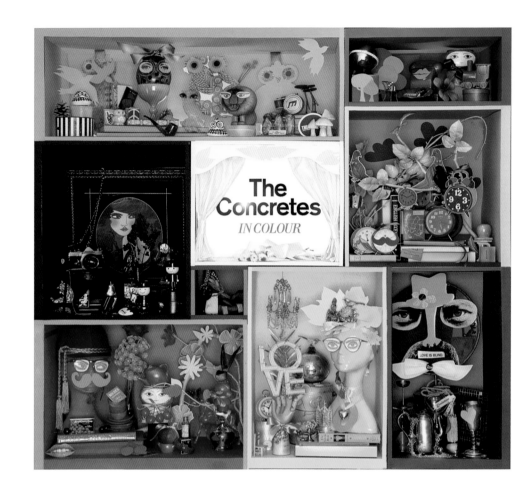

ADC LXXXVI

Interactive
Minisite—Games / Movies /
etc. / Single
Multiple Winner
see page 106

Merit
Guinness—Hands

363

GUINNESS—HANDS
Art Director
Michael Durban,
Mauricio Carrasco,
Damion Parsons,
Cesar Santos,
Stuart Woodall
Copywriter
Tony Strong, Erica Boynton,
Sean Vrabel
Creative Director
Paul Brazier
Agency
Abbott Mead Vickers BBDO
Client
DIAGEO
Country
United Kingdom

ADC LXXXVI

Interactive
Wireless—Product / Service
Promotion / Single

Merit
On Treo Bus Shelter

364

ON TREO BUS SHELTER

<u>Executive Creative Director</u>
Adam Lau, Bob Pullum,
PJ Pererira, Rei Inamoto
<u>Art Director</u>
Bob Pullum
<u>Copywriter</u>
Adam Lau,
Michelle Hirschberg
<u>Programmer</u>
Alex Fernandez, Ryan
Brock, Russell Bolme
<u>Designer</u>
Bob Pullum
<u>Producer</u>
Olivia Murray
<u>Other</u>
QA: Paul Liszewski,
Production Artist:
Justin Fedewa
<u>Agency</u>
AKQA
<u>Client</u>
Palm
<u>Country</u>
United States

When we showed the Treo
to people they were always
intrigued by the things it
could do. So that's what
inspired this idea—show
people how much better a
Treo is by allowing them to
interact with it with their
own cell phone. SMS-
enabled bus shelters and
wallscapes in NYC, L.A and
S.F. were able to give non-
Treo owners a taste of what
life is like through SMS-
triggered Flash demos that
showed live feeds of weather, news, sports, and local
relevant content through
the screen of a large
Treo. Each of the shelters
were engineered and built
from scratch.

ADC LXXXVI

Interactive
New Media Innovation and
Development / Single

Merit
On Treo Kiosk

365

ON TREO KIOSK
Executive Creative Director
Adam Lau, Bob Pullum,
PJ Pererira, Rei Inamoto
Art Director
Bob Pullum
Copywriter
Adam Lau,
Michelle Hirschberg
Programmer
Alex Fernandez, Ryan
Brock, Russell Bolme
Designer
Bob Pullum
Producer
Olivia Murray
Other
QA: Paul Liszewski
Agency
AKQA
Client
Palm
Country
United States

ADC LXXXVI

Interactive
Minisite—Product / Service
Promotion / Campaign

Merit
Action City Campaign

366

ACTION CITY CAMPAIGN: THE STUNTMAN

Art Director
Miguel Calderon

Copywriter
Ivan Gonzalez

Creative Director
Miguel Calderon

Designer
Jezreel Gutierrez, Miguel Calderon, Sebastian Mariscal, Roberto Espero

Programmer
Homero Sousa, Raul Uranga, Edgar Ortiz, Daniel Granatta

Producer
Polo Pliego

Production Company
La Central

Multimedia Production
Ulises Valencia, Sebastian Mariscal, N-Render, Subsuelo Audio,

Agency
GrupoW

Client
Unilever, Rexona

Country
Mexico

The interactive campaign of Action City is conformed by 3 elements: a viral game, a microsite and a web game. The viral game Stuntman, gives the user the opportunity to live the experience of a beating and throw the main character against different places in the interface without making him any harm or even sweat. Action City gives the user the experience of living in the most dangerous city in the world and knowing more about the deodorant in a different and entertaining way. In the 13th Avenue, the user will have to go from his house to his work by the most risky route doing the less time possible to win attractive prizes.

*
Interactive
Minisite—Product / Service Promotion / Campaign
Merit
Action City Campaign
+
Interactive
Viral and Email—Product / Service Promotion / Single
Merit
The Stuntman

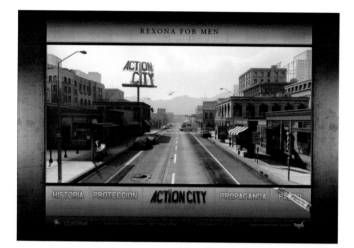

ADC LXXXVI   **Interactive**
Viral and Email—Product /
Service Promotion / Single

Merit
Fingerskilz

368

FINGERSKILZ

Art Director
Pedro Garcia, Dave Birss
Copywriter
Dave Birss
Creative Director
Dave Birss
Designer
Pedro Garcia
Producer
Ed Robinson
Production Company
The Viral Factory
Director
Ben Wheatley, The Viral
Factory
Programmer
Andrew Leszczynski, Sergio
Pedio, Sune Kaae
Account Team
Angelia Newell, Adam
Plater
Agency
MRM Worldwide
Client
HP
Country
United Kingdom

We created a new activity
to rival the 2006 World Cup
action. It was the entirely
new sport of fingerball. This
was fronted by a fanatical
HP user who made videos
of his amazing moves and
posted them on his blog.
His blog also showed you
how to get started with the
sport. The activity started
before the World Cup and
continued afterwards with
more films and content
appearing every few days.
During this time it was seen
by over 8 million people and
was featured on TV, news-
papers and countless web-
sites around the world.

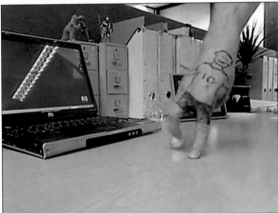

ADC LXXXVI

Interactive
Viral and Email—Product /
Service Promotion / Single

Merit
Tea Partay

369

TEA PARTAY
Art Director
Amee Shah
Copywriter
Matt Ian, Clay Weiner
Creative Director
Kevin Roddy
Designer
Matt Ian
Editor
Crandall Miller
Producer
Lisa Gatto, Melissa Bemis
Production Company
HSI Productions
Director
Julian Christian Lutz
Agency
BBH
Client
Smirnoff Raw Tea
Country
United States

The brief was simple: tea
with attitude. And since the
product launch was set for a
Northeast US test market,
we asked ourselves: what is
"tea with attitude" to people in the Northeast? That's
how we came up with
Prepstas and the Tea Partay.

ADC LXXXVI

Interactive
Viral and Email—Self-
Promotion / Single

Merit
Feliz 2007

370

FELIZ 2007

<u>Art Director</u>
Frédéric Sanz

<u>Creative Director</u>
Xavi Caparrós

<u>Designer</u>
Lisi Badia, Natalie Long

<u>Other</u>
Emma Pueyo, Marc de la
Cruz, Enric Juvé

<u>Agency</u>
DoubleYou

<u>Client</u>
DoubleYou

<u>Country</u>
Spain

ADC LXXXVI

Interactive
Website Design—Product /
Service Promotion / Single

Merit
Adidas Y-3 Reflections

371

**ADIDAS Y-3
REFLECTIONS**
Art Director
Bejadin Selimi
Creative Director
Elke Klinkhammer
Designer
André Bourguignon
Production Company
Effekt-Etage Berlin
Programmer
Heiko Schweickhardt,
Thomas Junk
Account Manager
Katrin Bergfeld
Agency
Neue Digitale GmbH
Client
Adidas AG
Country
Germany

ADC LXXXVI

Interactive
Website Design—Product /
Service Promotion / Single

Merit
Feel Volvo C70

372

FEEL VOLVO C70
Art Director
Chris Pacetti
Copywriter
Daniel Lutz
Creative Director
Sicco Beerda
Designer
Feike Kloostra, Roland
Lamers
Production Company
FramFab Gothenburg
Account Director
Sander Volten
Account Manager
Janette Decaire
Project Manager
Noora Repo
Agency
Euro RSCG 4D
Client
Volvo Cars Corporation
Country
Netherlands

For a car that's so gorgeous
and so much anticipated as
the Volvo C70, you don't
want to build a site that
sells. You need a site that
entertains in the exact right
way—a remarkable site for
a remarkable campaign: an
online invitation to Feel. The
Volvo C70 Guidebook to
Feel is a journey in itself.
Each new page a little surprise, a very entertaining
way to meet a new car and
its campaign. Just see the
pages turn in its awkward
way. Enjoy the moments
where the content breaks
the boundaries of the physical book. Keep an eye open
for extremely well animated
crash test dummies, relax
and charge your battery for
a couple of seconds, read
the floating poetry and
experience a campaign
come to life.

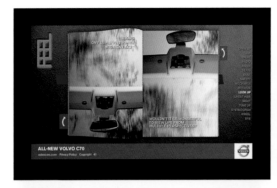

ADC LXXXVI

Interactive
Website Design—Product /
Service Promotion / Single

Merit
Vodafone Journey

373

VODAFONE JOURNEY
Art Director
Robert Lindström
Copywriter
Gabriele Dangel
Creative Director
David Eriksson
Designer
Charlotta Lundqvist, Mikael
Forsgren
Producer
Roger Stighäll, Monica
Harding
Programmer
Klas Kroon
Other
Daniel Wallström, Mathias
Lindgren, Tomas
Westermark
Agency
North Kingdom
Client
Vodafone Group
Country
Sweden

ADC LXXXVI

Interactive
Website Design—Product /
Service Promotion / Single

Merit
Lebron James IV

374

LEBRON JAMES IV

Executive Creative Director
Rei Inamoto, PJ Pereira
Creative Director
Neil Robinson
Associate Creative
Director
David Lee
Copywriter
Bob Hall
Designer
Kevin Hsieh
Producer
Jamie Kim
Production Company
Tronic, Palma VFX
Programmer
Terry Lee, Mike Knott
Other
QA: Paul Liszewski,
Technology Manager:
Charles Duncan
Agency
AKQA
Client
Nike
Country
United States

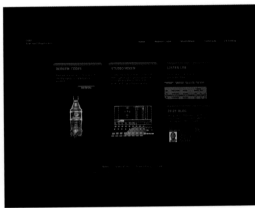
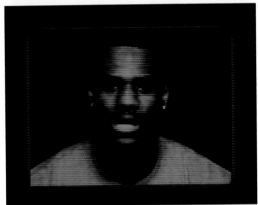

AKQA treated LeBron like
an artist who uses the court
as his canvas. On the court
he continually creates
unique moments in time
that can't be duplicated by
anyone else. We wanted to
exhibit the unique moments
he creates on the site. Each
creation is titled in the
same way a traditional artist
would name a painting. Like
LeBron, the LBJ IVs are
unique and make a state-
ment. Their performance
and style cannot be replicated by any other shoe—
and the LBJ IV takes shoe
design to bold new places.

ADC LXXXVI   **Interactive**   **Merit**   375
Website Design—Self-   10 Ways
Promotion / Single

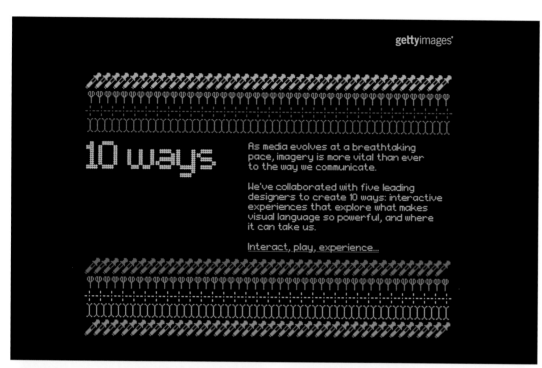

10 WAYS

<u>Art Director</u>
Mark Fraser

<u>Copywriter</u>
Joe Moore, John O'Reilly

<u>Creative Director</u>
Chris Ashworth

<u>Designer</u>
Sumona, The Barbarian
Group, Tomato, Less Rain,
Great Works

<u>Editor</u>
Larry White

<u>Programmer</u>
Jay del Rosario

<u>Project Manager</u>
Helen Tapping

<u>Agency</u>
Getty Images

<u>Client</u>
Getty Images

<u>Country</u>
United States

As media evolves at a
breathtaking pace, imagery
is more vital then ever to the
way we communicate. We've
collaborated with five leading designers (Sumona, The
Barbarian Group, Tomato,
Less Rain, and Great Works)
to create 10 ways: interactive experiences that explore
what makes visual lan-
guages so powerful, and
where it can take us.
Interact, play, experience.

ADC LXXXVI

Interactive
Interactive Website Design—
Self-Promotion / Single

Merit
Scholz & Volkmer
Geschenkedenken

376

SCHOLZ & VOLKMER
GESCHENKEDENKEN

Art Director
Dominik Lammer

Copywriter
Andreas Henke, Tim
Sobczak, Eva Kümml

Creative Director
Heike Brockmann

Designer
Melanie Lenz, Matthias
Zosel

Production Company
Scholz & Volkmer

Technical Director
Peter Reichard

Flash Programmer
Robert Fred Corporaal

Project Manager
Tobias Scholz

Concept
Andreas Henke, Peter
Reichard

Camera and Video
Production
Steffen Bärenfänger

Agency
Scholz & Volkmer GmbH

Client
Scholz & Volkmer

Country
Germany

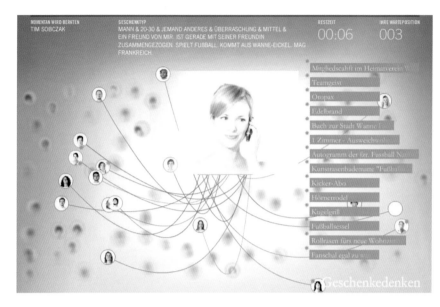

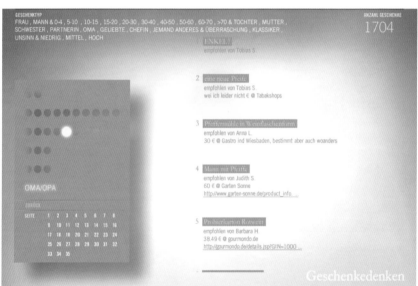

ADC LXXXVI

Interactive
Website Design—Games /
Movies / Webisodes /
Entertainment / Single

Merit
Verizon Beatbox Mixer

377

**VERIZON
BEATBOX MIXER**

Art Director
Seth Jablon

Copywriter
Nicole Possin

Creative Director
Douglas Dauzier, Jay Zasa

Designer
Mehmet Irdel, Mark
Corotan, Kiril Yeretsky

Editor
Laura Pence

Producer
Mitch Wegner, Peter Blitzer

Programmer
Russ Alderson, Hector
Larios, Bob Hoffman

Project Manager
Tobias Scholz

Concept
Andreas Henke, Peter
Reichard

Camera and Video
Production
Steffen Bärenfänger

Agency
R/GA

Client
Verizon

Country
United States

A mix between a music
video, a video game, and a
drum machine, featuring
five of the world's best
human beat-boxers. Users
can create a custom video
mix out of trillions of possible combinations, tweak it,
then e-mail it to friends. The
site also contains some
awesome "making of" video
footage. The goal is to build
brand awareness of Verizon
as a broadband and enter-
tainment company by pro-
viding a highly entertaining
broadband experience.

ADC LXXXVI

Interactive
Web Application / Single

Merit
Kuler

378

KULER

Other
Emerging Markets and
Technologies (EM+T) Team,
a group inside the Adobe
Creative Solutions
Business Unit
Agency
Adobe Systems,
Incorporated
Client
Adobe Systems, Inc.
Country
United States

A brainchild of Adobe Labs,
kuler.adobe.com, provides
users with a bevy of color
combinations to inspire
their creative projects.
Combating the color chal-
lenges faced by designers
and creatives alike, kuler
allows users to quickly create, share and export harmonious color themes over
the Internet and compose
custom themes via kuler's
interactive color wheel. For
those seeking creative color
inspiration, kuler also har-
bors a communal environ-
ment where users can tag,
comment on and share cre-
ations with others. kuler
fosters a communitarian
experience that delivers on
the promise of Web 2.0.
Recently updated, kuler now
features clickable tags and
RSS subscriptions of the
most popular, the highest
rated and the newest
themes. A space where creatives congregate, kuler
gives users room to inspire.

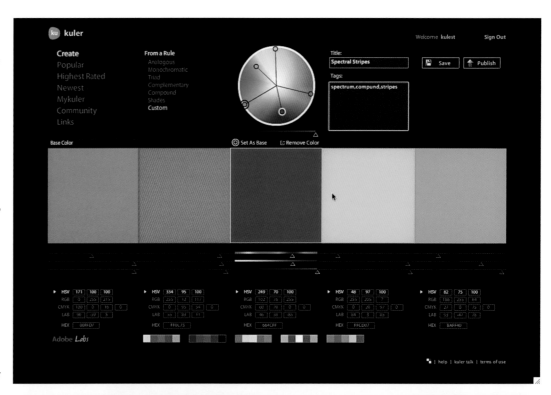

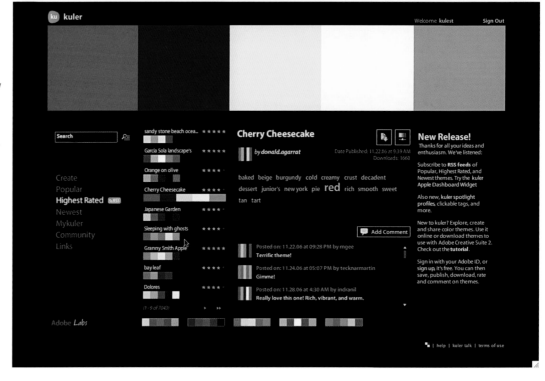

ADC LXXXVI

Interactive
New Media Innovation and
Development / Single

Merit
Cisco Boooming

379

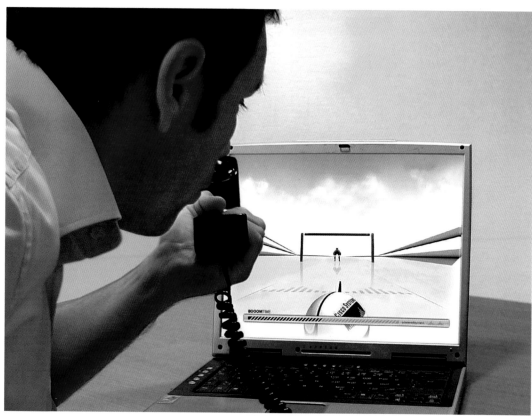

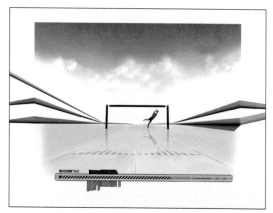

CISCO BOOOMING

Art Director
Uwe Jakob

Copywriter
Dr. Ulf Schmidt

Creative Director
Michael Kutschinski,
Dr. Ulf Schmidt

Designer
Serena Stoerlein,
Nicole Holzenkamp

Producer
Silke Gehrmann,
Martin Molter

Other
Sound: Sinus AV Studio

Agency
Ogilvy Frankfurt

Client
Cisco Systems Germany

Country
Germany

The Task: Create awareness
for Cisco Unified Communications Solutions during the
FIFA World Cup 2006 in
Germany. The main goal was
to make business decision-
makers aware of the possibility to fully integrate the
telephone system into the
existing company data network and to profit from highly innovative communication
applications. The Solution:
Use your telephone to call a
website, shoot penalties—
and shake the net with the
power of your voice. This is
the idea of booming—the
world's first voice-controlled
online soccer game. Users
connected to a website and
were able to shoot penalties
on their PC screen, con-
trolled solely by the power
of their voice. Telephone
and IT connected, soccer
integrated, fun guaran-
teed—and innovation
shown with a technical
breakthrough. Booom!

ADC LXXXVI

Interactive
Minisite—Product / Service
Promotion / Single

Merit
The New Volvo C30:
A Product of Free Will

380

**THE NEW VOLVO C30:
A PRODUCT
OF FREE WILL**

Art Director
Feike Kloostra

Copywriter
Darren Reynoldson

Creative Director
Sicco Beerda

Designer
Antonio Costa, Vanesa
Abajo Perez, Feike Kloostra

Production Company
FramFab Gothenburg

Account Director
Sabine Steinhaus

Account Manager
Janette Decaire

Project Manager
Noora Repo

Agency
Euro RSCG 4D

Client
Volvo Cars Corporation

Country
Netherlands

How do you change the
youth market preconception
that Volvos are "that boxy
car your Dad drives"? With
a highly interactive card-
board box that plays with
the "boxy" myth while
housing sixteen highly
interactive games and
gadgets that immerse site
visitors into the fantastic
environments of the ATL
animations. Less an information site than a fun fair
for C30 fans, visitors can
throw tomatoes or blow
kisses at the C30, express
themselves with a Big
Mouth voice generator,
unbox their own personal-
ized C30, design 'real
man' tattoos or funky
dance steps.

ADC LXXXVI

Interactive
Online Branded Content—
Product / Service Promotion /
Single

Merit
Friends of Bright

381

FRIENDS OF BRIGHT

Art Director
Jose Luis Martinez

Copywriter
Associate Creative
Director: Alexandra Tyler

Executive Creative Director
Jason Zada (EVB)

Chief Creative Officer
Marty Orzio (Energy BBDO)

Group Creative Directors
Bobby Pawar, Miles Turpin
(Energy BBDO)

Interactive Creative
Director
Sean Donohue (Energy
BBDO)

Designer
Kevin Hsieh, Jacob Hawley

Producer
Amanda Cox, Laurale
Wunsch

Production Company
Rock Fight

Production Designer
Lisi Howell

Programmer
Flash Developer: Justin
Peterson

Other
Account Supervisor:
Justin Acuff, After
Effects Artist: Andrew
Whitelaw, Matt Petrocci,
3D Animation: Keytoon,
Director: Joe Cole,
Paul Roy

Agency
EVB

Client
Orbit White

Country
United States

We know Orbit White users
indulge in activities that
stain their teeth—coffee,
red wine, smoking. They
want to believe that whiten-
ing gums work, but they
needed more reason to
believe. Meet the Friends of
Bright, a group of smile-
obsessed individuals
who've "seen the bright"
and made it their mission to
spread the word about Orbit
White. The group's charis-
matic leader encourages
visitors to explore the quirky
desert landscape—and ultimately become a "Friend".
Pushing Flash8 to the limit
with original video content,
a unique sing-a-long and
more, we once again found
ourselves stretching cre-
ative boundaries and exploring fresh new territory.

STUDENT /
ADC LXXXVI

THE JUDGES HAVE AWARDED 1 SILVER CUBE / 2 DISTINCTIVE MERIT WINNERS / 18 MERIT WINNERS IN THIS CATEGORY.

Perfect / Silver / see page 384

Take a Stand / Merit / see page 397

clean.

Clean. / Merit / see page 400

i love
the tension
between
myself and
these posters
next to me.

Lyrical Moments / Merit / see page 405

Commercial Free / Merit / see page 396

Syphilis / Merit / see page 403

Radiograph / Distinctive Merit / see page 388

A Good Tattoo Can Save a Bad Boy / Merit /
see page 392

Truck & Type - Transit Graphics in Europe / Merit / see page 390

Liebes Buch (Dear Book Full of Love) / Merit /
see page 399

Wish I Was 3 / Merit / see page 401

ADC LXXXVI

Student
Graphic Design Book Design
Limited Edition, Private Press
or Special Format Book /
Single

Silver
Perfect

384

PERFECT

Copywriter
Sarah Cohen

Designer
Sarah Cohen

Editor
Sarah Cohen

Illustrator
Sarah Cohen

Photographer
Sarah Cohen

Production Company
Sarah Cohen

Instructors
Michael Vanderbyl, Leslie
Becker

School
California College of the
Arts

Country
United States

This project appeared a tall
order, to say the least—
make something on some
topic and make it good. The
first challenge was to pick a
subject I actually cared
about—a lot. After picking a
hyper-personal subject, I
was faced with revealing a
lot about myself—well, facing myself, honestly. It was
hard. The actual construction of the book, however,
proved a ridiculous obstacle—to perfect bind an 800
page book was a task that
no bindery would take on.
Somehow I made it work in
the end. I let every design
decision stem from what
the project needed in order
to convey my state of mind
at that very moment.

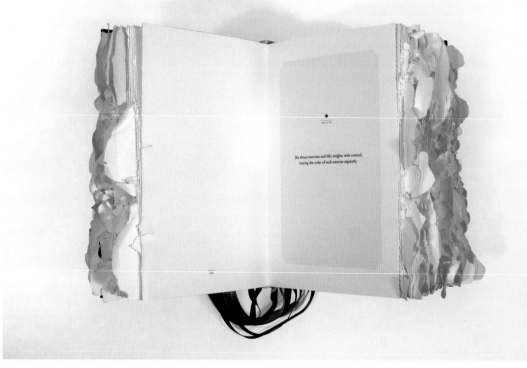

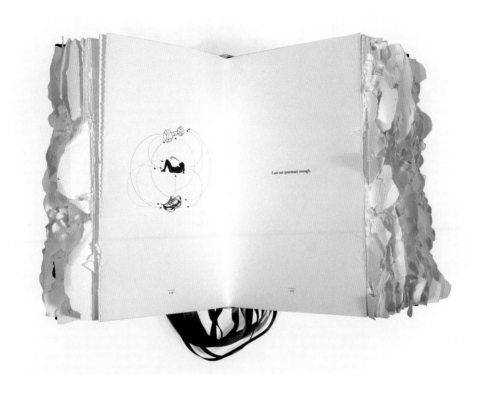

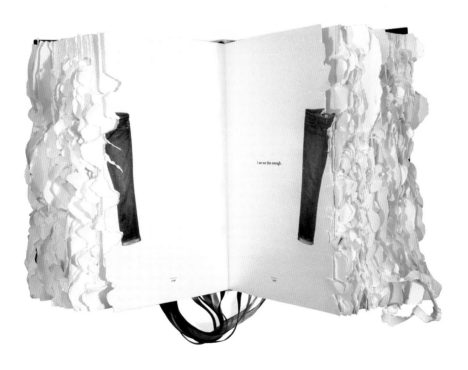

ADC LXXXVI

Student
Graphic Design Book Design
Special Trade Book (Image-
Driven) / Single

Distinctive Merit
Vom Rechten Pfad

386

VOM RECHTEN PFAD

<u>Art Director</u>
Duc Nguyen
<u>Copywriter</u>
Duc Nguyen
<u>Designer</u>
Duc Nguyen
<u>Photographer</u>
Duc Nguyen
<u>Illustrator</u>
Duc Nguyen
<u>Production Company</u>
The Asia Snack Company
<u>School</u>
University of Applied
Sciences Wiesbaden
<u>Client</u>
Fachhochschule Wiesbaden
<u>Country</u>
Germany

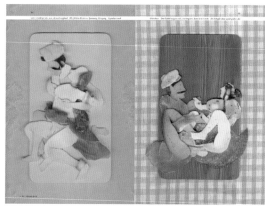

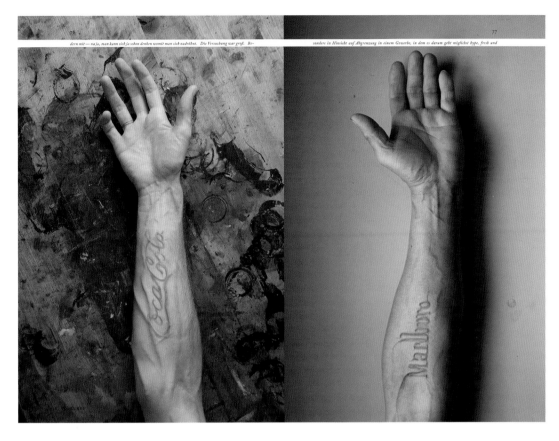

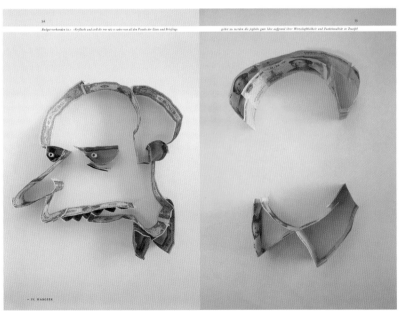

ADC LXXXVI

Student
Print Advertising Magazine,
Consumer, Full Page /
Campaign

Distinctive Merit
Radiograph

388

RAPIDOGRAPH
<u>Art Director</u>
Chase Quarterman
<u>Copywriter</u>
Derek Bishop
<u>Creative Director</u>
Sean Thompson,
David Horridge
<u>School</u>
Texas Creative, The
University of Texas at
Austin
<u>Country</u>
United States

What looks like a nice illustration is emphasized by subtle cues that these drawings are miniscule, and done by hand with the Rapidograph, a pen made for detailed drawings and fine lines.

ADC LXXXVI

Student
Print Advertising Newspaper,
Consumer, Less Than a Full
Page / Campaign

Merit
Madlib

389

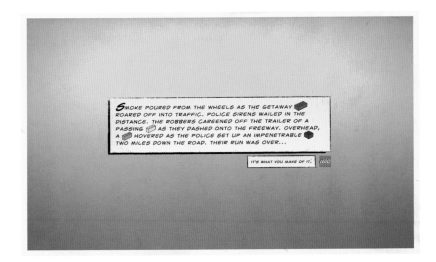

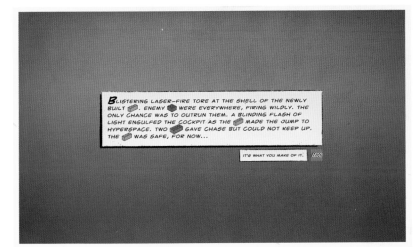

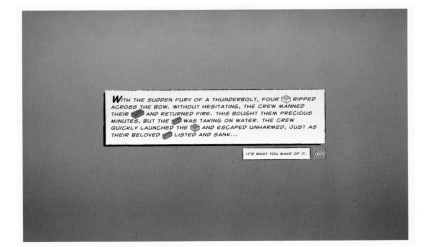

MADLIB
Art Director
Croix Gagnon, Siavosh
Zabeti
Copywriter
Croix Gagnon
Creative Director
Adam Kerj
Designer
Croix Gagnon, Siavosh
Zabeti
School
Miami Ad School Europe
Client
Lego
Country
United States

We wanted parents to
understand the real attraction of Lego lies in it's limit-
less nature. The use of copy,
rather than imagery, affords
readers the opportunity to
use their own imaginations,
placing them for a moment
in their kids' shoes.

ADC LXXXVI

Student
Book Design Special Trade
Book (Image-Driven) / Single

Merit
Truck & Type - Transit
Graphics in Europe

390

**TRUCK & TYPE -
TRANSIT GRAPHICS
IN EUROPE**
Art Director
Michael Diebold
Copywriter
Michael Diebold
Creative Director
Michael Diebold
Designer
Michael Diebold
Illustrator
Michael Diebold
Photographer
Michael Diebold
School
Bauhaus-University Weimar
Client
Bauhaus University Weimar,
Germany
Country
Germany

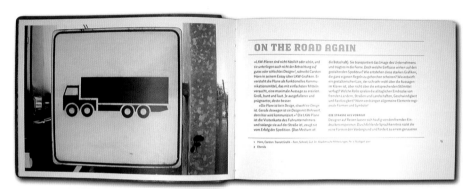

ADC LXXXVI

Student
Print Advertising Insert,
Newspaper / Magazine,
Multi-Page / Campaign

Merit
Aquafina

391

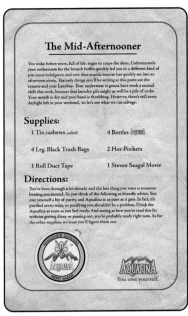

(front)

(back)

(front)

(back)

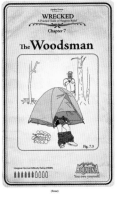

(front)

(back)

AQUAFINA
Art Director
Jeremy Diessner
Copywriter
Nathan Dills, Tara Lawall
School
Miami Ad School
Country
United States

How do you get noticed in a category overwrought with sameness? You tell the truth. To do this, you first throw out imagery of mountain springs or glacial ice flows. Toss out the urge to talk about how great your brand of water tastes (nobody cares). Then you get down to the business of why your customer might actually buy your product. You acknowledge that young males do in fact get hangovers. Then you talk to them in a familiar tone, give them instructions for survival, and recognize their effort with a merit badge sticker. Done.

ADC LXXXVI

Student
Print Advertising Magazine,
Consumer, Full Page /
Campaign

Merit
A Good Tattoo Can Save a
Bad Boy

392

**A GOOD TATTOO CAN
SAVE A BAD BODY**
Art Director
Sebastian Kaufmann
Copywriter
Ricardo Wolff
Instructor
Dörte Spengler-Ahrens,
Jan Rexhausen
School
Miami Ad School Europe
Client
Tattoo Banzai
Country
Germany

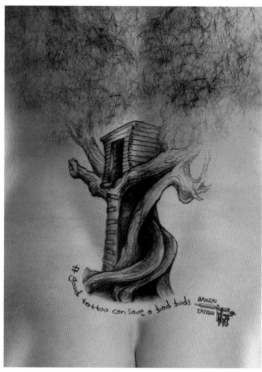

Merit
3M Point of Purchase

**3M POINT OF
PURCHASE**
<u>Art Director</u>
Ryan Fluet
<u>Copywriter</u>
Mandy Osterhout
<u>Creative Director</u>
Sean Thompson
<u>School</u>
Texas Creative, The
University of Texas at
Austin
<u>Country</u>
United States

ADC LXXXVI

Student
Advertising Posters &
Billboards Outdoor /
Billboard / Single

Merit
Versatile Options

394

VERSATILE OPTIONS
<u>Art Director</u>
Carrie Ammermann
<u>Copywriter</u>
Rebecca Hasskamp
<u>Creative Director</u>
Wayne Gibson
<u>School</u>
VCU Adcenter
<u>Client</u>
U-Haul
<u>Country</u>
United States

A problem for U-Haul cus-
tomers is that they never
know what size truck
will properly fit all of their
stuff. To make it simple, U-
Haul labeled each
of their trucks and trailers
according to how many bed-
rooms each one would
hold. To make it even sim-
pler, this execution visually
demonstrates it.

ADC LXXXVI

Student
Advertising Posters &
Billboards Outdoor /
Billboard / Campaign

Merit
Puma

395

PUMA
<u>Art Director</u>
Shawna Laken, Tony
Kalathara
<u>School</u>
Miami Ad School
<u>Country</u>
United States

These outdoor posters are
designed to promote Puma
during the summer
Olympics. Since we were
not allowed to mention the
Olympics by name or sym-
bol, this visual relays athletic performance on the track
while retaining the fashion
essence of Puma's brand.

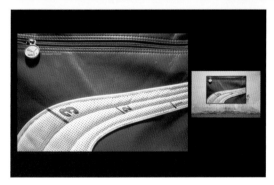

ADC LXXXVI

Student
Advertising Posters &
Billboards Outdoor /
Billboard / Single

Merit
Commercial Free

396

COMMERCIAL FREE
Art Director
Moyeenul Alam, Lucas
Napolitano
Copywriter
Moyeenul Alam
School
Miami Ad School
Client
Sirius Satellite Radio
Country
United States

ADC L̲X̲X̲X̲V̲I̲

Student
Advertising Posters &
Billboards Outdoor /
Billboard / Campaign

Merit
Take a Stand

397

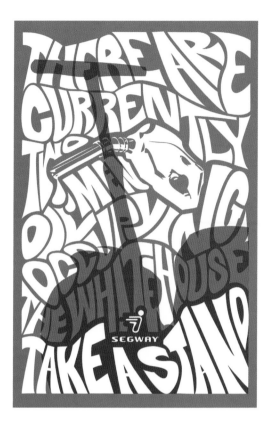

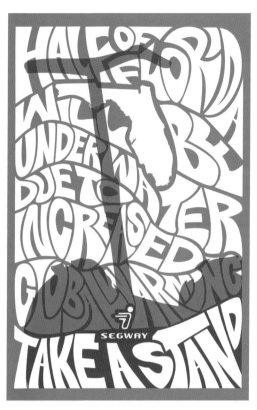

TAKE A STAND
A̲r̲t̲ ̲D̲i̲r̲e̲c̲t̲o̲r̲
Alison Chan
C̲o̲p̲y̲w̲r̲i̲t̲e̲r̲
Alison Chan
S̲c̲h̲o̲o̲l̲
Parsons the Newschool for
Design
C̲l̲i̲e̲n̲t̲
Segway Inc.
C̲o̲u̲n̲t̲r̲y̲
United States

Segway Inc. is all about
innovation and ignoring conventional thinking. With the
belief that science and engineering can be harnessed to
improve people's daily lives,
the Segway HT is designed
to be an environmentally
conscious alternative to
short distance travel by car.
Inspired by the radical
posters from the 60s, this
campaign aims to communi-
cate serious political issues
of present day through
evoking an immediate
nostalgia to take a stand.

ADC LXXXVI

Student
Collateral Guerrilla /
Unconventional / Single

Merit
Product Demo

398

PRODUCT DEMO
Art Director
Moyeenul Alam & Jessica
Maittre
Copywriter
Niklas Kristensen
School
Miami Ad School
Client
Hoover Vacuums
Country
United States

Stickers are placed on airplane windows to show the
product benefit of Hoover
Vacuums.

ADC LXXXVI

Student
Illustration Book
(Commercially Published
Volumes Only) / Single

Merit
Liebes Buch, (Dear Book Full
of Love)

399

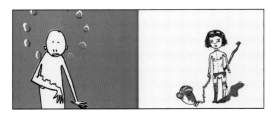

LIEBES BUCH, (DEAR BOOK FULL OF LOVE)
<u>Art Director</u>
Class of Prof. Girst and
Prof. Felten
<u>Illustrator</u>
Class of Prof. Girst and
Prof. Felten
<u>School</u>
Akademie der Bildenden
Kuenste in Nuernberg
<u>Country</u>
Germany

"Risks and adverse effects
with love." A class project.
Class of Prof. Holger Felten
and Prof. Friederike Girst in
collaboration with associate
lecturer Monika Aichele ,
Academy of Fine Arts in
Nuremberg, Germany.
Contributing Students:
Friedrich Bischoff, Tobias
Bittermann, Christoph
Kienzle, Harms Kraa,
Sabine Kraus, Dominik
Krauss, Hyo Jung Kwag,
Suvi-Erika Häring, Karsten
Petrat, Georg Reinhardt,
Juliane Scheib, Rainer
Schenk, Philipp Seis, Tobias
Tilgner, Frank Weidenfelder,
Marek Zdarsky.

ADC LXXXVI

Student
Graphic Design Book Design
Limited Edition, Private Press
or Special Format Book /
Single

Merit
Clean.

400

CLEAN.

<u>Copywriter</u>
Walter Baumann
<u>Designer</u>
Walter Baumann
<u>Illustrator</u>
Walter Baumann
<u>Photographer</u>
Walter Baumann
<u>School</u>
California College of the
Arts
<u>Country</u>
United States

I explored "clean" from as
many angles as I could,
given the time constraint of
15 weeks. Given the seem-
ingly prosaic quality of
"clean," what better way to
explore the topic than to
give the viewer exactly what
they expect. Then show
them that their expectations
are not based on fact or
reality but emotion and the
ugly side of capitalism. With
so much information I maxi-
mized the impact of the data
and thoughts I had collected through scale shifts and
visual explanations. Type
became a character that
cloaked a message in familiar clothes, but whose message undermined the view-
er's expectations and con-
sequently their beliefs. The
cover was hand screen-
printed with thermochro-
matic ink that changes to
clear with the heat of the
reader's hands intended to
create another level of
doubt in the reader's mind,
"Is this book clean, or are
my hands dirty?"

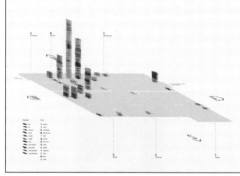

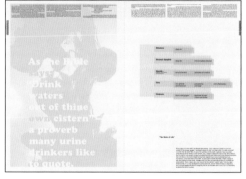

ADC LXXXVI

Student
Graphic Design Book Design
Limited Edition, Private Press
or Special Format Book /
Single

Merit
Wish I Was 3

401

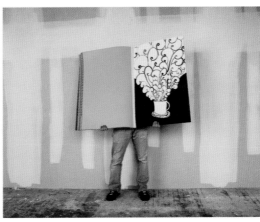

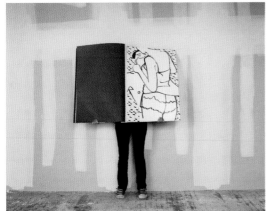

WISH I WAS 3
Designer
Marc Rabinowitz,
Zeynep Orbay
Instructor
Stefan Sagmeister
School
School of Visual Arts
Country
United States

"Wish I Was 3" was a 24 x 36
inch coloring book created
to touch the hearts of a
community. We went around
New York with a huge coloring book and spent time coloring with people, attempting to reconnect them with
their youth by giving them a
chance to turn objects and
events from their daily lives
into celebrated and colorful
self-expressive experiences.
Themes from the coloring
book include couples and
sex, alcohol, cars, fashion,
coffee and elements from
old advertisements.

ADC LXXXVI

Student
Graphic Design Book Design
Museum, Gallery or Library
Book / Single

Merit
Ruedi Baur Exhibition
Brochure

402

**RUEDI BAUR
EXHIBITION
BROCHURE**

Art Director
Jin yeoul Jung

Copywriter
Helen Ku

Designer
Jin yeoul Jung

Producer
Joon hee Lee

Publisher
Zeroone design center

School
Yale School of Art

Client
Zeroone Design Center

Country
United States

Brochure design for the
Ruedi Baur exhibition in
Seoul, South Korea. I con-
sider this brochure as a
small exhibition that can be
hung anywhere. I designed
it to look like a set of
posters. If you open the
poster set and hang it on
the wall, you can see large-
scale type (RUEDI BAUR).
It works two ways, as a
poster (small exhibition)
and as a brochure.

SYPHILIS

Designer
Thomas Geisler, Christof
Nardin
Photographer
Kramar
School
University of Applied Arts
Vienna
Client
Homed.at
Country
Austria

Lass dir nichts anhaengen!

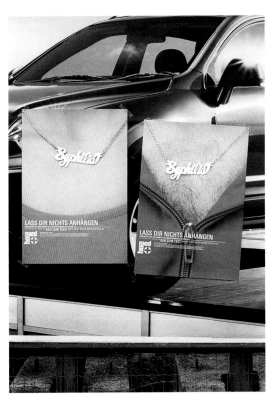

ADC LXXXVI

Student
Graphic Design Poster
Design Public Service / Non-
Profit / Educational /
Campaign

Merit
The Hurricane Poster Project

404

**THE HURRICANE
POSTER PROJECT**
Art Director
Joshua Gomby
Copywriter
Joshua Gomby
Creative Director
Joshua Gomby
Designer
Joshua Gomby
School
Rochester Institute of
Technology
Client
The Hurricane Poster
Project
Country
United States

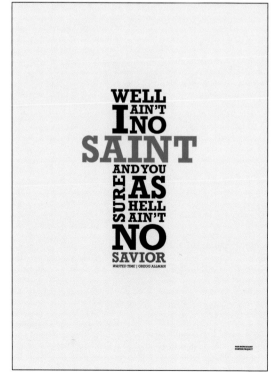

Student
Graphic Design Poster
Design Public Service / Non-
Profit / Educational /
Campaign

Merit
Lyrical Moments

405

her long,
beautiful,
wrinkly face
makes me
feel ok about
growing old.

www.weputthingshere.com

i love
the tension
between
myself and
these posters
next to me.

www.weputthingshere.com

LYRICAL MOMENTS
Art Director
Alexandra Brand
Instructor
William Morissey
School
School of Visual Arts
Country
United States

With the contents of my
poster being so open-
ended, my exploration was
wide spread. Ultimately,
they stemmed from the
simple, beautiful moments
of a regular day. The final
posters are some of my
most sincere thoughts.
Simple, honest, open:
like kids can be, like the
Dick & Jane books are.

her smile
makes me
wish i were
a regular.

www.weputthingshere.com

ADC LXXXVI

Student
Graphic Design Poster
Design Billboard / Campaign

Merit
Greener New York

406

GREENER NEW YORK

<u>Art Director</u>
Jeanne Lee
<u>Copywriter</u>
Jeanne Lee, Juan Moreno
<u>Creative Director</u>
Jeanne Lee
<u>Designer</u>
Jeanne Lee
<u>Instructor</u>
Alisa Zamir
<u>School</u>
Pratt Institute
<u>Client</u>
Trees New York
<u>Country</u>
United States

Trees New York is a non-profit organization situated in Lower Manhattan. This organization concentrates on preserving, pruning and protecting trees in the Five boroughs. The purpose of this campaign is to "Plant a seed for a Greener Apple." To demonstrate the idea, the forms of New York icons such as the Statue of Liberty, Chrysler Building, Empire State Building and the New York skyline were applied to die-cut billboards.

ADC LXXXVI

Student
Graphic Design Package
Design Cosmetics / Perfume /
Single

Merit
Tazaa Brand Soap

407

TAZAA BRAND SOAP
Art Director
Jesse Kirsch
Designer
Jesse Kirsch
Instructor
Chad Roberts
School
School of Visual Arts
Country
United States

Strong typography and a
sharp color pallet define
this packaging system for a
line of six scented soaps.
The bright white of the
sleeve evokes a feeling of
cleanliness, while the interi-
or box conveys the color of
the ingredients used to
make the soap. The initials
of each scent's name, die
cut on the outside sleeve,
allow the color of the box
below to show through. A
small narrow opening at
either end invites the consumer to smell the soap
without having to open the
box. The product itself
echoes its packaging with
matching initials recessed
into the surface of each bar.

ADC LXXXVI

MEMBERSHIP AND ADMINISTRATION /
INDEX /
OTHER INDICES /

MEMBERSHIP AND ADMINISTRATION

Corporate Members

2.gc, Inc.
Adobe Systems, Inc.
Alchemy Creative Studios
Bloomingdale's
Charlex, Inc.
Corbis
Eliran Murphy Group
Foote Cone & Belding
Frankfurt Kurnit Klein & Selz
G2Worldwide
Getty Images
Hachette Book Group USA
HBO—Off Air Creative Services
Hill Holliday
Image Source
Janou Pakter Inc.
Kraftworks Ltd.
L.P. Thebault Company
Little, Brown and Company
Manhattan Marketing Ensemble
Marks Paneth & Shron LLP
Martha Stewart Omnimedia
Merkley + Partners
OPIUMeffect GmbH
Parade Publications
Pentagram
@radical.media
Reuters
Saatchi & Saatchi
Situation Marketing LLC
St. Martin's Press
Taxi NYC
Trinity Church—St Paul's Chapel
Trollback & Company
X-Rite

ADC MEMBERS

United States

Karen Abrams
Ruba Abu-Nimah
Lymari Acevedo
Rea Ackerman
Ron Acquavita
Cornelia Adams
Gaylord Adams
Malcolm Louis Adams
Sean Adams
Peter Adler
Charles S. Adorney
Shig Ahn
Frank Aldorf

Barbara Alexander
Julie Alperen
Gordana Andejelic-Davila
Melanie Andersen
Emily Anderson
Jack Anderson
Matthew Anderson
Mats Andersson
Gennaro Andreozzi
Victor Anselmi
Ariel Apte
Chie Araki
Lia Aran
Ron Arnold
Rashi Arora
Noel Artiles
Michael Ash

Blanca Aulet
Alma Grace Avanzado
Matthew Axe
Katherine Babanovsky
Robert O. Bach
Kristina Backlund
Ronald Bacsa
Priscilla Baer
Patrick Baird
Kim Baker
Denise Banister
Matthew Bannister
Giorgio Baravalle
Sarah Barclay
Freya Barea
Mimi Bark
Don Barron

Robert Barthelmes
Hugh Barton
Tripp Bassett
Dawn Bauer
Mary K. Baumann
Matthew Baumlin
Damian Bazadona
Allan Beaver
Christop Becker
April Bell
Rhiannon Bell
Lois Bender
Edward J. Bennett
Nneka Bennett
TJ Bennett
Michael Benvenga
Richard Berenson

John Berg
Jennifer Bergamini
Robert Bergman
Walter L. Bernard
Alex Bershaw
Francesco Bertocci
Anthony Bianchi
Jennifer Binder
Mat Bisher
Debra Bishop
Christina Black
R.O. Blechman
Robert H. Blend
Barbara Bloemink
Joan Bodensteiner
Anastasia Bogdanova
Carol Bokuniewicz

Jean Bourges
Jeroen Bours
Harold A. Bowman
Patrick Bowyer
Rick Boyko
Barbara Boyle
Kevin Brainard
Al Braverman
Andrew R. Brenits
Kristi Bridges
Nathan Brockman
Jackie Brodley
Ed Brodsky
Ruth Brody
Barbara Brown
Bo Youn Brown
Claire Brown
Wendy Brown
Michael Bruce
Bruno E. Brugnatelli
Janice Brunell
Meghan Bryant
William H. Buckley
Gene Bullard
Christopher Buonocore
Sara Burke
Larry Burnett
Red Burns
Rodrigo Butori
Chris Byrnes
Amy Byron
Stephanie Cabrera
Mark Cacciatore
Jodi Cafritz
Patrick Cahalan
Christina Cahill
Brian Caiazza
Ivy Calahorrano
Nicholas Callaway
Jon Cammarata
David Caplan
Alberto Capolino
Ken Carbone
Marcelo Cardosa
Gregg Carlesimo
Thomas Carnase
EJ Carr
Roymieco Carter
Fraser Cassidy
Tina Marie Cecere-Hunter
Gabrial Ceslov
Andrew Chang
Rodd Chant
Anthony Chaplinsky Jr.
Delanie West Cheatam
Jack Chen
Peter Chen
Ivan Chermayeff
Deanne Cheuk
Mark Chew
Roberta Chiarella
Young Hee Choi
Richard Christiansen
Tom Christmann
Tim Chumley
Shelly Chung
Stanley Church
Seymour Chwast
Joseph Cipri
Douglas Clark
Herbert H. Clark
Thomas F. Clemente
John Clifford
Joann Coates

Colleen Cody
Michael Cohen
Peter Cohen
Rhonda Cohen
Jack Cohn
Karen Cohn
Alisa Coleman
Anthony Colletti
Brian Collins
James Collins
Solange Collins
Andreas Combuechen
Tom Connor
Mary Jane Conte
Christopher Cook
Ryann Cooley
Andrew Coppa
Dominick Correale
Andres Cortes
Gary Cosimini
Erminia Costantino
Sheldon Cotler
Susan Cotler-Block
Coz Cotzias
Michael Coulson
Phyllis Cox
Robert Cox
James Edward Craig
Meg Crane
Gregory Crossley
Bob Crozier
Joseph Crump
Sergio Cuan
Haozheng Cui
Tom Cunningham
Lisa Curesky
Ethel R. Cutler
Pier Nicola D'Amico
Shelagh D'Arcy-Hinos
Johan Dahlqvist
Kyle Daley
Jakob Daschek
David Davidian
Simone Davidson
J. Hamilton Davis
Paul Brookhart Davis
Randi B. Davis
Roland De Fries
Allison DeFord
Richard Degni
Joe Del Sorbo
Joy Delaney
Kathy Delaney
Kristofer Delaney
Nancy Delmerico
Venus Dennison
David Deutsch
Dennis Di Vincenzo
John F. Dignam
Eric Dilone
Christina Dittmar
Jason Dodd
Michael Donovan
Louis Dorfsman
Marc Dorian
Bruce Doscher
Kay E. Douglas
Sheila Doyle
Stephen Doyle
Christian Drury
Frank Dudley
Donald H. Duffy
Joe Duffy
Erica Duggan

Robin Duggan
Michael Dulligan
James Dunlinson
Rob Dybec
Bernard Eckstein
Noha Edell
Geoffrey Edwards
Andrew Egan
Yael Eisele
Nina Eisenman
Stanley Eisenman
Brad Eisenstein
Chris Elliott
David Epstein
Lee Epstein
Elke Erschfeld
Robert Evangelista
Ben Farber
Rachel Farley
Sally Faust
Michael Fenga
Mark Fenske
Andres Fernandez
Mary Fetters
Krista Noelle Finck
Stan Fine
Blanche Fiorenza
Andre Fiorini
Carl Fischer
Gill Fishman
Theresa Fitzgerald
Bernadette Fitzpatrick
Donald P. Flock
Patrick Flood
Marta Florin
Michael Fofrich
Amanda Ford
Kathy Formisano
Peter Fraioli
Polly Franchini
Cliff Francis
Michael Frankfurt
Stephen Frankfurt
C. Freed
Craig Freitag
Christina Freyss
Michael K. Frith
Stephen Fritz
Janet Froelich
Glen Fruchter
S. Neil Fujita
Leonard W. Fury
Danielle Gallo
Shallon Gammon
Brian Ganton Jr.
Maria Garffer
Gino Garlanda
Simona Gaudio
Einat Gavish
Tom Geismar
Steff Geissbuhler
Mike Gentile
Janet Giampietro
Rob Giampietro
Kurt Gibson
Claire Giddings
Justin Gignac
Monica Gilburt
Sharla Gillard
Tim Gilman
Matthew Gingrich
Frank C. Ginsberg
Sara Giovanitti
Bob Giraldi

Milton Glaser
Julia Glick
Marc Gobé
Greg Goings
Bill Gold
Roz Goldfarb
Bruce Goldstein
Daniel Gonzalez
Trent Good
Joanne Goodfellow
Scott Goodson
Josh Gordon
Michael W. Gottlieb
Jonathan Gouthier
Jean Govoni
William Graham
Anthony Granata
Tony Granger
Ali Grayeli
Jeff Greenbaum
Simon Grendene
Ben Griffin
Jack Griffin
Olga Grlic
Andrea Groat
Glenn Groglio
Raisa Grubshteyn
Victoria Grujicic
Vicky Guo
Frank Guzzone
Lori Habas
Robert Hack
Suzanne Hader
Bob Hagel
Jeseka Hahn
Kurt Haiman
Elisa Halperin
Everett Halvorsen
India Hammer
Sammi Han
Linda Hanick
Marie Nicole Haniph
Ann Harakawa
Jeff Harris
Lara Harris
Wade Harris
Laurel Hausler
Benson Hausman
Craig Hayes
Keith Hayes
Matt Healy
Marc Hedges
Karl Heine
Steven Heller
Kerri Helliwell
Debbie Hemela
Randall Hensley
Erin Herbst
Peiter Hergert
Lauren Herman
Craig Hern
Nancy Herrmann
Samantha Hickey
Lee Hilands Horswill
Chris Hill
Cheryl Hills
Sean Hills
Bill Hillsman
Carolyn Hinkson-Jenkins
Andy Hirsch
Marcel Hirschegger
Paul Ho
Dan Hoffmann
Marilyn Hoffner

Chad Hogan
Sandy Hollander
Janet Holmes
Michael Hong
Jane Hope
Daniel Hort
Michael Hortens
Anne Hrubala
Kim Huelsman
Karin Hug
Pia Hunter
Brian Hurewitz
Victoria I. Hyman
Cassandra Illidge Roberts
Manabu Inada
Rei Inamoto
Bob Isherwood
Adam Isidore
Jarard Isler
Edouard Israel
Joseph Issak
Sarah Jackson
Harry Jacobs
Jan Jacobs
Ashwini M. Jambotkar
Justin Jameyson
John E. Jamison
Ron Jautz
Lenlee Jenckes
Loretta Jeneski
Patricia Jerina
Paul Jervis
Dana Johnstone
Lindsey Jones
Eric Junker
Mirela Jurisic
Raquella Kagan
Kenneth Kaiser
Stephen Kallaugher
Jon Kamen
Lauren Kangas
Takako Kanzaki
Walter Kaprielian
Julieta Kattan
Stacey Katzen
Michael Ian Kaye
David Kegel
Iris Keitel
Sirpa Kela
Nancy Kent
Katherine Keogh
Candice Kersh
Sara Kidd
Elizabeth Kiehner
Thomas Kieren
Satoiro Kikutake
Chris Kim
June Kim
Will Kim
Amy Kindred
Caroline King
Nathalie Kirsheh
Susan Kirshenbaum
Alex Kirzhner
Judith Klein
Hilda Stanger Klyde
Andrew Kner
Henry O. Knoepfler
Kayako Kobayashi
Kurt Koepfle
Gary Koepke
Andrea Kohl
Tae Koo
Sanjay Kothari

Charlie Kouns
P. Koutsis
Justin Kovics
Damian Kowal
Dennis Koye
Neil Kraft
Veronique Krieger
David Krulik
Rick Kurnit
Julia Kushnirsky
Joseph Kuzemka
Ande La Monica
Anthony La Petri
Micah Laaker
Jason Lancaster
Robin Landa
Danika Landers
Dean Landew
David Langley
Jim Larmon
Lisa LaRochelle
Jeremy Lasky
Stacy Lavender
Paul Lavoie
Amanda Lawrence
Leonardo Lawson
Keshida Layone
David Lazarus
Sal Lazzarotti
Mary Leahy
Mortimer Lebigre
Julianna Lee
Saehee Lee
Estelle Leeds
Peter Leeds
Felipe Leite
Sebastian Lemm
Mark Levenfus
Adrienne Levin
Charlotte Lewis
Stefanie Lieberman
Thomas Lincoln
Andreas J.P. Lindstrom
Matthew Llewellyn
Douglas Lloyd
Rebecca Lloyd
George Lois
Jon Paul LoMonaco
Carolyn London
Jennifer Long
Miriam Lorentzen
Tom Lorenzo
George Lott
Robert Lowe
Diane Luger
Shane Luitjens
William Lukach
Ronnie Lunt
Yih Ma
Richard MacFarlane
David H. MacInnes
Carla Mackintosh
Victoria Maddocks
Vanessa Maganza
Lou Magnani
Lisa Maione
Jay Maisel
Romy Mann
David R. Margolis
Leo J. Marino, III
Jack Mariucci
Andrea Marquez
Christian Martillo
Charlene Martin

Flavio Masson
Stephen Mayes
Victor Mazzeo
Keith McCabe
William McCaffery
Brian Matthew McCall
Mei-Lu McGonigle
Kevin McKeon
Michael McQuade
Sean McQueen
Jeff Meglio
Nancy A. Meher
Lisa Mehling
Michael Meikson
Kevin Melahn
Kristin Meloche
Jose Mendez
Anastassios Mentis
Juliette Merck
Parry Merkley
Josh Merwin
Djiana Mesin
Jack Messina
Jeffrey Metzner
Jackie Merri Meyer
Alejandro Meza
Anna Michalski
Madeleine Michels
Eugene Milbauer
Eric Miller
Joan Miller
Lauren J. Miller
Mark Miller
Steven A. Miller
Trente Miller
John Milligan
Margaret Minnis
Wendell Minor
Amanda Mintz
Michael Miranda
Samantha Mitchell
Susan L. Mitchell
Tim Mitchell
Sam Modenstein
Christine Moh
Jose Molla
Sakol Mongkolkasetarin
Ty Montague
Allan Montaine
Mark Montgomery
Rachel Moog
Jacqueline C. Moorby
William Moore
Diane Moore Behrens
Anthony Morais
Dan Morales
Noreen Morioka
Minoru Morita
Donald Morrison
William R. Morrison
Barbara Moscarello Barbera
Shay Moscona
Louie Moses
Alexa Mulvihill
Yuki Muramatsu
Ann Murphy
Brian Murphy
S. Murphy
Wylie H. Nash
Bonnie Natko
James D. Nesbitt
Barbara Nessim
Okey Nestor
Noelle Newbold

Robert Newman
Darren Newton
Maria A. Nicholas
Mary Ann Nichols
Davide Nicosia
Joseph Nissen
Audrey Nizen
Barbara J. Norman
Roger Norris
George Noszagh
David November
John O'Callaghan
Kevin O'Callaghan
Wendy O'Connor
Rudi O'Meara
Bill Oberlander
Beverly Okada
John Okladek
Paula Oliosi
Amy Olsen
Bradley Olsen-Ecker
Carlos Onaindia
Lisa Orange
Soner Ormanbaba
Nina Ovryn
Jessica Owen-Ward
Onofrio Paccione
Paula Pagano
Frank Paganucci
Sheila Paige
Mike Pakalik
Janou Pakter
Jack Palancio
Brad Pallas
Richard Pandiscio
Lydia Paniccia
Mitchell Paone
Kelly Parrotto
Linda Passante
Terri Passick
Chee Pearlman
Stan Pearlman
Brigid Pearson
Ana Perez
Christine Perez
Dan Perlet
David Perry
Harold A. Perry
Christos Peterson
Jonathan Petley
Robert Petrocelli
Theodore D. Pettus
Allan A. Philiba
Eric A. Pike
Ebru Pinar
P. Pinedo
Ernest Pioppo
Michael Pirolo
Mary Pisarkiewicz
Carlos Pisco
Robert Pliskin
Peter Pobyjpicz
Simeon Poulin
Neil D. Powell
Tim Powell
Lea Ann Powers
Dan Poynor
Don Puckey
Mario J. Pulice
Liz Quinlisk
Ana Racelis
Ronaldo Ramirez
Peter Raymond
Diane Reed

Samuel Reed
Kendrick Reid
Geoff Reinhard
Herbert Reinke
Marie Reinoso
Joseph Leslie Renaud
Christa Renee
Sean Reynolds
Howard Rhee
Anthony Rhodes
David Rhodes
Sharon Richards
Stan Richards
Hank Richardson
Margaret Riegel
Michael Riley
Lianne Ritchie
Geoffrey Rittenmyer
Arthur Ritter
Jonathan Robbins
Nadine Robbins
Wayne Robins
Douglas Rockhill
Jonathan Rodgers
Roswitha Rodrigues
Cindy Rodriguez
Tamara Rodriguez
Andy Romano
Dianne M. Romano
Christopher Rosales
Jamie Rosen
Charlie Rosner
Peter Ross
Richard J. Ross
Tina Roth Eisenberg
David Baldeosingh Rotstein
Mort Rubenstein
Randee Rubin
Henry N. Russell
Don Ruther
Stephen Rutterford
Thomas Ruzicka
Kate Ryan
Jan Sabach
Stewart Sacklow
Randy Saitta
Robert Saks
Robert Salpeter
James Salser
Greg Samata
Steve Sandstrom
Yolanda Santosa
Nathan Savage
Robert Sawyer
Julie Sbuttoni
Sam Scali
Ernest Scarfone
Heide Schaffner
Wendy Schechter
Nicole Schembeck
Paula Scher
Randall Scherrer
David Schimmel
Klaus F. Schmidt
Jonathan Schoenberg
Maria Schriber
Michael Schrom
Stephen Schuler
Eileen Hedy Schultz
Deborah Schwartz
Gillian Schwartz
Joe Sciarrotta
Stephen Scoble
William Seabrook, III

J.J. Sedelmaier
Leslie Segal
Alison Segura
Christian Seichrist
Pippa Seichrist
Ron Seichrist
Sheldon Seidler
Don Seitz
Kimberly Selber
Audrey Shachnow
Jennifer Sherman
Allan Shoemake
Limore Shur
Patricia Silva
Jackie Silvan
Karen Silveira
Louis Silverstein
Rich Silverstein
Robert Simmons
Timothy Simmons
Todd Simmons
Milton Simpson
Scott Sindorf
Leila Singleton
Ploy Siripant
Leonard Sirowitz
Oscar Skelton
Robert Slagle
Spencer Slemenda
Gary Sloan
Abby Smith
Carol Lynn Smith
James C. Smith
Kevin Smith
Nancy Smith
Todd Smith
Virginia Smith
Eugene M. Smith Jr.
Christine Sniado
Steve Snider
DeWayne A. Snype
Jeronimo Sochaczewski
Russell L. Solomon
Ashley Sommardahl
Harold Sosnow
Courtney Spain
Harvey Spears
Jenya Spektor
Serena L. Spiezio
Russell Spina
Mindy Phelps Stanton
Hope Stehling
Doug Steinberg
Karl Steinbrenner
Alexej Steinhardt
Jeff Stevens
Monica Stevenson
Daniel E. Stewart
Colleen Stokes
Bernard Stone
Jimmie Stone
Michael Storrings
Lizabeth Storrs Donnelly
Lisa Strausfeld
Eric Striffler
Peter Strongwater
William Strosahl
Snorri Sturluson
Sandra Sumski
Fredrik Sundwall
Matt Sung
Kayoko Suzuki-Lange
Barbara Taff
KC Tagliareni

Elizabeth Talerman
Peijuan Tang
Penny Tarrant
Melcon Tashian
Jack G. Tauss
Sarah Tay
Mary Tchorbajian
Carlos Tejeda
Mark Tekushan
David Ter-Avanesyan
JP Terlizzi
Jonathan Tessler
Beau Thebault
Benjamin Thoma
Anne Thomas
Chris Thomas
Tessa M. Tinney
Jerry Todd
Pauline Tomko
Flamur Tonuzi
Nicholas E. Torello
Damian Totman
Gael Towey
Victor Trasoff
Marc Tremitiere
Rodrigo Trevino
Jakob Trollback
Linne Tsu
Joseph P. Tuohy
Patricia Turken
Jenny Turner
Mark Tutssel
Anne Twomey
Jamie Vance
Carlos Vazquez
Shruti Veeramachineni
Claudio Venturini
Frank Verlizzo
Amy Vernick
Jovan Villalba
Anthony Viola
Frank A. Vitale
John Vitro
Jurek Wajdowicz
Kay Wakabayashi
Glen Waldron
Clint Walkingstick
Richard Wallace
Helen Wan
George Wang
Jennifer Wang
Allison Warner
Shannon Washington
Jonathan Webb
Jessica Weber
Alex Weil
Joe Weil
Roy Weinstein
Courtney Weiss
Jeff Weiss
Clint Welsh
Renetta Welty
Wendy Wen
Robert Shaw West
Miriam White
Sabine Wieger
Richard Wilde
Justin Wilkes
Keith Williams
Maurice Williams
Melinda Williams
Mike Williams
Michael Wilson
Jay Michael Wolf

Nelson Wong
Tracy Wong
Tim Woods
Fred Woodward
Nina Wurtzel
Ping Xu
Chisa Yagi
Megumi Soleh Yamada
Can Yanardag
Paul Yeates
Henry Sene Yee
Ebru Yildiz
Ira Yoffe
Zen Yonkovig
Won You
Frank Young
Frank Zabski
Mark Zapico
Predrag Zdravkovic
Li Zhang
Lloyd Ziff
Bernie Zlotnick
John Zontini
Jonathan Zweifler
Alan H. Zwiebel

**ACADEMIC
MEMBERS**
College for Creative Studies
Miami AD School
School of Visual Arts
VCU Adcenter

**INTERNATIONAL
MEMBERS**

Australia
Chun Yi Chau
Jo Dalvean
Giuseppe Demaio
Kathryn Dilanchian
Neil Mallett
Ashley Ringrose

Austria
Tibor Bárci
Mariusz Jan Demner
Damir Krizmanic
Lois Lammerhuber
Silvia Lammerhuber
Franz Merlicek
Roland A. Reidinger

Brazil
Douglas Alves
Daniel da Hora

Canada
Jean-Francois Berube
Rob Carter, R.G.D.
Stephane Charier
Louis Gagnon
S. Jacqueline Kelly
Wally Krysciak
Lance Martin
Jason McCann
Zak Mroueh
Steve Mykolyn
Ric Riordon
Tom Rudman
Dominique Trudeau

China
Zhiwei Bai
Han JiaYing
Ge Liu
Wenjiang Tan
Cai Shi Wei
Lai Wei
Xia Wenxi
Gabriel Wong
Hui Zhang

Croatia
Davor Bruketa
Dubravka Perisa

Denmark
Soeren Kjaer
Lars Pryds

Finland
Kari Piippo

France
Fabrice Monier

Germany
Thomas Ernsting
Jan Peter Gassel

Roland Gloeckner
Jens Gutermann
Harald Haas
Oliver Hesse
Ralf Heuel
Michael Hoinkes
Armin Jochum
Matthias Kaeding
Amir Kassaei
Claus Koch
Olaf Leu
Andreas Lueck
Friederike Mojen
Ingo Mojen
Lothar Nebl
Gertrud Nolte
Friedhelm Ott
Andreas Rell
Achim Riedel
Alexander Rötterink
Sven Hedin Ruhs
Klaus Schaefer
Daniel Scheibel
Hans Dirk Schellnack
Holger Schmidhuber
Marc Oliver Schwarz
Andreas Uebele
Michael Volkmer
Oliver Voss
Gabriele Zuber
Joerg Zuber

Greece
Rodanthi Senduka

Hong Kong
David Chow
Tommy Li

Ireland
Eoghan Nolan

Italy
Sergio Calatroni
Angela D'Amelio
Titti Fabiani
Valerio Galli
Marta Oroni
Milka Pogliani

Japan
Ikegoshi Akihiro
Takashi Akiyama
Masuteru Aoba
Hiroyuki Aotani
Katsumi Asaba
Norio Fujishiro
Shigeki Fukushima
Osamu Furumura
Keiko Hirata
Kazunobu Hosoda
Kogo Inoue
Masami Ishibashi
Shoichi Ishida
Keiko Itakura
Yasuyuki Ito
Tetsuro A. Itoh
Toshio Iwata
Kenzo Izutani
Takeshi Kagawa
Hideyuki Kaneko
Satoji Kashimoto
Seijo Kawaguchi
Shun Kawakami

Fumio Kawamoto
Yasuhiko Kida
Katsuhiro Kinoshita
Takashi Kitazawa
Kunio Kiyomura
Pete Kobayashi
Ryohei Kojima
Akiko Kuze
Arata Matsumoto
Takao Matsumoto
Shin Matsunaga
Iwao Matsuura
Keisuke Nagatomo
Hideki Nakajima
Kazuto Nakamura
Shuichi Nogami
Sadanori Nomura
Yoshimi Oba
Kuniyasu Obata
Toshiyuki Ohashi
Gaku Ohsugi
Yasumichi Oka
Masato Okada
Akio Okumura
Toshihiro Onimaru
Nobumitsu Oseko
Hiroshi Saito
Kouzo Sasahara
Michihito Sasaki
Akira Sato
Hidemi Shingai
Norito Shinmura
Radical Suzuki
Zempaku Suzuki
Yutaka Takahama
Izumi Takahashi
Masami Takahashi
Satoshi Takamatsu
Shigeru Takeo
Masakazu Tanabe
Soji George Tanaka
Yasuo Tanaka
Norio Uejo
Katsunori Watanabe
Masato Watanabe
Yoshiko Watanabe
Yumiko Watanabe
Akihiro H. Yamamoto
Hiroki Yamamoto
Yoji Yamamoto
Kiyoka Yamazuki
Masaru Yokoi
Masayuki Yoshida

Korea
Bernard Chung
Kwang-Kyu Kim
Kum Jun Park

Mexico
Felix Beltran

New Zealand
Jason Dooris
Guy Pask

Puerto Rico
Marcelo DiFranco

Saudi Arabia
Atul Rajhans

Serbia
Dragan Sakan

Singapore
Hal Suzuki
Noboru Tominaga

Slovak Republic
Andrea Bánovská

Slovenia
Vesna Brekalo

Spain
Jaime Beltran
Manuel Estrada Perez

Sweden
Kari Palmqvist

Switzerland
Stephan Bundi
Bilal Dallenbach
Igor Masnjak
Manfred Oebel
Susanne Reimann
Dominique Anne Schuetz
Philipp Welti

Taiwan
Jack Chang

The Netherlands
Pieter Brattinga

Turkey
Sami Basut
Mete Gurgun

UAE
Nisreen El Lababidi Moghraby

UK
Domenic Lippa
Harry Pearce

STUDENT MEMBERS

Bambang Adinegoro
Rachel Adler
Sumayya Alsenan
Lukasz Antkiewicz
Rafi Bernstein
Joshua Carpenter
Steven Case
Armando Ceron
Alison Chan
Sue Won Chang
Mu-Ni Cheng
Jin Choi
Miae Choi
Angela Colley
Alex Cortani
Jordan Farkas
Douglas Fielder
Derek Gordon
Veronica Hamburger
Hai Ri Han
Esayuri Harsono
Jasmine Hernandez
Ixel Huerta-Velasco
Roman Jaster
Mike Keller
Daniel Kim
Shawna Laken
Rosey Lakos
Lester Lee
Li Juan Lin
Christopher Lyzcen
Michael MacDonald
Joanna Maj-Khan
Nasser McMayo
Eri Nagakubo
Wilfredo Otero
Jennifer Pi
Michael Raczy
Vidur Raswant
Christopher Rogan
Michael Romeo
Kaori Singer
Rozely Souza
Lauren Stewart
Manoj Swearingen
Kristine Sweep
Angela Tai
Anthony Tam
Michelle Testani
Kwan Ling Tin
Cathy Tippett
Natallia Tsynkevich
Wendy Walker Davis
Kevin Ward
Jungho Wi
Brittany Megan Wycoff
Changjing Xu
Erica Yamada
Karen Yeung

ADC ADMINISTRATION

Executive Director
Ami Brophy
Director of Operations
Olga Grisaitis
Annual Awards Manager
Chris Reitz
Interactive Manager
Jenny Synan
Education Coordinator
Kate Farina
Membership Coordinator
Ann Schirripa
Marketing Associate
Laura Des Enfants
Awards Program Associate
Kimberly Hanzich
Awards Program Associate
Glenn Kubota
Assistant to
the Executive Director
Danielle Epstein
Digital Archivist
Catherine Archias
Archive Assistant
Stephen Long
Financial Consultant
Tony Ziza
Certified Public Accountant
Winnie Tam & Co., P.C.
Waitstaff
Margaret Busweiler
Patricia Connors

2006-2007 ADC BOARD OF DIRECTORS

President
Paul Lavoie
TAXI NYC

Officers

Vice President
Brian Collins
Brand Innovation Group,
Ogilvy & Mather

Second Vice President
Jeroen Bours
Independent

Secretary
Chee Pearlman
Chee Company

Treasurer
Michael Donovan
D/G2, Inc.

Assistant Secretary /
Treasurer
Gael Towey
Marths Stewart Living
Omnimedia

Board

Ken Carbone
Carbone Smolan Agency

Chris Hacker
Johnson & Johnson

Ann Harakawa
Two Twelve Associates

Doug Jaeger
The Happy Corp. Global

Linus Karlsson
Mother

Gary Koepke
Modernista!

Rick Kurnit
Frankfurt, Kurnit,
Klein & Selz

Michael Royce
New York Foundation
for the Arts

Neil Powell
WeAreGigantic

Steve Smith
Stephen M. Smith & Co.

Lisa Strausfeld
Pentagram

Jakob Trollbäck
Trollbäck and Company

Kevin Wassong
Minyanville

Emeritus

Rick Boyko
VCU Adcenter

Jon Kamen
@radical.media

Parry Merkley
Merkley + Partners

Advisory Board President

Bob Greenberg
R/GA

86TH ANNUAL AWARDS

Special Thanks

Gold Sponsors
Corbis
YAHOO!

Silver Sponsors
Stora Enso
LP Thebault
MediaTemple

Distinctive Merit Sponsors
AdForum

Call for Entries
TBWA\Chiat\Day

Gala Invitation
TBWA\Chiat\Day

Winners' Souvenir
Moleskine

Exhibit Design
C&G Partners

Kiosk and DVD Design
C&G Partners

Photographer
EJ Carr

Gala A/V Presentation
Michael Andrews Audio Visual
Services

ADC PAST PRESIDENTS

Richard J. Walsh, 1920–21
Joseph Chapin, 1921–22
Heyworth Campbell, 1922–23
Fred Suhr, 1923–24
Nathaniel Pousette-Dart, 1924–25
Walter Whitehead, 1925–26
Pierce Johnson, 1926–27
Arthur Munn, 1927–28
Stuart Campbell, 1929–30
Guy Gayler Clark, 1930–31
Edward F. Molyneuz, 1931–33
Gordon C. Aymar, 1933–34
Mehemed Fehmy Agha, 1934–35
Joseph Platt, 1935–36
Deane Uptegrove, 1936–38
Walter B. Geoghegan, 1938–40
Lester Jay Loh, 1940–41
Loren B. Stone, 1941–42
William A. Adriance, 1942–43
William A. Irwin, 1943–45
Arthur Hawkins Jr., 1945–46
Paul Smith, 1946–48
Lester Rondell, 1948–50
Harry O'Brien, 1950–51
Roy W. Tillotson, 1951–53
John Jamison, 1953–54**
Julian Archer, 1954–55
Frank Baker, 1955–56
William H. Buckley, 1956–57**
Walter R. Grotz, 1957–58
Garrett P. Orr, 1958–60
Robert H. Blattner, 1960–61
Edward B. Graham, 1961–62
Bert W. Littman, 1962–64
Robert Sherrich Smith, 1964–65
John A. Skidmore, 1965–67
John Peter, 1967–69
Wiilliam P. Brockmeier, 1969–71
George Lois, 1971–73**
Herbert Lubalin, 1973–74
Louis Dorfsman, 1974–75**
Eileen Hedy Schulz, 1975–77**
David Davidian, 1977–79**
William Taubin, 1979–81
Walter Kaprielian, 1981–83**
Andrew Kner, 1983–85**
Edward Brodsky, 1985–87**
Karl Steinbrenner, 1987–89
Henry Wolf, 1989–91
Kurt Haiman, 1991–93**
Allan Beaver, 1993–95**
Carl Fischer, 1995–97**
Bill Oberlander, 1997–2000**
Richard Wilde, 2000–2002**
Bob Greenberg 2002-2005**

** Advisory Board

INDEX

OTHER INDICIES / 2007 AGENCIES

OTHER INDICIES /
2007 CLIENTS

WELCOME TO THE WORLD OF **LE BOOK**

A CUSTOM-MADE TRADESHOW FOR THE CREATIVE COMMUNITY

SHOWCASING MORE THAN 1000 PHOTOGRAPHERS' AND ILLUSTRATORS' PORTFOLIOS BY **LE BOOK**

CONNECTIONS

CONNECTIONS TOUR 2008 | PARIS - APRIL 08
NEW YORK - JUNE 08 | LONDON - OCTOBER 08

DESIGN SEE STUDIO

REGISTER ON WWW.LEBOOK.COM/CONNECTIONS BY INVITATION ONLY

What do you m
You're fired!

DON'T LET IT GO
TO YOUR HEAD

I'm fired?

A note on the numerals

Roman numerals appear to derive from notches on tally sticks, such as those used by Italian and Dalmatian shepherds into the 19th century. Thus, the I descends from a notch scored across the stick. Every fifth notch was double cut (V), and every tenth was cross cut (X), much like European tally marks today. This produced a positional system: Eight on a counting stick was eight tallies, IIIIVIII, but this could be abbreviated VIII, as the existence of a V implies four prior notches. Likewise, number four on the stick was the I-notch that could be felt just before the cut of the V, so it could be written as either IIII or IV. Thus the system was neither additive nor subtractive in its conception, but ordinal. When the tallies were later transferred to writing, the marks were easily identified with the existing Roman letters I, V, X.

The tenth V or X along the stick received an extra stroke. Thus 50 was written most often as a chicken-track shape like a superimposed V and I. This had flattened to an inverted T by the time of Augustus, and soon thereafter became identified with the graphically similar letter L. Likewise, 100 was written as any of the symbols for 50 above plus an extra stroke. A superimposed X and I came to predominate, was written variously as >I< or an I between back-to-back C's, with C finally winning out because, as a letter, it stood for the Latin centum, or 100.

Roman numerals are commonly used today for numbered lists (in outline format), clockfaces, pages preceding the main body of a book, chord triads in music analysis, successive political leaders or children with identical names, and the numbering of some sport events, such as the Olympic Games or the Super Bowl. They are also used widely in the sciences for The Periodic Table of the Elements, the numbering of planetary satellites, the designation of degrees on the Mercalli earthquake intesity scale, etc.

A note on the type

The design of Monotype Grotesque was supervised at the Monotype foundry in 1926 by F.H. Pierpont, a Connecticut engineer who moved to London and headed the Monotype Corporation matrix factory and drawing office from early in the century until 1936. Pierpont based his design for Monotype Grotesque on Ideal, an earlier and more idiosyncratic sans-serif by the H. Berthold AG foundry, and William Thorowogood's 1832 face titled "Grotesque." Uppercase characters are of near equal width, the G has a spur, and the M in the non-condensed weights is square. The lowercase characters a, e, g, and t follow the model of twentieth century English romans.

Aa Bb Cc Dd Ee Ff Gg Hh
Ii Jj Kk Ll Mm Nn Oo Pp Qq Rr
Ss Tt Uu Vv Ww Xx Yy Zz

RotoVision

Sales and Editorial Office
Sheridan House
114 Western Road
Hove, BN3 1DD UK
Tel: +44 (0) 1273 727268
Fax: +44 (0) 1273 727269
www.rotovision.com